JORDANS
COMPANY SECRETARIAL
PRECEDENTS

JORDANS COMPANY SECRETARIAL PRECEDENTS

HGM Leighton MA, FCA
Director, Jordan Group Ltd

JRM Lowe LLB
Jordans

JORDANS
1991

Published by
Jordan & Sons Limited
21 St. Thomas Street, Bristol BS1 6JS

British Library Cataloguing in Publication Data
Leighton, H. G. M.
Jordans company secretarial precedents.
1. Great Britain. Business enterprise. Secretaryship
I. Title
344.106664

ISBN 0 85308 153 0

Typeset by Mendip Communications, Frome
Printed by Bocardo Press, Didcot

CONTENTS

Introduction – How to Use this Book

This book aims to provide precedents to cover situations faced by a company secretary or professional adviser in relation to the management of a limited company under the Companies Acts 1985 to 1989. It is orientated towards the private company, of which some 800,000 are currently in business in the United Kingdom, compared with the public limited company, of which less than 10,000 are in use. Many of the precedents are suitable for both types of company and also for a company limited by guarantee – frequently used for charitable or property management purposes. It does not attempt to provide precedents for additional formalities which apply specifically to public limited companies either under the Companies Acts or, if the shares are traded in the securities market, under any Listing Agreement.

This work does not cover complicated situations where documentation needs to be specifically drafted; and professional advice will be necessary in the circumstances in which certain precedents are used.

Precedents are of greater value to the user if the context of their use is explained and examples completed with specimen entries. Therefore, an introduction to each set of precedents is provided dealing with general practice, but these should not be taken as exhaustive, nor do they deal with accountancy and taxation issues which may be relevant in some cases. Precedents can only be illustrations and may need adaptation to exact circumstances.

Precedents have been completed with fictitious names and transactions where it is felt that such details are necessary to show how they should be used. This applies particularly to the completion and narrative to be entered on forms prescribed by the Companies Acts. In cases where entries are obvious, the names, dates, and transaction details have been left blank, for to do otherwise would be tendentious.

Resolutions, whether for directors or company meetings, must be used within the context of the meetings at which they are proposed.

Directors' resolutions will form part of the minutes of a Board meeting, the procedures for which are covered in Chapter 10.

Shareholders' resolutions will form part of the record of the meeting; arrangements for their proposal, notice to members and filing with the Registrar of Companies when required, are dealt with in Chapter 14.

All shareholders' resolutions can be passed at a general meeting of the company, properly convened and with the necessary quorum. The particular requirements for the passing of different types of resolution are covered in Chapter 14. All such resolutions (other than to remove a director or auditor, when they have a right to make representations at a general meeting) can also be passed by a resolution in writing carried through in accordance with provisions introduced by the Companies Act 1989. A resolution in writing, organised under any enabling provision such as the articles of association, cannot be used in circumstances where the Companies Acts specifically, or impliedly, require a meeting (eg to alter the memorandum as for class meetings) and this is also discussed in Chapter 14.

These differing methods of dealing with shareholders' resolutions are not spelt out in the text against each separate precedent; the relevant sections of the book which cover these methods need to be consulted.

The Companies Act 1989 enables a company to dispense with the use of a seal and, coupled with The Land Registration (Execution of Deeds) Rules 1990, provides alternative methods for a company to execute deeds and documents in accordance with English law. These, together with the use of the seal, are covered in Chapter 12. In other parts of the book the precedents are drafted as if a seal continues to be used, which will be the practice of many, if not the majority, of existing companies. These precedents can be adjusted by reference to that chapter to execution without use of a seal, if so desired.

The 'elective regime' of the Companies Act 1989, which enables private companies to relax certain formalities subject to shareholder approval, is covered in Chapter 14C and is not repeated in detail against the separate transactions to which it applies.

The precedents are based on the office practice of Jordan & Sons Limited as company registration agents and as company secretaries. They use the drafts of memoranda and articles of association, revised for Jordans by leading counsel, to meet the circumstances of the Companies Act 1989, and cover the sections of that Act in force at 31 March 1991.

Where appropriate, an indication is given of the legislative changes that this Act will bring about as further sections are brought into force, but in the absence of prescribed forms or practice notes, which are unlikely to be promulgated before commencement dates, it is not at present possible to cover those areas definitively.

The book is not intended to be a study of company law. Where appropriate, reference is made to *Jordans Secretarial Administration* or to *Gore-Browne on Companies*, both of which are published by Jordans and give a fuller description of the legal position.

For the convenience of users the principal references to the Companies Acts 1985 and 1989 and to the 1985 Table A are cited in the margin of the explanatory text. Where the Companies Act 1989 has amended the 1985 Act, by repealing and replacing whole sections, the new sections are annotated 'ns'.

Prescribed forms required to be filed with the Registrar of Companies are listed in Appendix 4. In the Precedents the repetitive format at the foot of the prescribed forms, giving the presentor's address, is not always included.

The Companies Registry has executive agency status within the Department of Trade and is now called 'Companies House', but for simplicity all references in the text are to 'the Registrar of Companies' and included within that meaning is 'Companies House'.

It will be seen that occasions where fees are payable are noted in the text (eg registration or re-registration of a company, filing of annual returns, etc) but the amount of the fee is not given. These fees are subject to periodic alteration and the current scale of fees is published in *Jordans Journal*, which is distributed free of charge on application to the publishers. See also the Companies (Fees) (Amendment) No 2 Regulations 1990 (SI 1990 No 1368).

ABBREVIATIONS

BNA 1985: Business Names Act 1985.
CA 1985: Companies Act 1985.
IA 1985: Insolvency Act 1985.
FA 1986: Finance Act 1986.
FSA 1986: Financial Services Act 1986.
IA 1986: Insolvency Act 1986.
CA 1989: Companies Act 1989.

Chapter 1

INCORPORATION OF A PRIVATE LIMITED COMPANY

The Registration Process

Private limited companies are incorporated by the registration of the following documents and forms with the Registrar of Companies.

1. Memorandum of Association.
2. Articles of Association.

s 10 3. Form 10 (notice of address of registered office and details of first directors and secretary).

s 12 4. Form G 12 (statutory declaration of compliance with the Companies Acts).

These should be sent or delivered to the Registrar of Companies with the appropriate registration fee.

s 12 Assuming that the documents are in order, and the proposed company's name is
s 13 acceptable, the Registrar of Companies will, in due course, issue a certificate of incorporation, stating that the company is incorporated as a private limited company. The
company comes into existence as a legal entity on the date of this certificate.

Practical considerations

Name

Before any documents are prepared or submitted to the Registrar, it is important to establish that the proposed company name is available. This matter is covered in Chapter 3.

Notepaper

Because there is always some doubt whether a company name will be accepted for registration and because the company's registration number (stated on the certificate of incorporation) must be shown, notepaper should not be printed in advance of receipt of the certificate. The legal requirements for company notepaper are also covered in Chapter 3.

Limited liability

As noted above, the company does not come into existence until the date on the certificate of incorporation. It follows that the company cannot do any business, or enter into any transaction whatsoever, until that date. Any matter undertaken in the name of the company, or on its behalf before that date, will not be binding on the company when it is eventually incorporated, but the person or persons who purported to contract on its behalf will be personally liable for any obligations undertaken. If business, generally, is started before the date of incorporation, those conducting it will have unlimited liability.

Ready-made companies

There is, inevitably, a period of time between submission of the papers to the Registrar and the issue of the certificate by him. This varies from time to time, but is typically three to four weeks. If incorporation is required urgently, it may be more expeditious to acquire a ready-made company from a company registration agent of standing. Such companies are incorporated by agents for the purpose of resale and all the details of the company (such as its name, objects, authorised capital and articles of association) may be altered so as to convert the ready-made company into the company which would have been formed if time had allowed. This is a standard practice and approximately two-thirds of all companies are set up in this way.

Expedited incorporation

In March 1991, Companies House introduced a new service whereby a certificate of incorporation may be obtained on a 'same day' basis, at an increased registration fee and if all necessary documentation is complete. The service is also available upon change of name and re-registration of a company.

Companies House

Companies incorporated in England and Wales are registered by the Registrar of Companies, whose office is in Cardiff; Scottish companies are handled by a separate registry in Edinburgh. There are also registries in Northern Ireland, the Isle of Man, Jersey and Guernsey, although the documentation and legal rules applicable in these jurisdictions are different in many respects from those of England, Wales and Scotland.

The Documents and Forms

Memorandum and articles of association

Although these documents are usually referred to collectively, and are almost always printed and bound together, they are two separate documents which between them set out the constitution of the company.

s 7(3) The memorandum must contain the information set out in the Companies Acts (see below), while the articles, which contain the internal rules for running the company, can be drafted to suit the needs of the individual company. The Act also requires the memorandum and articles to be printed, although the Registrar will accept clear, typewritten
s 3 documents. They should be as close as possible in format to the specimen documents set
s 8 out in the Companies (Tables A to F) Regulations 1985 (SI 1985/805). These are: Table B for the memorandum of a private company limited by shares; Table F for the memorandum of a public company; and Table A for either company's articles. However, subject to any specific rules with which the articles must comply (such as Stock Exchange requirements), a company may freely choose to vary or disapply Table A. The Regulations are to
ns 8A be found in Appendix 1 and see there note on Table G created by CA 1989.

Memorandum of association

s 2 A private company's memorandum must contain the following:

(1) **Company's name.** (For regulations as to companies' names see Chapter 3.)

(2) **Situation of the registered office.** This is the country in which the company is registered (eg England and Wales, Scotland).

(3) **Objects.** Because of the common law *ultra vires* rule, that a company may only do those things which are expressly or impliedly authorised by the memorandum, it has long been the practice to set out a company's objects and powers at length. The convention is for the first paragraph to state all the activities which the draftsman considers the company may ever wish to undertake, and for the remaining paragraphs to be additional objects and powers which enable it to function in a suitable manner. These usually include an 'any other business' clause and a *Cotman v Brougham*[1] clause stating that the various paragraphs are to be given the widest possible interpretation, and not to be treated as independent objects, or interpreted by reference to any other object or the company's name.

CA 1989, ss 108, 109 s 110 ns 3A The Companies Act 1989 contains provisions enabling transactions outside the company's objects to be enforced against the company in most circumstances and for the company to be able to ratify what would otherwise be *ultra vires* acts. This Act also allows the memorandum to state that the company is a 'general commercial company', in which case:

> '(*a*) the object of the company is to carry on any trade or business whatsoever, and
>
> (*b*) the company has power to do all such things as are incidental or conducive to the carrying on of any trade or business by it.'

The intention behind this provision was to enable the practice of endowing companies with unduly prolix objects clauses to become a thing of the past. Unfortunately, the wording of the clause is not entirely clear, and for this reason the standard memorandum of association (see Appendix 2) is for a general commercial company – but a full range of subsidiary provisions is also included, which is current practice.

s 2(3) (4) **Statement of limited liability.**

s 2(5) (5) **Authorised share capital.** This must be expressed as a sum of money, divided into a number of shares of a fixed amount (eg £1,000 divided into 1,000 shares of £1 each). For a *private* company there is no minimum or maximum capital. The minimum authorised and issued capital for a *public limited* company which wishes to trade or borrow money is £50,000. The capital (or part of it) of a private company may be expressed in a currency other than sterling, eg US dollars. Subject to there being a part of the share capital amounting to at least £50,000 sterling, the remainder of the capital of a public company may also be expressed, by using a different share class, in a currency other than sterling. However, advice should be sought if any company is to have a multi-currency share capital.

[1] [1918] AC 514, 87 LJ Ch 379

The authorised capital is simply the upper limit to the amount of share capital which the company may issue, unless it goes through the procedure to increase its capital (see Chapter 7). Because at one time stamp duty was levied on the amount of the authorised capital, it became the practice for companies to be registered with the minimum possible amount. There is now little reason to keep the authorised figure low. The company may have a large authorised capital, much of which remains unissued indefinitely. The members' liability is not affected by this figure.

s 17 (6) **Additional items.** Additional items may be included, and this may be done in order to 'entrench' rights, as the memorandum may specify that these additional provisions are unalterable, or may lay down a special procedure for their alteration. This cannot be done in the articles. Such absolutely entrenched provisions can cause difficulties in changing conditions and commercial circumstances and it is not common practice nowadays to include them in the memorandum. They are more usually to be found in the articles where they may be changed by special resolution, although this may be restricted if class rights are affected.

s 2(6) **Subscription of the memorandum.** On the formation of a company the original memorandum must be signed by at least two subscribers, who must each agree to take at least one share in the company. The subscribers' signatures must be witnessed and the document dated. The subscribers are the founder members of the company and their names must be entered in the Register of Members when the company is formed (see Chapter 11). In many cases the subscribers are nominees of the registration agents or solicitors who formed the company and are not the intended founding shareholders. In these cases it is important that the subscribers' shares are transferred at the earliest opportunity (see Chapter 7 for share transfers) and usually while unpaid.

Articles of association

The articles contain the internal regulations for running the company. Although there are some provisions of the Companies Acts which impose regulations from which there may be no derogation in the articles, in many respects a company may have such regulations as its members consider appropriate. A company limited by shares can be registered
s 7(1) entirely without articles (in which case its regulations will be those of Table A), but this is most unusual and articles will normally be sent to the Registrar with the memorandum.
s 7(3)(c) In this case the articles must also be signed by the subscribers to the memorandum.

Most companies' articles adopt the specimen set of articles from the Companies (Tables A to F) Regulations 1985, known as Table A, with a small number of modifications. There have been successive versions of Table A in force and when dealing with the articles of an established company, care should be taken to ensure that the right version of Table A is referred to. On most occasions when a Table A is modified, the changes apply only to companies registered (or adopting new articles) after that date. Existing companies continue to operate under their original articles and the version of Table A applicable to those articles. Only the current (1985) version of Table A appears in this book.

General

Great care should be taken over the drafting of memorandum and articles and unless special terms are necessary it is preferable to use, as far as practical, a standard precedent.

See Appendix 1 for Table A and Appendix 2 for Jordans standard memorandum and articles for a private company limited by shares, which were settled by a leading company lawyer. This standard draft is for a general commercial company (with a full set of provisions) and with articles based on Table A, but with modifications suitable for a modest private company. A number of alternative provisions which are commonly included in the articles of such companies are also provided, including four alternative share transfer provisions.

For alteration of memorandum and articles, see Chapter 6.

Accompanying forms

Forms 10 and G 12 must be lodged with the memorandum and articles.

See Precedent 1.1 (p 13) FORM 10 STATEMENT OF FIRST DIRECTORS AND SECRETARY AND INTENDED SITUATION OF REGISTERED OFFICE

See Precedent 1.2 (p 16) FORM G 12 STATUTORY DECLARATION OF COMPLIANCE WITH REQUIREMENTS ON APPLICATION FOR REGISTRATION OF A COMPANY

Form G 12 is a statutory declaration which must be declared by either a solicitor engaged in the formation of the company or one of the officers of the company named in Form 10.

As the statutory declaration confirms that all the requirements of the Acts have been complied with, the statutory declaration may not be dated earlier than any of the other formation documents.

Company Limited by Guarantee

Companies limited by guarantee are used for various purposes including clubs, charities, community activities, property management and co-operative ventures. They are created by the same registration process as private companies limited by shares but have the following essential differences.

(1) The members' liability

Whereas the members of a company limited by shares are required to pay the agreed price for their shares, in a company limited by guarantee the memorandum of association states:

s 2(4) 'Every member of the company undertakes to contribute such amount as may be required (not exceeding £x) to the Company's assets if it should be wound up while he is a member or within one year after he ceases to be a member for payment of the company's debts and liabilities contracted before he ceases to be a member and of the costs, charges and expenses of winding up, and for the adjustment of the rights of the contributees among themselves.'

In other words, the members guarantee to contribute to the payment of the company's debts up to this fixed sum. The guaranteed sum is often £1.

(2) No share capital

s 1(4) A company limited by guarantee cannot now be registered with a share capital, or create a share capital. (Before the enactment of the Companies Act 1980 this was possible, but seldom done.) The absence of a share capital marks the essential differences in the relationship between a company limited by guarantee and its members, and the more common company limited by shares – that there are, of course, no shareholders. The members of the company will be the subscribers to the memorandum, together with such other persons who become members under the provisions of the memorandum and articles, and whose names are entered in the Register of Members.

As the members have no shares they cannot transfer their interests in the company to others. When they wish to leave the company, they resign their membership. Although the members cannot be said to have individual proprietary interests in the company the members collectively control the company by voting at general meetings. A company limited by guarantee may have different classes of membership, which may involve differences as to voting and other membership rights.

Distribution of profits

Most companies limited by guarantee are not set up for the purpose of making profits and, not having a share capital, they lack any ready mechanism for the distribution of profits among the members. Many such companies include in their memorandum a clause prohibiting the distribution of profits or capital, and this will be essential if the company is also to be registered as a charity or if the company is to include any of certain prescribed words in its name, such as 'Association' or if the company name is not to end with the word 'Limited' (see p 11).

Charities

Many registered charities take the form of companies limited by guarantee so as to obtain the benefits of corporate status. Others are not incorporated but are governed by the provision of a trust deed, in which case the governing body of the charity will be personally liable for the charity's debts. A charity which is also a company will have to comply with both the legislation governing charities and the Companies Acts.

Companies Acts apply

Apart from those parts of the Companies Acts which govern share capital and related matters (the issue of shares, prospectuses, maintenance of capital, etc) companies limited by guarantee are subject to the same statutory and common law rules as those limited by shares. So, for example, the laws governing directors, the company secretary, general meetings, statutory registers, accounts, liquidation, etc, generally apply with equal force to such companies. A company limited by guarantee is a private company and so those rules applicable only to public limited companies do not apply.

Registration procedure

The registration procedure is the same as for a private company limited by shares (see above), requiring the delivery to the Registrar of Companies of memorandum and articles of association, together with Forms 10 (Precedent 1.1) and G 12 (Precedent 1.2).

s 3(1) The form of the memorandum should be as near as circumstances permit to that laid out in Table C. This Table also contains specimen articles of association based on Table A (for a private company limited by shares) but with suitable modifications. See Appendix 1 for Table C and Appendix 2 for Jordans standard memorandum and articles of association for a company limited by guarantee, not having charitable purposes, and with articles based on Table A.

Many companies limited by guarantee have 'long form' articles that are not based on Tables A and C, especially where the company is also to be registered as a charity. In this case the Charity Commission will have to approve the documents, including the company's objects, which must comply with the strict legal requirements for a charity. Such an objects clause will usually require to be specially drafted.

Charities which also engage in non-charitable activities (eg trading to raise funds) commonly have such activities conducted by a separate company (usually limited by shares) which is controlled by the charity and which covenants its profits to the charity. Such a company should have memorandum and articles drafted so as to ensure that it remains under the control of the charity.

Company names

s 30 A company limited by guarantee whose objects are the promotion of commerce, art, science, education, religion, charity or any profession, or matters incidental thereto, and whose memorandum and articles require its profits to be applied only to those ends, and also prohibit the distribution of profits or capital among members, are exempt from the requirement to have 'limited' as the last word of the name. If the exemption is to be claimed on the formation of such a company, a statutory declaration on Form G 30(5)(a) must be delivered to the Registrar of Companies with the formation documents.

If such a company wishes to claim this exemption on a change of name, Form G 30(5)(c) should be lodged together with the special resolution. In other respects the regulations on names, applicable to companies limited by shares, apply also to those limited by guarantee.

See Precedent 1.3 (p 17) FORM G 30(5)(a) DECLARATION ON APPLICATION FOR THE REGISTRATION OF A COMPANY EXEMPT FROM THE REQUIREMENT TO USE THE WORD 'LIMITED' OR ITS WELSH EQUIVALENT

Unlimited Company

An unlimited company is incorporated by registration with the Registrar of Companies in the same way as companies limited by shares or guarantee. The same documents, ie memorandum and articles of association, Form 10 (Precedent 1.1) and Form G 12 (Precedent 1.2), must be lodged with the Registrar of Companies, with the registration fee. The company will be subject to general rules on company names (see above), save that its name may not end with 'limited' or 'public limited company' (or abbreviations of these).

The members of an unlimited company are liable, in the event of liquidation, to contribute such sums as are necessary to meet the company's debts and liquidation expenses. Such a company is a private company and will often have a share capital, but is not required to do so. As a private company, it may not offer shares or other securities for sale to the public. The main advantage of an unlimited company is that it is not required to file annual accounts with the Registrar provided the company has not, during the accounting reference period, been the subsidiary or holding company of a limited company. An annual return must be lodged (with the filing fee) as must other returns, except those relating to share capital.

If the company has a share capital this must be stated in the articles of association and, as such, may be increased, reduced or otherwise altered by special resolution. No returns of allotments need to be lodged.

The unlimited company is rarely used, but can be useful where corporate personality, perpetual succession or taxation as a company are required and limited liability is not essential, or is prohibited by the rules of a professional association. See Appendix 1 for Table E memorandum and articles of an unlimited company having a share capital.

Precedent 1.1

10

Statement of first directors and secretary and intended situation of registered office

This form should be completed in black.

	CN For official use
Company name *(in full)*	BILLBROOK ENTERPRISES LTD
Registered office of the company on incorporation.	**RO**
	25 STATION ROAD
Post town	NORRINGTON
County/Region	RUFFORDSHIRE
Postcode	UF9 71E
If the memorandum is delivered by an agent for the subscribers of the memorandum mark 'X' in the box opposite and give the agent's name and address.	X
Name	JORDAN & SONS LIMITED
	RA
	21 ST THOMAS STREET
Post town	BRISTOL
County/Region	
Postcode	BS1 6JS
Number of continuation sheets attached	1
To whom should Companies House direct any enquiries about the information shown in this form?	JORDAN & SONS LIMITED
	(as above)
	Postcode
Telephone	0272 230600 Extension

Company Secretary *(See notes 1 - 5)*

Name	*Style/Title	CS MR
	Forenames	JOHN GEORGE
	Surname	STICKATIT
	*Honours etc	FCA
	Previous forenames	NONE
	Previous surname	NONE
Address		AD 25 SOUTHVIEW CRESCENT
Usual residential address must be given. In the case of a corporation, give the registered or principal office address.		
	Post town	DILSBOROUGH
	County/Region	RUFFORDSHIRE
	Postcode	RU15 6AB — Country

I consent to act as secretary of the company named on page 1

Consent signature Signed J G Stickatit Date 28 JUNE 1990

Directors *(See notes 1 - 5)*

Please list directors in alphabetical order.

Name	*Style/Title	CD MR
	Forenames	JAMES
	Surname	BOTSEY
	*Honours etc	
	Previous forenames	NONE
	Previous surname	NONE
Address		AD FIELD CLOSE
Usual residential address must be given. In the case of a corporation, give the registered or principal office address.		BULLOCKS HILL
	Post town	DILSBOROUGH
	County/Region	RUFFORDSHIRE
	Postcode	RU15 8SE — Country ENGLAND
	Date of birth	DO 09 05 59 — Nationality NA BRITISH
	Business occupation	OC MARKETING EXECUTIVE
	Other directorships	OD BILLBROOK & BOTSEY LTD

* Voluntary details

I consent to act as director of the company named on page 1

Consent signature Signed J Botsey Date 28 JUNE 1990

Directors (continued)
(See notes 1 - 5)

Name	*Style/Title	CD MR
	Forenames	JOHN FRANK
	Surname	RUNCIMAN
	*Honours etc	
	Previous forenames	NONE
	Previous surname	NONE
Address		AD THE BUSH HOTEL
Usual residential address must be given. In the case of a corporation, give the registered or principal office address.		MARKET SQUARE
	Post town	DILSBOROUGH
	County/Region	RUFFORDSHIRE
	Postcode	RU15 3AB Country ENGLAND
	Date of birth	DO 0 8 0 9 5 8 Nationality NA BRITISH
	Business occupation	OC HOTELIER
	Other directorships	OD BUSH HOTEL (DILSBOROUGH) LTD
* Voluntary details		I consent to act as director of the company named on page 1
	Consent signature	Signed J. F. Runciman Date 28 JUNE 1990

FOR JORDAN & SONS LIMITED

Glynis Dyson

Signature of agent on behalf of all subscribers Date 28 JUNE 1990

Delete if the form is signed by the subscribers.

Delete if the form is signed by an agent on behalf of all the subscribers.

All the subscribers must sign either personally or by a person or persons authorised to sign for them.

SignedXXXXXXXXXXXXXXXXXXXXXXXXXXXXXXXXXXXXXXXXXDate

SignedXXXXXXXXXXXXXXXXXXXXXXXXXXXXXXXXXXXXXXXXXDate

SignedXXXXXXXXXXXXXXXXXXXXXXXXXXXXXXXXXXXXXXXXXDate

SignedXXXXXXXXXXXXXXXXXXXXXXXXXXXXXXXXXXXXXXXXXDate

SignedXXXXXXXXXXXXXXXXXXXXXXXXXXXXXXXXXXXXXXXXXDate

SignedXXXXXXXXXXXXXXXXXXXXXXXXXXXXXXXXXXXXXXXXXDate

Page 3

Precedent 1.2

Statutory Declaration of compliance with requirements on application for registration of a company

12

Please do not write in this margin

Pursuant to section 12(3) of the Companies Act 1985

To the Registrar of Companies

For official use | For official use

Please complete legibly, preferably in black type, or bold block lettering

Name of company

* insert full name of Company

* BILLBROOK ENTERPRISES LTD

I, JAMES BOTSEY

of FIELD CLOSE

BULLOCKS HILL

DILSBOROUGH

† delete as appropriate

do solemnly and sincerely declare that I am a ~~[Solicitor engaged in the formation of the company]†~~ [person named as director or secretary of the company in the statement delivered to the registrar under section 10(2)]† and that all the requirements of the above Act in respect of the registration of the above company and of matters precedent and incidental to it have been complied with,

And I make this solemn declaration conscientiously believing the same to be true and by virtue of the provisions of the Statutory Declarations Act 1835

Declared at 20 LONG LANE

DILSBOROUGH

the 21 day of JULY

One thousand nine hundred and 90

before me James Morris

~~A Commissioner for Oaths or Notary Public or Justice of the Peace or~~ Solicitor having the powers conferred on a Commissioner for Oaths.

Declarant to sign below

J Botsey

Presentor's name address and reference (if any):

For official Use

New Companies Section | Post room

Precedent 1.3

Declaration on application for the registration of a company exempt from the requirement to use the word "limited" or its Welsh equivalent

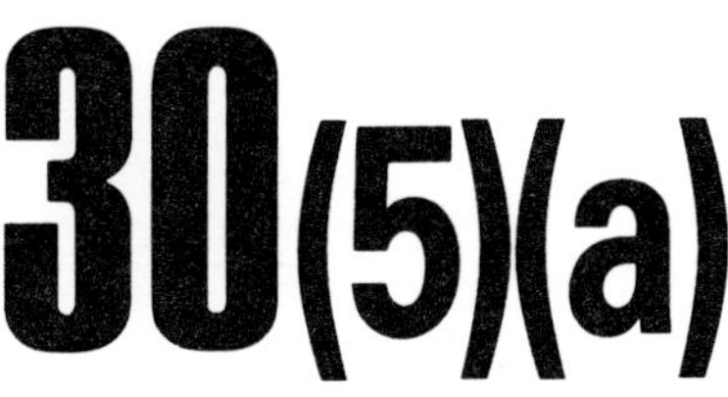

Please do not write in this margin

Pursuant to section 30(5)(a) of the Companies Act 1985

Please complete legibly, preferably in black type, or bold block lettering

Note
This declaration should accompany the application for the registration of the company

* insert full name of company

† delete as appropriate

For official use

Company number: 4 500 250

Name of company

* THE MELMOTTE TRUST

I, JOHN SAMUEL DOCKWRATH

of 25 MARKET SQUARE, BARCHESTER

a [Solicitor engaged in the formation of the above-named company]~~[person named as director or secretary of the above company in the statement delivered under section 10 of the above Act]†~~ do solemnly and sincerely declare that the company complies with the requirements of section 30(3) of the above Act.

And I make this solemn Declaration conscientiously believing the same to be true and by virtue of the Statutory Declarations Act 1835.

Declared at 3 HIGH ST
BARCHESTER

the 20 day of FEBRUARY

One thousand nine hundred and NINETY

before me John Jones

~~A Commissioner for Oaths or Notary Public or Justice of the Peace or~~ Solicitor having the powers conferred on a Commissioner for Oaths

Declarant to sign below

Samuel Dockwrath

Presentor's name address and reference (if any):

For official Use
New Companies Section | Post room

Chapter 2

ALTERATION TO MEMORANDUM AND ARTICLES OF ASSOCIATION

Alteration to Memorandum

Change of name

See Chapter 3 on company names.

Change of situation of registered office

A company registered in one jurisdiction cannot move the situation of its registered office outside that jurisdiction, so that a company registered in England and Wales must maintain a registered office there and cannot change its situation to Scotland. Scottish companies are similarly prevented from moving south of the border. (See Chapter 9, 'Registered Office'.)

Alteration of objects

s 4 A company may alter its objects by special resolution. The procedure for calling an extraordinary general meeting (EGM), passing the special resolution and sending a copy of the special resolution in the correct format to the Registrar of Companies within 15 days, is set out in Chapter 14. Also set out in that chapter is the written resolution procedure which, under the provisions of the Companies Act 1989, may now be used as an alternative.[1]

See Precedent 2.1 (p 21) DIRECTORS' RESOLUTION TO CALL EGM AND RECOMMEND CHANGE OF OBJECTS

See Precedent 2.2 (p 21) SPECIAL RESOLUTION TO ADOPT NEW OBJECTS

It will be observed that Precedent 2.2 will enable the company to adopt general commercial objects in accordance with the Companies Act 1989.

A printed copy of the memorandum as altered must also be lodged with the Registrar within 15 days. No fee is payable. The change of objects takes effect on the date of the resolution.

ss 4–6 CA 1989, s 110(2) It is unusual for a change of objects to be contentious but the Acts confer a right on the holders of 15 per cent of the shares, or of any class of shares, to object to the court within 21 days of the special resolution, whereupon the court has a wide discretion to either prevent the company making the alteration, or to permit it, with or without conditions.

For increase of authorised (nominal) capital, see Chapter 5.

[1] See Chapter 14

s 17 Other provisions in the memorandum, which otherwise could have been included in the company's articles of association, may be altered by special resolution, unless the memorandum itself provides a different procedure, or prohibits the alteration, or the memorandum contains class rights and does not provide a procedure for their alteration.

Alteration to Articles

s 9 A company may alter or add to its articles by special resolution and such alterations are as valid as if contained in the company's original articles.

See Precedent 2.3 (p 21) DIRECTORS' RESOLUTION TO CALL EGM TO RECOMMEND ALTERATION TO ARTICLES

See Precedent 2.4 (p 22) SPECIAL RESOLUTION TO ALTER ARTICLES

The procedure for calling an extraordinary general meeting, passing the special resolution and sending a copy of the special resolution in the correct format to the Registrar of Companies within 15 days, is set out in Chapter 14. Alternatively, the written resolution procedure, also set out in that chapter, may be used.

A printed copy of the articles as altered must also be lodged with the Registrar of Companies within 15 days of the special resolution. No fee is payable. The change in the articles takes effect on the date of the resolution.

Care should also be taken to ensure that the articles as altered do not infringe the Act in any way (eg by specifying periods of notice shorter than the statutory minimum) and also that the alteration does not amount to a variation of class rights (ie the special rights attached to a class of shares) for which an additional procedure is required. (See Chapter 14.)

Objecting members

A member of the company who disagrees with the alteration may ask the court to set it aside, which the court will do if the objector can show that the alteration was not made bona fide for the benefit of the company as a whole.

Adoption of New Articles

Often the simplest way of effecting alterations is to encompass them in a complete set of new and up to date articles matched to the current Table A, and to have the company adopt the new articles by one resolution. This is a simple procedure for adopting a number of alterations all at once, but if there are going to be objections to particular alterations it may be necessary to take the amendments one at a time in separate resolutions. Care should be taken to take account of any resulting change in the version of Table A applicable to the company in consequence of adopting the new articles.

See Precedent 2.5 (p 22) DIRECTORS' RESOLUTION TO CALL EGM TO RECOMMEND THE ADOPTION OF NEW ARTICLES

See Precedent 2.6 (p 23) SPECIAL RESOLUTION TO ADOPT NEW ARTICLES

Precedent 2.1

Directors' Resolution to Call EGM and Recommend Change of Objects

It was resolved to convene an extraordinary general meeting of the company forthwith to consider the alteration of the objects of the company in accordance with the draft produced to this meeting and approved thereby.

The appropriate notice to convene such a meeting on [*date*] was produced by the secretary and was approved.

Precedent 2.2.

Special Resolution to Adopt New Objects

That the objects set forth in paragraph [ ] of the document produced to this meeting, and for the purposes of identification signed by the chairman hereof, be approved and adopted as the objects of the company, in substitution for, and to the exclusion of, all the existing objects thereof, and the memorandum of association be altered accordingly.

Precedent 2.3

Directors' Resolution to Call EGM to Recommend Alteration to Articles

It was resolved to convene an extraordinary general meeting of the company forthwith to consider the alteration of the articles in the following manner:

(a) By the deletion of Articles [ ] and [ ] and the renumbering of subsequent articles accordingly.

(b) By the addition of the following new articles to be numbers [ ] and [ ].

The appropriate notice to convene such a meeting on [*date*] was produced by the secretary and was approved.

Precedent 2.4

Special Resolution to Alter Articles

That the articles of association be altered in the following manner:

(a) By the deletion of Articles [ ] and [ ] and the renumbering of subsequent articles accordingly.
(b) By the addition of the following new articles to be numbered [ ] and [ ].

[*here set out new articles in full*]

Precedent 2.5

Directors' Resolution to Call EGM to Recommend the Adoption of New Articles

It was resolved to convene an extraordinary general meeting of the company to consider the adoption of new articles of association of the company in accordance with the draft produced to this meeting and approved thereby.

The appropriate notice to convene such a meeting on [*date*] was produced by the secretary and was approved.

Precedent 2.6

Special Resolution to Adopt New Articles

That the regulations set forth in the printed document produced to this meeting and for the purposes of identification signed by the chairman hereof, be approved and adopted as the articles of association of the company, in substitution for, and to the exclusion of, all existing articles thereof.

Chapter 3

COMPANY NAMES

Requirements as to Names

s 27 Every registered company must have a name which is different from that of every other
s 28 registered company. Companies may change their names, however, and the only precise way of identifying a company is by its registered number.

s 30 A private company, limited by shares, must have the word 'Limited' as the last word of its name, unless it is exempt from this requirement (see below).

s 26 The words 'Limited', 'Unlimited' and 'Public Limited Company' (and their abbreviations and Welsh equivalents) may not be used as part of a company name except at its end.

A proposed company name must not be offensive or such that its use would constitute a criminal offence.

The Registrar will not accept a name which is the same as one already registered.

s 26 To ensure that the proposed company name will be acceptable it should be checked
s 29 against the index of companies held by the Registrar of Companies to see that the name is not the same as one already registered and that it does not contain any of the 'sensitive' words or expressions contained in the Company and Business Names Regulations (see Appendix 3). Such names may be used only with the consent of the Registrar or the body or person specified in the Regulations.

The proposed name should also be avoided if it appears to be *too like* a name already in use by another company, or the business name of a sole trader, partnership or foreign company. A name which is similar to such a name, but which is not the same as a name on the index, will be accepted for registration, but may later cause difficulties (see below).

Exemption from using 'Limited'

To be exempted from the use of 'Limited' or 'Ltd' in the name, the company's objects must be the promotion of commerce, art, science, education, religion, charity or any profession, and anything incidental or conducive thereto, and the memorandum or articles must require the company's profits or income to be applied to those objects and must prohibit the payment of dividends to members and provide that, on winding up, the assets must not be distributed among the members but must be transferred to another body having similar objects. On formation of a new company, or on change of name, the exemption can be claimed provided a statutory declaration of compliance is delivered to the Registrar of Companies (Form G 30(5)(a) on formation (see Precedent 1.3) and Form G 30(5)(c) on change of name.

Power of Registrar to change the name

s 28(2) The Registrar may, within 12 months of a company's name being accepted, order a company to change its name if it has been registered with one which is too like a name already on the index.

Objection by existing companies to newly registered company name

s 28 A company already registered may object to the Registrar of Companies if another company is incorporated with, or changes its name to, a name which is the same as or too like its own. The Registrar has power to make an order, within 12 months of incorporation or change, that the second company alters its name. Since the order must be made within the statutory time-limit, any objection must be lodged at an early date to enable due consideration by the Registrar.

Objection is made by a letter to the Registrar. Since this is usually the only opportunity for the objector to make its case the letter must cover all relevant issues for consideration and a company may regard it wise to take advice from a Company Registration Agent or professional advisor with requisite practical experience. Care must be taken that the objection letter deals with the exact registered name of each company on the certificate of incorporation, or on change of name, and the Registrar of Companies' files should be carefully checked first.

Orders to change name are made sparingly.

See Precedent 3.1 (p 30) OUTLINE LETTER OF OBJECTION TO 'TOO LIKE' COMPANY NAME

The submission should cover:

1. Name confusion:
   - (a) phonetic similarity;
   - (b) qualifying or distinguishing words.

An objection will not succeed if the name contains words which indicate a different business or a different trading area, but words such as 'group' 'holdings' and 'service' are not usually considered distinctive.

2. Other factors leading to confusion will include:
   - (a) any overlap in the nature of the businesses carried on by each company;
   - (b) any overlap in the geographical area within which each company operates;
   - (c) any overlap between the customers and suppliers of each company;
   - (d) any common advertising medium (such as Yellow Pages, trade directories) used by each company;
   - (e) any common source of employees (employment agencies, etc);
   - (f) any similarity in logo, symbol or trading name used by each company, and the appearance of stationery or promotional literature;
   - (g) any similarity in the appearance, livery or 'get up' of the premises of each company, or their vehicles or uniforms, or of their tools, plant and machinery;
   - (h) any similarity in the appearance or 'get up' of the products of each company.

Evidence of the occurrence of actual confusion is very important. A classic example of confusion arose when the Registrar received an objection from Company A in respect of Company B. Company B was operating in the same street. The Registrar duly wrote to Company B seeking its comments. His letter was delivered to Company A, and the objection was upheld.

Passing off

The company could also be sued by an established trader for using a name in circumstances which amount to passing off. Passing off is a common law action brought by an established business (whether a sole trader, partnership, registered company or even a foreign trader which has established a reputation in the UK) against a newcomer who conducts business in such a way that potential customers may confuse the two businesses. Using a similar name is the most obvious way of causing such confusion. The established trader must show that he has a reputation to protect in that name and that the new trader's activities are likely to cause damage to the established business. In most circumstances the two traders must be in the same general type of business and the same or overlapping locations. Because of the risks of such an action, great care should be taken in selecting a new trading name and searches made of such sources as trade directories and Yellow Pages.

The adoption of a name by a company can also lead to an infringement of another's registered trade or service mark, and in many cases the company should undertake a search of the trade marks register before adopting a name.

s 32 The Secretary of State for Trade may, at any time, order a company to change its name if it gives so misleading an indication of the company's activities as to be likely to cause harm to the public.

Change of Name

s 28 A company may change its name by special resolution, but the change takes effect only on the issue of a certificate of incorporation on change of name by the Registrar. The Registrar will issue such a certificate only if the proposed name meets the same requirements as would the name of a *new* company on registration. It follows that, before taking steps to change the name, the same enquiries should be taken to ascertain the acceptability of the name that would need to be taken when forming a new company. The risks of being ordered to change the name by the Registrar, or of passing off, apply equally to a new name adopted by this procedure as on initial registration (see above).

See Precedent 3.2 (p 31) DIRECTORS' RESOLUTION TO CALL EGM AND RECOMMEND CHANGE OF NAME

See Precedent 3.3 (p 31) SPECIAL RESOLUTION TO CHANGE THE NAME OF COMPANY

The procedure for calling an extraordinary general meeting, passing the special resolution and sending a copy of the special resolution in the correct format to the Registrar of Companies within 15 days, or the alternative written resolution procedure (see Chapter 14) may be used. The resolution must be lodged with the appropriate registration fee (see Introduction).

If the name is accepted, the Registrar will issue a certificate of incorporation on change of name. The name change is effective on the date of the certificate. No rights or obligations of the company are affected by the name change. The company's registered number does not change and can be used to identify the company as the same entity, despite the change of name.

Having effected a change of name, the company must have its memorandum and articles reprinted in the new name, and submit a copy as altered to the Registrar. It should obtain a new company seal if necessary and display the new name outside every place of business and the registered office. It should also ensure that all company stationery bears the correct name.

Business Names

A company may use one or more business names in addition to its registered name. Such names are not required to be registered, but are subject to the following provisions of the Business Names Act 1985.

The name must not suggest connection with the government or any local authority.

Sensitive words and expressions specified in the Company and Business Names Regulations (see Appendix 3) may not be used without consent.

s 349 The company's registered name must appear on all business letters, orders for goods,
s 348 invoices, receipts, demands for payment, etc. (For other matters which must appear on
BNA 1985, company stationery, see below.)
ss 4, 7

See Precedent 3.4 (p 32) NOTICE OF PARTICULARS OF OWNERSHIP

In addition to these statutory restrictions, a company using a business name must take care to avoid using a name which is too similar to that of an existing business (so rendering it liable to an action for passing off) and must not infringe any registered trade mark. (For passing off and trade marks, see above.)

Displaying the Name

s 2 A company's name must appear in its memorandum of association, outside its registered
ss 348, 349, 350 office and other places of business, on its stationery and on its company seal if it has one.

Company stationery

s 349 The requirement to state the company's name in legible characters applies to all business letters, notices and official publications, bills of exchange, promissory notes, endorse-
s 349(4) ments, cheques, orders for money or goods, bills of parcels, invoices, receipts and letters of credit. Failure to comply can render the company and its officers liable to a fine, but can also have the sometimes unfair effect of making a director or other agent personally liable on a document in which the company is misnamed.

If the company uses a trade or business name, its full registered name must still appear on all stationery.

s 351 Apart from the company's name, the stationery must also show the company's place (ie country) of registration, its registered number and the address of its registered office. If the company is registered for VAT, its VAT registration number must be shown on VAT invoices and receipts.

s 351(1) An investment company (as defined by s 266) must state this fact on its stationery, and a company which is exempt from using the word 'Limited' as the last word of its name must state that it is a limited company.

CA 1989, s 111 A company which is a registered charity must state the fact on its notepaper and other documents, if such is not apparent from its name.

s 351(2) If any reference is made to the company's share capital, it must be paid up share capital.

s 305 There is no requirement to state the names of the directors, but if *any* are named (other than as signatory to a letter) they must *all* be named.

See Precedent 3.5 (p 33) SPECIMEN COMPANY NOTEPAPER

Approval of Name for Registration under the Consumer Credit Act 1974

The Consumer Credit Act 1974 requires companies or businesses trading within the categories of consumer credit* in the Act to obtain a licence to trade from the Office of Fair Trading (OFT).

An application for a licence will be refused if the OFT is not satisfied as to the company or business name. Although the licence cannot be issued before the company is incorporated, nor on change of name before the company has received the certificate of incorporation on change of name, the OFT will give preliminary clearance.

See Precedent 3.6 (p 34) APPLICATION TO OFT FOR APPROVAL OF NAME FOR LICENSING UNDER THE CONSUMER CREDIT ACT 1974

A name cannot be 'reserved' as it may not necessarily be available when application is made for a licence. It is, therefore, important to proceed with all possible speed once the OFT has indicated that a name is available. It will usually do so within seven working days of the application.

Applicants for a licence should obtain the necessary forms, CC 1/86 and CC 2/86, together with the explanatory booklet CCP 22 as to licensing under the Act, from: OFT, Government Building, Bromyard Avenue, Acton, London W3 7BD.

The procedures for licensing are beyond the scope of this work.

*Categories of credit business requiring a licence are:
1. Consumer credit;
2. Consumer hire business;
3. Credit brokerage business;
4. Debt adjusting and debt controlling;
5. Debt collecting;
6. Credit reference agency.

Precedent 3.1

Outline Letter of Objection to 'Too Like' Company Name

The Registrar of Companies,
Companies House,
Crown Way, Maindy, Cardiff CF4 3UZ

Dear Sir,

. . . . Ltd, Reg No:. ('ourselves')
. . . . Ltd, Reg No:. (new company)

We request through you that the Secretary of State directs, under the provisions of s 28 of the Companies Act 1985, that the new company change its name [with which it was incorporated on (*date*)]* [for which a Certificate of Incorporation on Change of Name was issued on (*date*)]* on the grounds that its name is too like that of ourselves. Our name is that [with which this company was incorporated on (*date*)]* [for which a Certificate of Incorporation on Change of Name was issued on (*date*)]*.

We append a memorandum setting out the position and submit that the name of the new company is too like that of ourselves which at the time of registration of the new company's name was a name appearing in the Registrar's index of company names and the similarity is a cause of confusion to those persons and businesses dealing with ourselves to an extent that an order under s 28 is appropriate.

If you require any further information or have any questions we would be pleased to attend to such.

Yours faithfully,

For Ltd.

Director

MEMORANDUM

Reasons why the name of. . . . . Ltd, Reg No: . . . . (new company) is too like the name of . . . . Ltd, Reg No: . . . . (ourselves).

[*Here set out the reasons which will cover the issues listed in the text.*]

EDITOR'S NOTE

* Delete as appropriate.

Precedent 3.2

Directors' Resolution to Call EGM and Recommend Change of Name

It was resolved to convene an extraordinary general meeting of the company to consider the change of the name of the company from Bush Hotel (Dilsborough) Ltd to Dilsborough Hotels Ltd.

Precedent 3.3

Special Resolution to Change the Name of Company

That the name of the company be changed to

DILSBOROUGH HOTELS LTD.

Precedent 3.4

NOTICE OF PARTICULARS OF OWNERSHIP

AS REQUIRED BY SECTIONS 4 AND 7 OF THE BUSINESS NAMES ACT 1985

THE BUSH HOTEL

PROPRIETOR

DILSBOROUGH HOTELS LTD

ADDRESS WITHIN GREAT BRITAIN AT WHICH DOCUMENTS MAY BE EFFECTIVELY SERVED ON THE PROPRIETOR IN RELATION TO THE BUSINESS

10 MARKET PLACE
DILSBOROUGH
RUFFORDSHIRE
RU15 3AB

Precedent 3.5

Specimen Company Notepaper

The Bush Hotel

10 Market Place Dilsborough Ruffordshire RU15 3AB
Telephone 0456 830789

Dilsborough Hotels Ltd
Registered office: 10 Market Place Dilsborough Ruffordshire
Registered in England and Wales No 1234567
VAT Reg. No. 200:200:220

Precedent 3.6

Application to the Office of Fair Trading for Approval of Name for Licensing under the Consumer Credit Act 1974

Office of Fair Trading,
Consumer Credit Licensing Branch,
Government Building,
Bromyard Avenue,
Acton,
London W3 7BB

Dear Sirs,

Re: RUFFORD HIRE PURCHASE LTD.

We would be obliged if you would give a preliminary opinion on the above name as to whether it is available for registration under the Consumer Credit Act.

It is wished to incorporate a company with this name and then apply for a Consumer Credit Licence. It is, therefore, desired to obtain your opinion prior to the company being incorporated in order to mitigate problems on the name at licence application stage.

It is fully understood that you reserve the right to refuse a name when the application itself is considered. The registered office will be at [*address*].

We would be grateful for a reply within the next seven days as we are anxious to proceed with the incorporation as a matter of urgency.

Yours faithfully,

Chapter 4

RE-REGISTRATION

Introduction

ss 43–55 A company must be registered either as a private company limited by shares or by guarantee, as a public limited company or as an unlimited company. Provision is made in the Companies Acts for re-registration from one type to another, except that a company limited by guarantee cannot be re-registered as one limited by shares, or vice versa.

If a public limited company wishes to re-register as unlimited it must first re-register as a private company limited by shares and then convert from private limited company to unlimited company; and vice versa if an unlimited company wishes to become a public limited company.

s 51(2) An unlimited company which was originally formed as a limited company and re-registered cannot re-register back again into a limited company and vice versa.

On any re-registration, and in particular if alterations to the memorandum and articles are proposed which are beyond the essentials for the purpose of registration, a careful explanatory letter must be sent to shareholders with the notice of meeting.

The above procedures are fully described in *Jordans Secretarial Administration*, at §§ 2.12 to 2.18.

A fee is charged by the Registrar of Companies for re-registration (see Introduction).

4A Re-registration of a Private Company Limited by Shares as a Public Limited Company

ss 43–47 **The steps are as follows.**

(1) Prepare a 'relevant balance sheet' (ie made up to a date not more than seven months prior to the application for re-registration) which must have an 'unqualified
s 43 report' by the auditors attached. The auditors are also required to state that in their opinion the net assets are not less than the share capital and undistributable reserves.

See Precedent 4A.1 (p 37) SPECIMEN UNQUALIFIED AUDITORS' REPORT ON BALANCE SHEET AND STATEMENT OF NET ASSETS UPON RE-REGISTRATION

(2) Board meeting to approve and confirm arrangements.

See Precedent 4A.2 (p 38) MINUTES OF BOARD MEETING

(3) Extraordinary general meeting to pass special resolution to re-register and make consequential alterations to the memorandum and articles of association.

See Precedent 4A.3 (p 39) SPECIAL RESOLUTION TO RE-REGISTER AND MAKE CONSEQUENTIAL ALTERATIONS TO MEMORANDUM AND ARTICLES OF ASSOCIATION

(4) Complete application for re-registration (Form G 43(3)) and declaration of compliance with requirements (Form G 43(3)(e)).

See Precedent 4A.4 (p 40) FORM G 43(3) APPLICATION BY A PRIVATE COMPANY FOR RE-REGISTRATION AS A PUBLIC COMPANY

See Precedent 4A.5 (p 41) FORM G 43(3)(e) DECLARATION OF COMPLIANCE WITH REQUIREMENTS BY A PRIVATE COMPANY ON APPLICATION FOR RE-REGISTRATION AS A PUBLIC COMPANY

s 44 If the company has issued any shares for a non-cash consideration between the date of the balance sheet and the application to re-register, such shares must be valued and a valuation report lodged with the application to re-register. A bonus issue is not treated as a non-cash consideration in this context.

(5) Arrange for memorandum and articles to be re-printed in a manner suitable for filing with Registrar of Companies.

(6) Board meeting to approve documentation of application for re-registration.

See Precedent 4A.6 (p 42) BOARD MINUTES APPROVING DOCUMENTATION OF APPLICATION FOR RE-REGISTRATION

(7) Registrar of Companies will issue a certificate of re-registration. Re-registration is effective from the date of that certificate.

Following re-registration the company will need to:

ns 36A, CA 1989, s 130

(1) Alter the name displayed at the registered office, other places of business, notepaper and other documentation (see Chapter 3).
(2) Adopt a new seal (if a seal is used) with its name as altered (ending with Plc) (see Chapter 12).
(3) Advise shareholders and either issue new share certificates with name altered or a sticker to be placed on existing certificate (see Precedent 4B.4).

It will also need to comply with the provisions of the Companies Acts which attach to public limited companies but not to private companies, eg maintain register of substantial shareholdings, minimum number of directors is two, not one, etc.

Precedent 4A.1

Specimen Unqualified Auditors' Report on Balance Sheet and Statement of Net Assets upon Re-registration

[AUDITORS' REPORT TO THE MEMBERS OF LIMITED]

We have audited the accounts on pages to in accordance with auditing standards.

In our opinion the accounts of Limited give a true and fair view of the company's affairs at [*date*] and of its profit and source and application of funds for the year then ended and have been properly prepared in accordance with the Companies Act 1985. It is also our opinion that the net assets of Limited were not less than the aggregate of the called up share capital and undistributable reserves of the company at [*date*].

Chartered Accountants

[*date*]

Precedent 4A.2

Minutes of Board Meeting

IT WAS RESOLVED that:

1. It was desirable in the interests of the company to seek re-registration as a public company, within the meaning of s 1(3) of the Companies Act 1985.
2. The balance sheet and unqualified report produced to the meeting and dated as at [*date*] be approved as the relevant balance sheet and unqualified report required by s 43(3)(c) of the Companies Act 1985, provided that application to re-register be made not later than [*date*]*.
3. The nominal value of the allotted share capital of the company was not less than the minimum £50,000 required by the Companies Act 1985 and that all the shares comprised therein had been paid up as required by s 45 of the Companies Act 1985.
4. Changes be made to the memorandum of association pursuant to s 43 of the Companies Act 1985 [and in addition it would be appropriate to alter the objects of the company; particulars of the proposed new objects were produced].
5. ** It would be appropriate to adopt new articles of association in the form produced to the meeting.
6. An extraordinary general meeting of the company be convened to consider the relevant matters resolved upon and minuted above. The appropriate notice to convene such a meeting on [*date*] was produced by the secretary and approved.

EDITOR'S NOTES

* Not more than seven months after date of balance sheet.

** Include or omit according to the circumstances. It may be desirable to alter provisions of the articles essentially suitable for a private company, eg restrictions on transfers of shares.

Precedent 4A.3

Special Resolution to Re-register and Make Consequential Alterations to Memorandum and Articles of Association

That the company be re-registered as a PUBLIC COMPANY as defined in s 1(3) of the Companies Act 1985, and

(a) the company's memorandum be altered so that:

(i) it states that the name of the company is 'Dilsborough Hotels Plc'; and

(ii) it states that the company is to be a 'Public Company'; and

* (iii) the objects set forth in Clause 4 of the printed document produced to this meeting be approved and adopted as the objects of the company, in substitution for, and to the exclusion of, all the existing objects thereof, with effect from the date of re-registration of the Company as a Public Company,

*
** and the print of the memorandum of association of the company, as so altered, produced to the meeting and for the purpose of identification signed by the chairman thereof, be approved and adopted as the memorandum of association of the company;

** (b) that the Regulations set forth in the printed document produced to this meeting and for the purpose of identification signed by the chairman hereof, be approved and adopted as the articles of association of the company, in substitution for, and to the exclusion of, all the existing articles thereof, with effect from the date of re-registration of the company as a Public Company.

NOTE: A copy of the memorandum and articles of association in the form referred to in the resolution will be available for inspection at the registered office of the company during business hours on any weekday (Saturdays and public holidays excepted) until the day of the meeting and at the meeting.

EDITOR'S NOTES

* Include if appropriate and match items 4 and 5 in Board minutes.

** Include if the memorandum or articles are altered.

Precedent 4A.4

Application by a private company for re-registration as a public company

43(3)

Please do not write in this margin

Pursuant to section 43(3) of the Companies Act 1985

Please complete legibly, preferably in black type, or bold block lettering

To the Registrar of Companies

For official use

Company number: 5 367 028

Name of company

* insert existing full name of company

* DILSBOROUGH HOTELS LTD

ø insert full name of company amended to make it appropriate for this company as a public limited company

applies to be re-registered as a public company by the name of ø

DILSBOROUGH HOTELS PLC

and for that purpose delivers the following documents for registration:

1 Declaration made by a director or the secretary in accordance with section 43(3)(e) of the above Act (on Form No 43(3)(e)).

2 Printed copy of memorandum and articles as altered in pursuance of the special resolution under section 43(1)(a) of the above Act.

3 Copy of auditors written statement in accordance with section 43(3)(b) of the above Act

4 Copy of relevant balance sheet and of auditors unqualified report on it

§ delete if section 44 of the Act does not apply

~~[5 Copy of any valuation report.]§~~

† delete as appropriate

Signed J. F. Runciman [Director]~~[Secretary]†~~ Date 24 AUGUST 1990

Presentor's name address and reference (if any):

For official Use	
General Section	Post room

Precedent 4A.5

Declaration of compliance with requirements by a private company on application for re-registration as a public company

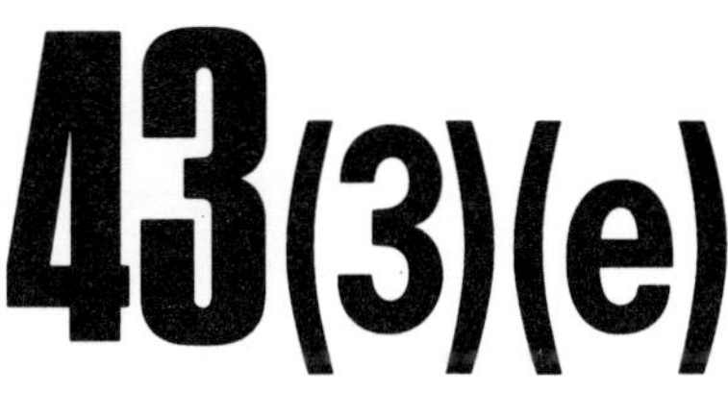

Please do not write in this margin

Pursuant to section 43(3)(e) of the Companies Act 1985

Please complete legibly, preferably in black type, or bold block lettering

To the Registrar of Companies

For official use

Company number: 5 367 028

Name of company

* insert full name of company

* DILSBOROUGH HOTELS LTD

I, JOHN FRANK RUNCIMAN

of THE BUSH HOTEL, DILSBOROUGH IN THE COUNTY OF RUFFORDSHIRE

† delete as appropriate

§ insert date

[XXXXXXXXXX][a director]† of the company, do solemnly and sincerely declare that:

1 the company, on 24 AUGUST 1990 §, passed a special resolution that the company should be re-registered as a public company;

2 the conditions of sections 44 and 45 of the above Act (so far as applicable) have been satisfied;

3 between the balance sheet date and the application for re-registration, there has been no change in the company's financial position that has resulted in the amount of its net assets becoming less than the aggregate of its called-up share capital and undistributable reserves.

And I make this solemn declaration conscientiously believing the same to be true and by virtue of the provisions of the Statutory Declarations Act 1835.

Declared at 75 HIGH STREET DILSBOROUGH

the 24 day of AUGUST

One thousand nine hundred and 90

before me G Masters

A Commissioner for Oaths or Notary Public or Justice of the Peace or Solicitor having the powers conferred on a Commissioner for Oaths.

Declarant to sign below

J. F. Runciman

J F Runciman

Presentor's name address and reference (if any):

For official Use

General Section | Post room

Precedent 4A.6

Board Minutes Approving Documentation of Application for Re-registration

Minutes of a meeting of the Board of directors held on the day of 19 , at .

Present:

1. It was noted that at the extraordinary general meeting of the company held on 19 , a resolution had been duly passed to re-register the company as a public company.

2. It was confirmed that the company satisfied the conditions as to share capital specified in s 45 of the Companies Act 1985.

3. It was further confirmed that since the date to which the balance sheet, approved by the general meeting, was prepared, namely 19 , there had been no change in the financial position of the company that had resulted in the amount of the company's net assets becoming less than the aggregate of its called up share capital and undistributable reserves.

4. There were produced:

   (a) the special resolution to re-register the company as a public company and alter memorandum and articles of association;
   (b) printed copies of the memorandum and articles of association as altered in pursuance of the resolution;
   (c) prescribed application form (G 43(3));
   (d) prescribed statutory declaration in support (G 43(3)(e));
   (e) copy of the 'relevant balance sheet' and the auditors' 'unqualified report' thereon;
   (f) copy of a written statement of the auditors that in their opinion the balance sheet shows that at the balance sheet date the amount of the company's net assets was not less than the aggregate of its called up share capital and undistributable reserves.

* 5. It was resolved that the seal, an impression of which is placed below, be adopted as the new common seal of the company forthwith upon the date of issue by the Registrar to the company of a Certificate of Incorporation evidencing that the company is a public company.

It was resolved that the secretary be authorised:

   (i) to make a Declaration of Compliance in Form G 43(3)(e); and
   (ii) to sign Form G 43(3) and to deliver this form with other requisite documents listed thereon and re-registration fee to the Registrar of Companies.

EDITOR'S NOTE

* Include if a seal is adopted.

4B Re-registration of a Public Limited Company as a Private Company Limited by Shares

ss 53–55 **The steps are as follows.**

(1) Board meeting to approve and confirm arrangements.

See Precedent 4B.1 (p 44) MINUTES OF BOARD MEETING

(2) Extraordinary general meeting to pass special resolution to re-register and make consequential alterations to the memorandum and articles of association.

See Precedent 4B.2(1) (p 45) SPECIAL RESOLUTIONS TO RE-REGISTER AND MAKE CONSEQUENTIAL ALTERATIONS TO MEMORANDUM AND ARTICLES OF ASSOCIATION

s 54 Dissident shareholders who have not voted in favour of this special resolution may apply within 28 days to the court for its cancellation[1]. Upon receipt of notice of such an application the company must immediately file with the Registrar of Companies on Form G 54.

See Precedent 4B.2(2) (p 46) FORM G 54 NOTICE OF APPLICATION MADE TO THE COURT FOR THE CANCELLATION OF A SPECIAL RESOLUTION REGARDING RE-REGISTRATION

(3) Complete application for re-registration (Form G 53) which, accompanied by the documents listed thereon, is sent to the Registrar of Companies.

See Precedent 4B.3 (p 47) FORM G 53 APPLICATION BY A PUBLIC COMPANY FOR RE-REGISTRATION AS A PRIVATE COMPANY

(4) Registrar of Companies will issue a certificate of re-registration. Re-registration is effective from the date of that certificate.

Following re-registration the company will need to:

(1) Alter the name displayed at registered office, other places of business, notepaper and other documentation (see Chapter 5 and Precedent 4B.4).

(2) Adopt a new seal (if a seal is used) with its name altered (ending with limited) (see Chapter 13 and Precedent 4B.1).

(3) Advise shareholders and either issue new share certificates with name altered or a sticker to be placed on the existing share certificate.

See Precedent 4B.4 (p 48) STICKER FOR SHARE CERTIFICATE FOLLOWING RE-REGISTRATION

[1] See *Jordans Secretarial Administration*, at §2.14.

Precedent 4B.1

Minutes of Board Meeting

IT WAS RESOLVED that:

1. The company being a public company be registered as a private company as defined in s 1 of the Companies Act 1985 ('the Act').
2. The company's name, memorandum and articles of association be appropriately amended and the print of the memorandum and articles produced to the meeting and for the purpose of identification initialled by the chairman be approved for submission to shareholders.*
3. An extraordinary general meeting of the company be called on [*date*] at for the purpose of considering and if thought fit, passing, the requisite special resolutions to re-register and amend the memorandum and articles of association.
4. Subject to the passing of the aforesaid special resolutions the secretary was asked to complete the other requisite procedures to enable the company to be re-registered as private.

**5. It was resolved that the seal, an impression of which is placed below, be adopted as the new common seal of the company forthwith upon the date of issue by the Registrar to the company of a Certificate of Incorporation evidencing that the company is not a public company.

EDITOR'S NOTES

* The memorandum change must include substitution of Limited or Ltd instead of Public Limited Company or Plc in the name of the company. It is usual to adopt entirely new articles appropriate to a private company (see Appendix 2).

** Include if a seal is adopted.

Precedent 4B.2

(1) Special Resolutions to Re-register and Make Consequential Alterations to Memorandum and Articles of Association

That the company, being a public limited company, be re-registered under s 53 of the Companies Act 1985 as a private company limited by shares and accordingly:

(a) that the memorandum of association, with respect to its objects, be altered in accordance with the printed document produced to this meeting and for the purpose of identification signed by the chairman thereof, with effect from the date of re-registration of the company as a private company. *[and;]

[* (b) that the regulations set forth in the printed document produced to this meeting and for the purpose of identification signed by the chairman thereof, be approved and adopted as the articles of association of the company to the exclusion of and in substitution for the existing articles, with effect from the date of re-registration of the company as a private company.]

NOTE:
Copies of the existing and proposed memorandum *[and articles of association] are available for inspection at the registered office of the company from the date of this notice until the date of the meeting and will be available at the meeting. The alterations to the memorandum comprise the alteration of the name to .... Ltd and the deletion of clause 2 stating that the company is a public limited company.

*[Alterations to the articles are summarised in the attached note.]

EDITOR'S NOTE

* Alterations to the articles are not necessary for the purpose of re-registration, but it is usual to adopt new articles aligned to private company status and covering such matters as instructions on transfers of shares.

Delete these sections of the precedent if new articles are not adopted.

Precedent 4B.2(2)

Notice of application made to the Court for the cancellation of a special resolution regarding re-registration

Please do not write in this margin

Pursuant to section 54(4) of the Companies Act 1985

Please complete legibly, preferably in black type, or bold block lettering

To the Registrar of Companies

For official use

Company number: 8 765 432

Name of company

* insert full name of company

* DILSBOROUGH GOLF CLUB PLC

gives notice that an application has been made to the Court under section 54(1) of the above Act for the cancellation of the special resolution dated 20 JUNE 1990 that the company be re-registered under section 53(1) as a private company.

‡ Insert Director, Secretary, Administrator, Administrative Receiver or Receiver (Scotland) as appropriate

Signed J. F. Runciman Designation‡ (DIRECTOR) Date 28 JUNE 1990

Presentor's name address and reference (if any):

For official Use

General Section	Post room

Precedent 4B.3

Application by a public company for re-registration as a private company

Please do not write in this margin

Pursuant to section 53 of the Companies Act 1985

Please complete legibly, preferably in black type, or bold block lettering

To the Registrar of Companies

For official use

Company number 8 765 432

Name of company

* insert existing full name of company

* DILSBOROUGH GOLF CLUB PLC

§ insert full name of company amended to make it appropriate for this company as a private limited company

applies to be re-registered as a private company by the name of§

DILSBOROUGH GOLF CLUB LIMITED

and, for that purpose, delivers the following document(s) for registration:

ø delete if previously presented for registration

[1 Copy of the special resolution that the company be re-registered as a private company.]ø

2 Printed copy of the memorandum and articles of association as altered by the special resolution that the company be re-registered

† delete as appropriate

Signed John Brown [Director]~~[Secretary]~~† Date 20 JUNE 1990

Presentor's name address and reference (if any):

For official Use	
General Section	Post room

Precedent 4B.4

Sticker For Share Certificate Following Re-registration

The company has re-registered as **Dilsborough Golf Club Limited** on 20 June 1990.

EDITOR'S NOTE

This precedent can be adapted to meet the circumstances of other types of re-registration.

4C Re-registration of a Limited Company as Unlimited

ss 49–50 **The steps are as follows.**

(1) Board meeting to approve and confirm arrangements.

See Precedent 4C.1 (p 50) MINUTES OF THE DIRECTORS TO COMMENCE RE-REGISTRATION AS UNLIMITED

(2) Extraordinary general meeting to pass special resolution to make the requisite alterations to the memorandum and articles effective as from date of re-registration.

See Precedent 4C.2 (p 50) SPECIAL RESOLUTION TO MAKE REQUISITE ALTERATIONS TO MEMORANDUM AND ARTICLES OF ASSOCIATION

See Precedent 4C.5 for details of alterations.

Frequently, if there is a small number of shareholders, the special resolution will be passed by a written resolution instead of at a meeting (see Chapter 2).

(3) Signature by all members of an assent to the company being re-registered as unlimited (Form G 49(8)(a)). This may be a single document or a series of documents in like form.

See Precedent 4C.3 (p 51) FORM G 49(8)(a) MEMBERS' ASSENT TO COMPANY BEING RE-REGISTERED AS UNLIMITED

(4) Statutory declaration on Form G 49(8)(b) by all directors that all members of the company have assented to re-registration on Form G 49(8)(a).

See Precedent 4C.4 (p 52) FORM G 49(8)(b) FORM OF STATUTORY DECLARATION BY DIRECTORS AS TO MEMBERS' ASSENT TO RE-REGISTRATION OF A COMPANY AS UNLIMITED

(5) Complete application for re-registration on Form G 49(1) which, duly completed and accompanied by the documents listed thereon, is sent to the Registrar of Companies.

It will be noted that in addition to this form the special resolutions altering the memorandum and articles will have to be filed (see Chapter 14) and a print of the memorandum and articles as altered must accompany this form and details of the alterations entered on the reverse of the form.

See Precedent 4C.5 (p 53) FORM G 49(1) APPLICATION BY A LIMITED COMPANY TO BE RE-REGISTERED AS UNLIMITED

(6) Registrar of Companies will issue a certificate of re-registration. Re-registration is effective as from the date of that certificate.

Following re-registration the company will need to:

(1) Alter the name displayed at registered office and other places of business, notepaper and other documentation (see Chapter 5 and Precedent 4B.4).

(2) Adopt a new seal (if a seal is used) (see Chapter 13).

Precedent 4C.1

Minutes of the Directors to Commence Re-registration as Unlimited

It was resolved that it was in the best interests of the company to re-register as an unlimited company, and to alter its memorandum and articles accordingly.

The secretary was instructed to prepare and circulate forthwith a form of resolution in writing to be signed by every member of the company in lieu of a general meeting of the company, and to obtain requisite signatures on Forms G 49(1), G 49(8)(a) and G 49(8)(b).

Precedent 4C.2

Special Resolution to Make Requisite Alterations to Memorandum and Articles of Association

That the provisions of the memorandum of association set forth in the printed document produced to the meeting and for the purpose of identification signed by the Chairman thereof, be approved and that, with effect from the date of re-registration of the company as an unlimited company, the memorandum of association of the company be altered in accordance with the said printed document.

That the regulations set forth in the printed document produced to the meeting and for the purposes of identification signed by the Chairman thereof, be approved and, with effect from the date of re-registration of the company as an unlimited company, adopted as the articles of association of the company in substitution for and to the exclusion of the existing articles of association of the company.

EDITOR'S NOTES

(1) See Precedent 4C.5 for suitable alterations to memorandum and articles in this context.
(2) The note at the foot of the resolutions in Precedent 4A.3 should be included similarly in any notice of meeting at which a resolution to alter the memorandum and articles are proposed (as above).

Precedent 4C.3

Members' assent to company being re-registered as unlimited

Please do not write in this margin

Pursuant to section 49(8)(a) of the Companies Act 1985

Please complete legibly, preferably in black type, or bold block lettering

To the Registrar of Companies

For official use

Company number: 7 891 234

Name of company

* insert full name of company

* MORTON & CO LTD

We, being all the members of the company assent to the company being re-registered as unlimited

		Signature of member (or person lawfully authorised to sign on his behalf)
1 Full name of member	REGINALD MORTON	R Morton
Address	HOPPET HALL	
	HOBBS GATE	
	DILSBOROUGH, RUFFORDSHIRE	
2 Full name of member	GREGORY MASTERS	G Masters
Address	75 HIGH STREET	
	DILSBOROUGH	
	RUFFORDSHIRE	
3 Full name of member		
Address		
4 Full name of member		
Address		

Presentor's name address and reference (if any):

For official Use

General Section | Post room

Precedent 4C.4

Form of Statutory Declaration by directors as to members' assent to re-registration of a company as unlimited

Note. This form is not prescribed but has been prepared for those who wish to use it

Please do not write in this margin

Pursuant to section 49(8)(b) of the Companies Act 1985

Please complete legibly, preferably in black type, or bold block lettering

To the Registrar of Companies

For official use

Company number: 7 891 234

Name of company

* insert full name of company

* MORTON & CO LTD

I/We REGINALD MORTON

of HOPPET HALL HOBBS GATE DILSBOROUGH RUFFORDSHIRE

and GREGORY MASTERS

of 75 HIGH STREET DILSBOROUGH RUFFORDSHIRE

† delete as appropriate

~~[the sole director]~~ [all the directors]† of the above company do solemnly and sincerely declare

that the persons by whom or on whose behalf assent has been given on the attached Form No.49(8)(a) to the company being re-registered as unlimited constitute the whole membership of the company, and

that where any of these persons has not himself subscribed the form of assent, I/we have taken all reasonable steps to satisfy myself/ourselves that each person who subscribed it on behalf of a member was lawfully empowered to do so.

And I/we make this solemn declaration conscientiously believing the same to be true and by virtue of the provisions of the Statutory Declarations Act 1835

Declared at 75 HIGH STREET DILSBOROUGH

the ______ day of ______

one thousand nine hundred and ______

before me S Nickleson

A Commissioner for Oaths or Notary Public or Justice of the Peace or Solicitor having the powers conferred on a Commissioner for Oaths.

Declarant[s] to sign below

R Morton

G Masters

Presentor's name address and reference (if any):

For official Use

General Section

Post room

Precedent 4C.5

Application by a limited company to be re-registered as unlimited

Please do not write in this margin

Pursuant to section 49(1) of the Companies Act 1985

Please complete legibly, preferably in black type, or bold block lettering

To the Registrar of Companies

For official use

Company number: 7 891 234

* insert full name of company

Name of company

* MORTON & CO LTD

NOTE
Alterations in the memorandum and articles should be set out overleaf

applies to be re-registered as unlimited.

The following documents are attached in support of this application for the company to be re-registered as unlimited:

1. Signed assents by or on behalf of all the members of the company (Form No. 49(8)(a))
2. A statutory declaration made by the directors of the company in compliance with section 49(8)(b) of the above Act§
3. A printed copy of the company's memorandum incorporating the alterations set out overleaf
4. [A printed copy of the company's articles incorporating the alterations set out overleaf]†

§ a non-prescribed form of Statutory Declaration (Form No. 49(8)(b)) is available

Nominal share capital (if any) provided for in the articles as altered
£1,000

† delete as appropriate

Signed R Morton [Director]~~[Secretary]~~† Date 20 June 1990

Presentor's name address and reference (if any):

For official Use
General Section | Post room

Please do not write in this margin

Please complete legibly, preferably in block type, or bold block lettering

Alterations in the memorandum

1 HEADING
Deleting the words 'COMPANY LIMITED BY SHARES' and substituting the words 'UNLIMITED COMPANY HAVING A SHARE CAPITAL'.

2 SUB-HEADING
Deleting the word 'LIMITED' in the existing company name.

3 CLAUSE 1
Deleting the word 'LIMITED' in the existing company name.

4 CLAUSE 3
Deleting the existing objects of the company and substituting the objects set forth in the authenticated printed document adopted by special resolution.

5 CLAUSES 4 & 5 **
Deleted.

Alterations in the articles

1 HEADING
Deleting the words 'COMPANY LIMITED BY SHARES' and substituting the words 'UNLIMITED COMPANY HAVING A SHARE CAPITAL'.

2 SUB-HEADING
Deleting the word 'LIMITED' in the existing company name.

3 ARTICLES OF ASSOCIATION
Deleting the existing Regulations of the company and substituting the Regulations set forth in the authenticated printed document adopted by special resolution.

4 SECTION 49 AMENDMENTS
The following alterations are included in the adopted articles to comply with s 49 of the Companies Act 1985:

(a) Clause 2, regarding the share capital of the company;
(b) Clause 6, regarding the power of the company to alter its share capital, and the exclusion of Regulations 32, 34 and 35 in Table A.

** f/n

4D Re-registration of an Unlimited Company as a Private Limited Company

s 51 IA 1986, s 77 An unlimited company may re-register as a private limited company. Protection is given to creditors in a winding up within three years of the date of re-registration in respect of debts contracted by the company prior to that date.

s 51(2) A company originally formed with limited liability and subsequently re-registering as unlimited, cannot re-register back to limited status. An unlimited company which seeks to become a public limited company must first re-register as a private limited company and re-register again to public status.

The steps are as follows.

(1) Board meeting to approve and confirm arrangement.

See Precedent 4D.1 (p 56) MINUTES OF BOARD MEETING

(2) Extraordinary general meeting to pass special resolutions to re-register and make consequential alterations to the memorandum and articles of association. The re-registration resolution must state the manner in which liability is to be limited (ie by shares or by guarantee). Limitation by shares will be the usual course, in which case share capital must also be stated.

See Precedent 4D.2 (p 57) SPECIAL RESOLUTION TO RE-REGISTER AND MAKE CONSEQUENTIAL ALTERATIONS TO MEMORANDUM AND ARTICLES OF ASSOCIATION

(3) Complete application for re-registration (Form G 51) and send to the Registrar of Companies accompanied by printed copies of the memorandum and articles as altered.

See Precedent 4D.3 (p 58) FORM G 51 APPLICATION BY AN UNLIMITED COMPANY TO BE RE-REGISTERED AS LIMITED

(4) Registrar of Companies will issue a certificate of re-registration. Re-registration is effective from the date of the certificate.

Following re-registration the company will need to:

(1) Add the word 'limited' to the display of the company's name at its registered office, places of business, notepaper and other documentation including share certificates (see Chapter 5 and Precedent 4B.5).

(2) Adopt a new seal (if a seal is used) (see Chapter 13).

Precedent 4D.1

Minutes of Board Meeting

IT WAS RESOLVED that:

1. The company be re-registered with liability limited by shares.
2. The nominal share capital of the company remain unchanged at £1,000, divided into 1,000 ordinary shares of £1 each.
3. The changes to the memorandum and articles of association of the company, consequent upon this re-registration as set out in the print produced to the meeting, be approved for submission to shareholders.
4. An extraordinary general meeting of the company be called at which special resolutions be proposed to give effect to the re-registration and associated arrangements.
5. Upon such special resolutions being passed, an authority is given to any one director and the secretary to sign the application for re-registration to be submitted to the Registrar of Companies and take all steps necessary to carry the matter to completion.

* 6. It was resolved that the seal, an impression of which is placed below, be adopted as the new common seal of the company forthwith upon the date of issue by the Registrar to the company of a Certificate of Incorporation evidencing that the company is a limited company.

EDITOR'S NOTES

It is assumed in these precedents that no alteration is being made on the occasion of re-registration to the nominal share capital of the company or its classification.

* Include if a seal is adopted.

Precedent 4D.2

Special Resolution to Re-register and Make Consequential Alterations to Memorandum and Articles of Association

1. The company be re-registered as a company with liability limited by shares.
2. The memorandum and articles of association of the company be altered as necessary to give effect to limited liability and the documents produced to the meeting containing such amendments initialled by the chairman for purpose of identification be adopted as the memorandum and articles of association of the company with effect from the date of re-registration of the company with limited liability.

   [*The alterations to the memorandum and articles of association referred to in resolution 2 (above) will normally be as follows (although the wording will depend on the circumstances).*]

Alterations to the Memorandum

In Clause 1

The word 'Limited' be added to the name of the company.

The following additional clauses be added:

4. The liability of members is limited.

5. The company's share capital is £1,000 divided into 1,000 shares of £1 each.

Alterations to the Articles of Association*

EDITOR'S NOTES

* (1) In effect, Table A as amended by any special articles (apart from those in relation to unlimited liability) will be appropriate. Specifically, Clauses 2, 32, 34, and 35 in Table A, which will have been disapplied for the purpose of unlimited liability, will now be re-applied and the alteration usually made to alter 14 days' notice to seven days' notice in reg 38 of Table A.

  The standard clause in the articles of an unlimited company covering alterations to share capital (see Precedent 4C.5) must be deleted.

(2) The note at the foot of the resolutions in Precedent 4A.3 should be included similarly in any notice of meeting at which a resolution to alter the memorandum and articles are proposed (as above).

Precedent 4D.3

Application by an unlimited company to be re-registered as limited

Please do not write in this margin

Pursuant to section 51(4) of the Companies Act 1985

Please complete legibly, preferably in black type or, bold block lettering

To the Registrar of Companies

For official use

Company number: 8 234 567

Name of company

* insert full name of company

* BRAGTON ESTATE

applies to be re-registered as limited.

NOTE
If the company is to have a share capital the application should be accompanied by the appropriate Inland Revenue form PUC6 on which the capital duty has been paid, or a letter of dispensation

A Special Resolution authorising the re-registration of the company as limited was passed on 20 AUGUST 1990. The following documents are attached in support of this application for the company to be re-registered as limited

1 A copy of the Special Resolution (unless previously presented for registration)

2 A printed copy of the memorandum as altered in pursuance of the Special Resolution

3 A printed copy of the articles as altered in pursuance of the Special Resolution

Nominal share capital (if any) provided for in the memorandum as altered
£ 1,000

† delete as appropriate

Signed R Morton [Director]~~[Secretary]~~† Date 24 August 1990

Presentor's name address and reference (if any):

For official Use	
General Section	Post room

Chapter 5

SHARES AND SHARE CAPITAL

5A Allotment of Shares

Subscribers' shares

s 22
s 106 When a company is registered the subscribers to the memorandum of association (at least two) agree to take at least one share each in the company. On incorporation the subscribers become the first members of the company and are both entitled and bound to take the shares mentioned in the memorandum. The subscribers' shares should either be formally allotted or noted that they were subscribed at the first Board meeting. Subscribers' shares must be allotted for cash, if a public company, or cash or other consideration, if a private company.

Preconditions to allotment

Increase of authorised capital

s 121 Before any shares may be allotted the company must have unissued authorised capital sufficient to cover the allotment. The authorised capital is stated in the company's memorandum of association. If the authorised capital is not sufficient, it must be increased.

Table A, reg 32 This is done by an ordinary resolution in general meeting, or by written resolution, provided the company's articles permit this. (Table A does so.)

See Precedent 5A.1 (p 65) ORDINARY RESOLUTION TO INCREASE AUTHORISED CAPITAL

s 123 A copy of the resolution together with a Form G 123 must be filed with the Registrar of Companies within 15 days.

See Precedent 5A.2(1) (p 65) FORM G 123 NOTICE OF INCREASE IN NOMINAL CAPITAL

As the authorised capital is stated in the company's memorandum of association, a printed copy of the memorandum as altered must also be filed with the Registrar of Companies.

See Precedent 5A.2(2) (p 66) REPRINTED CLAUSE STATING ALTERED AUTHORISED SHARE CAPITAL

Authority to allot

s 80 It is for the company's directors to allot shares, but, apart from subscribers' shares, they may do so only to the extent that they are authorised by either the general meeting or the company's articles. Table A confers no such authority.

s 80A CA 1989, s 115 Whether the authority is conferred by the articles or the general meeting it must specify a maximum number of shares that may be allotted and must state either the date on which the authority expires or that it is of indefinite duration. Under the Companies Act 1985, such date must be not later than five years after the date of the resolution or when the articles become effective, which is the date of incorporation if within the original articles. By virtue of the Companies Act 1989, however, a private company may pass an elective resolution in general meeting or by written resolution to extend the authority either for a longer fixed period or indefinitely. See Chapter 14, Precedent 14C.7.

The authority to allot may be general or confined to a specific allotment, and may, but need not, impose conditions. The authority may be renewed or revoked at any time by ordinary resolution (even if in the articles), although not so as to invalidate an allotment already effected or any rights to shares already granted.

See Precedent 5A.3 (p 66) GENERAL MEETING RESOLUTION AUTHORISING DIRECTORS TO ALLOT SHARES

If the authorised share capital has to be increased, the resolutions to (a) increase capital and (b) authorise the directors to allot the shares, can be passed at the same meeting, but they should be passed in that order.

s 380 A copy of a resolution authorising the allotment of shares must be registered with the Registrar of Companies within 15 days.

An example of an authority included in the original articles of a company is to be found in Jordans standard articles of association for a private company (see Appendix 2).

Pre-emptive rights

Pre-emptive rights on allotment may arise by statute or under the company's memorandum and articles.

ss 89–96 The statutory pre-emptive rights apply to all allotments made wholly for cash unless these rights are (in a private company) excluded by, or are inconsistent with, the company's memorandum or articles, or are excluded by a special resolution, or the shares to be allotted are part of an employee share participation scheme.

See Precedent 5A.4 (p 67) PROVISION IN ARTICLES EXCLUDING PRE-EMPTIVE RIGHTS

s 91(2) A provision in the memorandum or articles containing a pre-emption scheme different from that in the Act will exclude the statutory scheme. Such a provision may be required where the share capital is divided into different classes.

See Precedent 5A.5 (p 67) (1) SPECIAL RESOLUTION TO EXCLUDE PRE-EMPTIVE RIGHTS FROM A PARTICULAR ALLOTMENT

(2) DIRECTORS' STATEMENT IN RECOMMENDATION

NB: Only statutory pre-emptive rights may be excluded or varied by special resolution.

Pre-emption provisions in the memorandum or articles may be varied only in accordance with their own terms, or by alteration of the memorandum or articles.

s 380 The special resolution in Precedent 5A.5(1) may be passed at the same meeting or in the same written resolution as any resolutions to increase authorised capital or confer authority to allot. Like all special resolutions, a copy must be sent to the Registrar of Companies within 15 days. If the resolution in Precedent 5A.5(1) is amended to exclude pre-emptive rights in relation only to one particular allotment, or is used in conjunction with a resolution which authorises the directors only to make one particular allotment of shares (see note (1) to Precedent 5A.3), such resolution cannot be proposed unless it is recommended by the directors and there is circulated with the notice of meeting a written
s 95(5) statement by the directors setting out:

(a) their reasons for the recommendations;
(b) the amount to be paid to the company in respect of the equity allotment;
(c) their justification of that amount (see Precedent 5A.5(2)).

ss 89–96 If the statutory pre-emptive rights are not excluded or varied by any of the above means, they will have to be complied with before the allotment is made. The company must offer, in writing, a number of shares to each shareholder, in proportion to the number of shares in the company already held by him. The offer only has to be made as nearly as is practicable and need not involve the offer of fractions of shares. The offer must state a latest date for acceptance of the shares, which must not be less than 21 days after delivery of the notice.

See Precedent 5A.6 (p 68) (1) NOTICE TO SHAREHOLDER OF PRE-EMPTIVE RIGHTS

(p 69) (2) SHAREHOLDER'S REPLY LETTER

Allotments for cash

The terms of payment for the shares will be fixed at the time at which they are offered. It is usual in a private company for the full amount to be payable on application or by a stated date. If, however, payment by instalments is proposed, or part of the consideration is to be left unpaid until called in by the directors, the shares are described as partly paid until the full amount, including any premium, has been received by the company.

s 100 Shares may not be allotted at a discount, ie at less than their nominal value. If this is
ss 130–134 attempted the shareholder becomes liable to pay the full nominal amount. If the price at which the shares are allotted is greater than their nominal value the excess is a premium and credited to the share premium account, which forms part of the non-distributable reserves of the company.

To summarise the procedures on allotment given above, before any shares may be allotted there must be sufficient unissued authorised capital, the directors must be authorised to allot shares and the statutory pre-emptive rights must either be excluded or modified (generally or for this particular issue) or followed, by making a rights issue in favour of existing shareholders.

Before embarking on such an allotment the secretary should check the memorandum and articles to ascertain the authorised capital, whether they contain any authority to the directors to allot shares and if the statutory pre-emptive rights have been excluded or modified. The company's minutes and statutory filing records should also be checked to see if any resolutions affecting these matters have been passed.

A typical procedure would involve:

(a) a first Board meeting to resolve that the increase in capital, share allotment and, if necessary, disapplication of pre-emptive rights, be put to the members, and that an extraordinary general meeting be called (the business could be conducted at an annual general meeting if convenient);
(b) an extraordinary general meeting called to pass all or some of the following:
    (i) ordinary resolution to increase authorised capital (see Precedent 5A.1 and Precedent 5A.2);
    (ii) elective resolution to permit directors' authority to allot to exceed five years (see Chapter 14, Precedent 14C.7);
    (iii) ordinary resolution to authorise directors to allot (see Precedent 5A.3);
    (iv) special resolution excluding pre-emptive rights (see Precedent 5A.4 and Precedent 5A.5);
(c) notice to the members of their pre-emptive rights (assuming the pre-emptive rights have not been excluded) (see Precedent 5A.6(1));
(d) having allowed sufficient time for the exercise of the pre-emptive rights and on receipt of the applications for the shares (and payment) a second Board meeting to resolve to allot the shares to the various applicants and issue share certificates;
(e) the issue of share certificates (see p 103), the completion of statutory registers (see Chapter 13) and the making of a return of allotments to the Registrar of Companies (see below).

While the above procedure appears cumbersome, in many private companies the general meeting may be held on short notice and, assuming there are no complications about pre-emptive rights, all the meetings may be held on the same day in rapid succession (see Chapter 14).

See Precedent 5A.7 (p 69) MINUTES OF FIRST BOARD MEETING TO CONSIDER ALLOTMENT OF SHARES

See Precedent 5A.8 (p 70) RESOLUTIONS FOR THE GENERAL MEETING TO INCREASE AUTHORISED SHARE CAPITAL AND GIVE DIRECTORS GENERAL AUTHORITY TO ALLOT

See Precedent 5A.9 (p 71) MINUTES OF SECOND BOARD MEETING – ALLOTMENT OF SHARES

Return of allotments

A return of allotments must be filed with the Registrar of Companies within one month of allotment on the prescribed form. No capital duty is payable. If there is any provision for renunciation of the shares by the allottees this return will be completed at the end of the renunciation period with the list finalised showing the names and shares taken by the renouncees as opposed to the original allottees who have renounced. See further the section on 'Renunciation of shares' in Chapter 5B (at p 84).

See Precedent 5A.10 (p 73) FORM G 88(2) RETURN OF ALLOTMENTS OF SHARES

Notification by director of interest in shares

s 324 A director must notify the company of any interest he has in the shares or debentures of that company or a related company, or of any change in such interest, within five days (see Chapter 10). A notification must be made if any additional shares are allotted so as to add to an existing disclosure.

Allotments for consideration other than cash

When shares are allotted wholly or partly for consideration other than cash the procedure is the same as that for a cash allotment, except:

s 89 (a) the statutory pre-emptive rights of existing members do not apply. (Pre-emptive rights in the company's articles will depend on their terms);

(b) care must be taken if the allottee is a director or connected with a director as the rules relating to contracts in which directors have an interest may apply (see Chapter 10);

s 88(3) (c) parts D and E of the return of allotments (Form G 88(2)) must be completed and this must be accompanied by either a copy of the contract, under which the assets are transferred, or, if there is no such contract, Form G 88(3);

(d) stamp duty may be payable on the contract to transfer the assets to the company and there may be legal formalities on such transfer, on which professional advice should be sought. This transfer of assets may require separate documentation (eg a share transfer form for the transfer of shares in another company so acquired) in which case this other document will be subject to stamp duty and duty will not be paid on Form G 88(3). The Certificate of Value at the foot of Form G 88(3) requires completion (if applicable). The figure entered is the amount on which duty is payable.

See Precedent 5A.11 (p 75) FORM G 88(3) PARTICULARS OF A CONTRACT RELATING TO SHARES ALLOTTED AS FULLY OR PARTLY PAID UP OTHERWISE THAN IN CASH

Bonus issues

The bonus or capitalisation issue of shares is a method of aligning the share capital of the company more closely to its net assets by converting reserves into share capital.

Professional advice is necessary in relation to the reserves utilised for such purposes and the associated effects. The following precedents cover the procedures and assume that the Table A, reg 110 articles of association apply Table A or contain the requisite enabling powers similar to Table A and there is adequate unissued authorised share capital for the purpose.

A bonus issue is treated for most purposes as an allotment of shares for non-cash consideration and this section should be read in conjunction with the section above, 'Allotments for consideration other than cash'.

The directors will first determine that reserves be capitalised by a bonus issue and the appropriate resolution be put to shareholders.

See Precedent 5A.12 (p 78) DIRECTORS' MINUTE TO CONVENE EGM TO DECLARE BONUS ISSUE

The resolution will be proposed as an ordinary resolution unless otherwise provided in the articles.

See Precedent 5A.13 (p 78) ORDINARY RESOLUTION TO CREATE BONUS ISSUE

This precedent assumes that the share capital of the company consists of one class of equity shares. If there is more than one class of shares the class(es) to receive bonus shares must be specified and it must be ensured that the respective rights of each class under the articles are correctly treated.

The precedent also assumes that the bonus issue is made from distributable revenue reserves and gives alternative wording if share premium or capital reserves are to be utilised. If such exist they should be used.

As with any other issue of shares it is important to make clear what dividend and other rights attach to the newly allotted shares. The phrase 'pari passu in all respects with existing shares' means there will be no difference between old and new shares and new shares will carry the right in full to all dividends subsequently declared, regardless of the accounting period to which they relate.

After the ordinary resolution has been passed the directors will meet to allot the bonus shares in accordance with the resolution.

See Precedent 5A.14 (p 79) MINUTES OF DIRECTORS' MEETING TO ALLOT SHARES ON A BONUS ISSUE

A certified copy of the ordinary resolution declaring the bonus issue and Forms G 88(2) and G 88(3) must be filed with the Registrar of Companies.

See Precedent 5A.15 (p 80) ENTRIES ON FORMS G 88(2) AND G 88(3) IN CIRCUMSTANCES OF A BONUS ISSUE

If so desired, provision may be made for the allottees of bonus shares to renounce them (see Precedent 5B.3).

Precedent 5A.1

Ordinary Resolution to Increase Authorised Capital

That the capital of the company be increased from £1,000 to £100,000 by the creation of 99,000 new shares of £1 each to rank pari passu in all respects with the existing shares in the capital of the company.

Precedent 5A.2(1)

Notice of increase in nominal capital

123

Please do not write in this margin

Pursuant to section 123 of the Companies Act 1985

Please complete legibly, preferably in black type, or bold block lettering

To the Registrar of Companies

For official use

Company number: 9 236 452

Name of company

* insert full name of company

BILLBROOK ENTERPRISES LIMITED

gives notice in accordance with section 123 of the above Act that by resolution of the company dated 24 JULY 1990 the nominal capital of the company has been increased by £ 99,000 beyond the registered capital of £ 1,000.

A copy of the resolution authorising the increase is attached.§

§ the copy must be printed or in some other form approved by the registrar

The conditions (eg. voting rights, dividend rights, winding-up rights etc.) subject to which the new shares have been or are to be issued are as follow:

RANKING IN ALL RESPECTS PARI PASSU WITH THE 1,000 EXISTING SHARES OF £1 EACH IN THE CAPITAL OF THE COMPANY.

‡ Insert Director, Secretary, Administrator, Administrative Receiver or Receiver (Scotland) as appropriate

Please tick here if continued overleaf ☐

Signed J. F. Runciman Designation‡ Director Date 24 JULY 1990

Precedent 5A.2(2)

Reprinted Clause Stating Altered Authorised Share Capital

5.* The share capital of the company is [100,000] shares of £1 each.

* Following resolution passed [24 July 1990].

EDITOR'S NOTE

This altered clause may be typed separately and pasted over the original clause and a copy of the memorandum so amended will be filed with the Registrar of Companies.

Precedent 5A.3

General Meeting Resolution Authorising Directors to Allot Shares

THAT the directors be and they are hereby generally and unconditionally authorised pursuant to s 80 of the Companies Act 1985 to exercise any power of the company to allot and grant rights to subscribe for or to convert securities into shares of the company up to a maximum nominal amount [equal to the nominal amount of the authorised but unissued share capital at the date of the passing of this resolution] (1) provided that the authority hereby given shall expire [five years] (2) after the passing of this resolution unless previously renewed or varied [save that the directors may, notwithstanding such expiry, allot any shares or grant any such rights under this authority in pursuance of an offer or agreement so to do made by the company before the expiry of this authority] (3).

EDITOR'S NOTES

(1) A specific amount may be inserted in place of the words in square brackets, eg '. . . of £10,000', but care should be taken to comply with s 95(5) of the Companies Act 1985 if such a resolution is coupled with a special resolution to exclude pre-emptive rights.
(2) A period less, but not more than, five years may be inserted. An elective resolution to authorise allotments during a period of more than five years or for an indefinite period may be passed. See Chapter 14, Precedent 14C.7.
(3) These words may be deleted or other conditions attached.

Precedent 5A.4

Provision in Articles Excluding Pre-emptive Rights

In accordance with s 91(1) of the Companies Act 1985, ss 89(1) and 90(1) to (6) (inclusive) of the Act (relating to shareholders' rights of pre-emption on the allotment of shares) shall not apply to the company.

Precedent 5A.5

(1) Special Resolution to Exclude Pre-emptive Rights from a Particular Allotment

'That in accordance with s 95 of the Companies Act 1985, s 89(1) of that Act shall not apply to the allotment of equity securities pursuant to the general authority given for the purposes of s 80 of that Act [in resolution 2 above]* and the directors may allot, grant options over or otherwise dispose of such shares to such persons, on such terms and in such manner as they see fit for as long as this resolution shall have effect.'

EDITOR'S NOTE

* See Precedent 5A.3.

(2) Directors' Statement in Recommendation*

[A draft note covering the disapplication of pre-emptive rights on issue of equity shares pursuant to Companies Act 1985, s 95(5).]

Notice is enclosed for a special resolution to be proposed on the recommendation of the directors to exclude the rights of shareholders to subscribe pre-emptively for the 20,000 ordinary shares of £1 each in the capital of the company which it is proposed to issue.

The proposal is to issue these shares which will represent 20 per cent of the capital of the company to XYZ Ltd who specialise in the provision of long-term capital to private companies. This issue of ordinary shares is part of a larger transaction in which XYZ Ltd will provide the company with a loan at a fixed rate of interest for a term of 15 years secured on its fixed assets.

The shares will be issued at a premium of 50p per share which will equate the issue price with the net assets' value after the issue has been made.

EDITOR'S NOTE

* This is an outline of the form that such a statement might take. Of course, it must be related to the specific circumstances.

Precedent 5A.6

(1) Notice to Shareholder of Pre-emptive Rights

To [shareholder's name and address]

RIGHTS ISSUE OF ORDINARY SHARES

Dear Sir or Madam,

Your directors have decided to issue ordinary shares of £ each by way of a rights issue and you have been provisionally allotted the number of new ordinary shares set out against your name in box 2 below. Allotments have been made to ordinary shareholders on the register at the close of business on [*date*] in the proportion of one new ordinary share for every ordinary share(s) then held. You have the right to subscribe for these shares at a price of £ per new ordinary share payable in full on acceptance not later than am/pm on [*date*]. The new shares will rank pari passu in all respects with the existing issued ordinary shares.

If you wish to accept all the new ordinary shares provisionally allotted to you this letter must be returned to the secretary of the company at the above address, accompanied by a remittance for the full amount shown in box 3 below and Section A [*overleaf*] completed, to arrive not later than am/pm on [*date*]. Such remittance when received will constitute acceptance of this provisional allotment in accordance with the terms hereof and subject to the memorandum and articles of association of the company. If this letter is not so returned, with cheque attached, the provisional allotment will be deemed to have been declined and will lapse.

Any new ordinary shares not taken up by am/pm on [*date*] will be offered at the same price as the present offer to those members who have taken up those shares. Please indicate below whether you wish to take advantage of any such additional offer by completing section (B) below.

Yours faithfully

Chairman

1	2	3
EXISTING SHAREHOLDING	NEW SHARES PROVISIONALLY ALLOTTED	AMOUNT PAYABLE FOR PROVISIONAL ALLOTMENT £

(2) Shareholder's Reply Letter

To the Directors of Limited

Section A

In reply to your letter dated [*date*] I hereby agree to take the shares provisionally allotted to me and enclose herewith payment of the full allotment price mentioned in that letter.

Section B

I hereby apply for the right to subscribe for any additional shares which may become available up to a maximum of ordinary shares of £1 each at the offer price.

Yours faithfully

Precedent 5A.7

Minutes of First Board Meeting to Consider Allotment of Shares

Present:

In attendance: Secretary
Auditors

It was resolved to convene an extraordinary general meeting to be held on [*date*] to consider the following:

(1) to increase the authorised share capital of the company from £ to £ by the creation of shares of £1 each, ranking pari passu in all respects with the existing share capital of the company;

(2) to authorise the directors generally and unconditionally to allot all or any such shares at any time during the five years after the date of the meeting;

(3) to pass a special resolution under s 95 of the Companies Act 1985 exempting any allotment of shares from application of the statutory pre-emptive rights under s 89 of the Companies Act 1985.

The appropriate notice to convene such a meeting was produced by the secretary and was approved.

Precedent 5A.8

Resolutions for the General Meeting to Increase Authorised Share Capital and Give Directors General Authority to Allot

ORDINARY RESOLUTIONS:

1. THAT the capital of the company be increased from £[1,000] to £[100,000] by the creation of [99,000] shares of £1 each to rank pari passu in all respects with the existing shares in the capital of the company.

2. THAT the directors be and they are hereby generally and unconditionally authorised pursuant to s 80 of the Companies Act 1985 to exercise any power of thc company to allot and grant rights to subscribe for or to convert securities into shares of the company up to a maximum nominal amount equal to the nominal amount of the authorised but unissued share capital at the date of the passing of this resolution. Provided that the authority hereby given shall expire five years after the passing of this resolution unless previously renewed or varied save that the directors may, notwithstanding such expiry, allot any shares or grant any such rights under this authority in pursuance of an offer or agreement so to do made by the company before the expiry of this authority.

EDITOR'S NOTE

This precedent combines Precedents 5A.1 and 5A.3. It is given in this form so as to set out, with 5A.7 and 5A.8, a complete procedure.
See notes to 5A.3 in respect of Resolution 2.

Precedent 5A.9

Minutes of Second Board Meeting – Allotment of Shares

Minutes of a second meeting of the Board of Directors held on the day of 19

Present:

In attendance: Secretary
Auditor

(FIRST ALTERNATIVE)

The secretary reported that the extraordinary general meeting held immediately prior to this meeting had passed the ordinary and special resolutions recommended by the Board and that the following persons had applied for £1 ordinary shares in the company, as set against each person's name:

NAME	NO OF SHARES
1.	
2.	
3.	

Those persons were all present and paid in full for the respective shares.

Accordingly, it was resolved that these shares should be allotted, ranking pari passu in all respects with the existing ordinary shares in issue and credited as fully paid and the secretary was to issue share certificates to those persons for their respective shares and to file with the Registrar of Companies copies of the ordinary and special resolutions and Forms G 123 and G 88(2).

(SECOND ALTERNATIVE)

Pursuant to the offer to allot additional shares in the capital of the company in accordance with Minute it was reported that applications had been received for shares set out in the Register of Applications produced to the meeting. It was therefore resolved that a total of ordinary shares be and are hereby allotted at [a price of £ per share inclusive of premium] [par]* to the persons listed in the aforesaid Register of Applications initialled by the chairman for identification, each respectively taking the number of shares entered against their name.

[These shares will rank for dividends declared in respect of the accounting period ending   but not for any earlier distributions.]*

[These shares will rank pari passu in all respects with the existing share capital of the company.]*

EDITOR'S NOTE

* As applicable. It is important to be precise about first entitlement to dividend.

Precedent 5A.10

Return of allotments of shares

88(2)

Pursuant to section 88(2) of the Companies Act 1985 (the Act)

Please do not write in this margin

(REVISED 1988)
This form replaces forms PUC2, PUC3 and 88(2)

To the Registrar of Companies **(address overleaf)** (see note 1)

Please complete legibly, preferably in black type, or bold block lettering

Company Number: 9 236 452

1. Name of company

* insert full name of company

• BILLBROOK ENTERPRISES LTD

2. This section must be completed for all allotments

† distinguish between ordinary preference, etc.

Descriptions of shares†	ORDINARY		
A Number allotted	10,000		
B Nominal value of each	£1	£	£
C Total amount (if any) paid or due and payable on each share (including premium if any)	£ 1.50	£	£

§ complete (a) or (b) as appropriate

Date(s) on which the shares were allotted

(a) [on 20 JULY 19 90]§, or

~~(b) [from 19 to 19]§~~

The names and addresses of the allottees and the number of shares allotted to each should be given overleaf

3. If the allotment is wholly or partly other than for cash the following information must be given **(see notes 2 & 3)**

D Extent to which each share is to be treated as paid up. Please use percentage.	100%		

E Consideration for which the shares were allotted: acquisition of share capital of Mary's Market (Dilsborough) Ltd from the allottee

NOTES

1. This form should be delivered to the Registrar of Companies within one month of the (first) date of allotment.

2. If the allotment is wholly or partly other than for cash, the company must deliver to the registrar a return containing the information at D & E. The company may deliver this information by completing D & E and the delivery of the information must be accompanied by the duly stamped contract required by section 88(2)(b) of the Act or by the duly stamped prescribed particulars required by section 88(3) (Form No 88(3)).

3. Details of bonus issues should be included only in section 2.

Presentor's name address, telephone number and reference (if any):

For official Use | Post Room

4. Names and addresses of the allottees

Please do not write in the margin

Please complete legibly, preferably in black type, or bold block lettering

Names and Addresses	Number of shares allotted		
	Ordinary	Preference	Other
REGINALD MORTON	10,000		
HOPPET HALL			
HOBBS GATE			
DILSBOROUGH			
RUFFORDSHIRE			
Total	10,000		

Where the space given on this form is inadequate, continuation sheets should be used and the number of sheets attached should be indicated in the box opposite:

‡ Insert, Director, Secretary, Administrator, Administrative Receiver or Receiver (Scotland) as appropriate.

Signed J. F. Runciman Designation‡ DIRECTOR Date 20 JULY 1990

Companies registered in England and Wales or Wales should deliver this form to:-

The Registrar of Companies
Companies House
Crown Way
Maindy
Cardiff
CF4 3UZ

Companies registered in Scotland should deliver this form to:-

The Registrar of Companies
Companies Registration Office
102 George Street
Edinburgh
EH2 3DJ

Precedent 5A.11

Particulars of a contract relating to shares allotted as fully or partly paid up otherwise than in cash

Pursuant to section 88(3) of the Companies Act 1985

Please do not write in this margin

Note: This form is only for use when the contract has not been reduced to writing

Please complete legibly, preferably in black type, or bold block lettering

To the Registrar of Companies

For official use

Company number: 9 236 452

Please do not write in the space below. For Inland Revenue use only

The particulars must be stamped with the same stamp duty as would have been payable if the contract had been reduced to writing. A reduced rate of ad valorem duty may be available if this form is properly certified at the appropriate amount.

Name of company

* insert full name of company

* BILLBROOK ENTERPRISES LTD

gives the following particulars of a contract which has not been reduced to writing

1 The number of shares allotted as fully or partly paid up otherwise than in cash	10,000
2 The nominal value of each such share	£1
3a The amount of such nominal value to be considered as paid up on each share otherwise than in cash	£10,000
b The value of each share allotted i.e. the nominal value and any premium	£1.50
c The amount to be considered as paid up in respect of b	£15,000
4 If the consideration for the allotment of such shares is services, or any consideration other than that mentioned below in 8, state the nature and amount of such consideration, and the number of shares allotted	N/A

Presentor's name address and reference (if any):

For official Use

Capital Section | Post room

5 If the allotment is a bonus issue, state the amount of reserves capitalised in respect of this issue	£	

6 If the allotment is made in consideration of the release of a debt, e.g., a director's loan account, state the amount released	£	

7 If the allotment is made in connection with the conversion of loan stock, state the amount of stock converted in respect of this issue	£	

8 If the allotment is made in satisfaction or part satisfaction of the purchase price of property, give below:

a brief description of property:

THE WHOLE OF THE ISSUED SHARE CAPITAL OF
MARY'S MARKET (DILSBOROUGH) LTD

b *full particulars of the manner in which the purchase price is to be satisfied*	£	p
Amount of consideration payable in cash or bills	15,000	
Amount of consideration payable in debentures, etc......		
Amount of consideration payable in shares		
Liabilities of the vendor assumed by the purchaser:		
Amounts due on mortgages of freeholds and/or leaseholds including interest to date of sale		
Hire purchase etc debts in respect of goods acquired ...		
Other liabilities of the vendor,..		
Any other consideration		
	15,000	

Please do not write in this margin

9 Give full particulars in the form of the following table, of the property which is the subject of the sale, showing in detail how the total purchase price is apportioned between the respective heads:

	£
Legal estates in freehold property and fixed plant and machinery and other fixtures thereon*	
Legal estates in leasehold property*	
Fixed plant and machinery on leasehold property (including tenants', trade and other fixtures)	
Equitable interests in freehold or leasehold property*	
Loose plant and machinery, stock-in-trade and other chattels (plant and machinery should not be included under this head unless it was in actual state of severance on the date of the sale)	
Goods, wares and merchandise subject to hire purchase or other agreements (written down value)	
Goodwill and benefit of contracts	
Patents, designs, trademarks, licences, copyrights, etc.	
Book and other debts	
Cash in hand and at bank on current account, bills, notes, etc	
Cash on deposit at bank or elsewhere	
Shares, debentures and other investments	15,000
Other property	
	15,000

* Where such properties are sold subject to mortgage, the gross value should be shown

‡ Insert Director, Secretary, Administrator, Administrative Receiver or Receiver (Scotland) as appropriate

Signed Designation‡ Date

Certificate of value§

§ This certificate must be signed by the persons to whom the shares have been allotted, as well as by an officer of the company.

It is certified that the transaction effected by the contract does not form part of a larger transaction or series of transactions in respect of which the amount or value, or aggregate amount or value, of the consideration exceeds £15,000

Signed J. F. Runciman Date 20/7/90

Signed R Morton Date 20/7/90

Precedent 5A.12

Directors' Minute to Convene EGM to Declare Bonus Issue

It was resolved to convene an extraordinary general meeting of the company forthwith to declare a bonus issue of one share for every five shares already held.

The appropriate notice to convene such a meeting on [*date*] was produced by the secretary and was approved.

Precedent 5A.13

Ordinary Resolution to Create Bonus Issue

THAT upon the recommendation of the directors the sum of £20,000* being part of the accumulated revenue reserves, be capitalised and appropriated as capital to and among the holders of the 10,000 shares of £1 each in the capital of the company as appearing in the Register of Members as at the close of business on [*date*] and that the directors be authorised and directed to apply such sum in paying up in full 10,000 shares of £1 each in the capital of the company and to allot and distribute such new shares, credited as fully paid, to and among the holders of the shares at the rate of [one] such new share(s) for every [ten] existing share(s) held by them.**

EDITOR'S NOTES

* If other than revenue reserves are utilised add appropriately 'being as to £ the [capital redemption reserve] [share premium account] and as to £ part of the accumulated revenue reserve'.

** This assumes the bonus entitlement is exactly allottable. If this is not so, add the following: [or as near as may be and any unallotted fractions of shares be allotted to the secretary to be sold as may be determined by the directors for the benefit of those shareholders entitled to them].

Precedent 5A.14

Minutes of Directors' Meeting to Allot Shares on Bonus Issue

1. The Secretary reported that at an extraordinary general meeting of the company, held immediately before this meeting, the following ordinary resolution had been passed:

[*here set out resolution.*]

2. It was thereupon resolved:

(a) that pursuant to the authority given by and the directions contained in that resolution, the sum of £20,000 therein referred to be capitalised and appropriated as therein set out;

(b) that 20,000 shares of £1 each credited as fully paid up be and they are hereby allotted ranking pari passu in all respects with the existing issued shares to the persons and in the amounts set out below.

NAME	PRESENT HOLDING	ALLOTMENT
(i) .... (ii)		

All shareholders indicated that they wished to accept their entitlement to the fully paid bonus shares allotted to them.

3. Accordingly the secretary was instructed to arrange the issue of share certificates for the shares so allotted and to file Forms G 88(2) and G 88(3) together with a copy of the ordinary resolution with the Registrar of Companies.

Precedent 5A.15

Entries on Forms G 88(2) and G 88(3) in Circumstances of a Bonus Issue

The completion of these forms is described in Precedent 5A.11 and Precedent 5A.12. The following specific entries will be made in the circumstances of a bonus issue.

Form G 88(2)

Although the allotment of bonus shares is wholly other than cash, box 3 should be left blank as instructed in note 3 of the Form.

Form G 88(3)

Since bonus shares are not allotted at a premium, 3(b) will be the nominal value of the share and 3(c) will be the nominal amount of the share capital allotted.

Box 5 will be completed as follows:

5 If the allotment is a bonus issue, state the amount of reserves capitalised in respect of this issue	£20,000	

No entries will be made in boxes 6 to 9 nor is it necessary to complete the certificate of value.

5B Transfer and Transmission of Shares

Transfer of shares

The transfer of shares is accomplished by the use of a standard form of stock transfer.

See Precedent 5B.1 (p 86) STOCK TRANSFER FORM

It is important that this form is accurately and exactly completed and particularly in respect of:

(a) the name of the company and the exact description of the shares;
(b) the name(s) of the transferor(s) which must correspond with those in the company's share register which will be evidenced by the transferor's share certificate;
(c) the name(s) of the transferee(s) which together with their address(es) will be entered in the company's share register on completion of the transaction.

This form must be signed by the transferor and, if it is in respect of a joint holding, by all joint holders. If a joint holder has died the death certificate must be registered before the holding is transferred (see page 83).

If the shares are not fully paid the form must also be signed by the transferee(s) to show acceptance of liability to meet the unpaid amount on the shares (in which case use the alternative form with provision for this – Jordans form J10).

The amount for which the shares are being sold must be entered under 'consideration money'.

If the transaction does not involve a sale, the entry should be 'NIL' and if necessary the appropriate certificate on the reverse of the form completed to claim the relevant stamp duty exemption (see *Jordans Secretarial Administration*, at FP 3.14).

In the 1990 budget statement it was indicated that stamp duty on transactions in shares would be abolished in 1991–92. Until such time the secretary of the company is responsible under the Stamp Act 1891 for ensuring that any transfer is duly stamped or exempted before it is registered and in particular if it is a transfer for value, stamp duty has been paid *ad valorem* on the price paid.

All stamping must be by Stamp Office impressed stamps (see *Jordans Secretarial Administration*, at § 3.19.2).

A share certificate covering the shares to be transferred should be attached to the stock transfer form, duly stamped and sent to the secretary of the company for registration.

If shares of more than one class registered in the same name are to be transferred, a separate form should be completed for each class.

Subject to the operation of any restrictive share transfer clause in the company's articles, or other bar on transfer such as a stop notice (see below), the secretary will enter the transfer in the transfer register.

This register is not required to be kept by law, but is an essential record behind the Register of Members. Its entries are self explanatory, but unless the secretary has been given a general authority to accept transfers within the terms of the articles he will first submit them to a Board meeting or appropriately constituted committee of directors.

The transfer, when approved for registration, will be recorded in the Register of Members. It is entry in this Register that makes the transferee a member of the company. See Chapter 5C for details of this Register.

See Precedent 5B.2 (pp 88–90) SPECIMEN PAGES OF REGISTER OF TRANSFERS AND REGISTER OF MEMBERS

A new share certificate is then issued to the transferee(s) for the shares acquired. See Chapter 5C.

The old share certificate should be filed away marked 'Cancelled' and the date of cancellation noted thereon.

If the certificate(s) tendered by the transferor are for a greater number of shares than that transferred, a certificate for the balance will be issued to him.

In the case of a new holding a dividend mandate may also be lodged, in which case it must be suitably recorded in the Register of Members.

Restrictions on share transfers

Table A, reg 24

If there are no restrictions in the memorandum and articles of the company then shares are freely transferable and the transferee is entitled to be registered as a member in respect of the shares. The only restriction in the 1985 version of Table A is in reg 24, which applies only to partly paid shares or where the company is in a position to exercise a lien on them. Earlier versions of Table A contain a restriction on transfer in the following terms (applicable to private companies only):

> 'The directors may, in their absolute discretion and without assigning any reason therefor, decline to register the transfer of any share, whether or not it is a fully paid share.'

Many companies are still operating under the Table A articles they adopted when this version was current and so will still have this restriction as an operative provision.

Private companies incorporated since 1985 with Table A based articles will not automatically have this restriction, but very many of them will have included it specifically in their articles. Jordans standard articles for a private company include this restriction (see Appendix 2, at p 391).

Even if the company has the provision set out above it should be noted that the transfer of the shares will be registrable unless the directors resolve to decline it within two months.

See Precedent 5B.3 (p 91) (1) RESOLUTION OF THE BOARD TO DECLINE TO REGISTER A SHARE TRANSFER
(2) LETTER TO SHAREHOLDER DECLINING REGISTRATION OF TRANSFER

Three examples of more elaborate restrictions on transfer can be found in Appendix 2 (at pp 392–399), as variations on Jordans standard articles for a private company. Typical elements in such provisions are:

(a) unrestricted transfer right to the shareholders' relatives or to beneficiaries under a family trust (see Transfer Article A);
(b) pre-emption rights in favour of existing members of the company (see Transfer Article B); or

(c) some combination of these, together with other provisions (see Transfer Article C).

The secretary must take great care to see that any such provision in the articles is met before a transfer is registered.

Stop notice

A stop notice is an order by the court, made on the application of a person claiming an interest in the shares. It will contain instructions from the court to the company requiring it to notify the person named in the order in the event that any request is made to transfer the shares, and to wait for seven days before registering the transfer. If such a notice is received the company secretary must ensure that the notice is endorsed against the appropriate page in the Register of Members, that a copy of the order is retained with the Register, and that the instructions in it are followed if any request for a transfer of the shares is made before the order is revoked.

See Precedent 5B.4 (p 92) NOTICE TO SERVER OF A STOP NOTICE

Death of a shareholder

Following the death of a shareholder the grant of probate or letters of administration evidencing who are his personal representatives should be exhibited to the company.

The company secretary will check that the document submitted, if a photocopy, is duly authenticated by a solicitor or other responsible person, annotate the share register and (after making a copy of the documents to keep in the company's file of registered documents) return it to the person who has lodged it, endorsed with a note that it has been exhibited to the company.

See Precedent 5B.5 (p 93) RECORD IN SHARE REGISTER OF GRANT OF PROBATE

If the deceased shareholder's share certificate(s) is (are) also submitted, a similar endorsement to that in the share register will be made on the certificate(s).

In respect of very small estates it is not obligatory to obtain probate or letters of administration. In such circumstances the secretary should obtain an appropriate statutory declaration and indemnity.

See Precedent 5B.6 (p 94) STATUTORY DECLARATION BY NEXT OF KIN IN A SMALL ESTATE

See Precedent 5B.7 (p 95) INDEMNITY BY NEXT OF KIN IN A SMALL ESTATE

Death of a shareholder in joint account

Only the personal representative named in the grant of probate or letters of administration can deal with a shareholding in the sole name of a deceased person. The holding is frozen until they have lodged the grant or letters with the company.

If, however, a shareholder in a joint account dies, the remaining shareholder(s) is (are) entitled to deal with the shares. In such circumstances it is only necessary for the company secretary to see the death certificate of the deceased shareholder, that should be dealt with in a similar fashion to a grant of probate.

See Precedent 5B.8 (p 96) RECORD IN SHARE REGISTER OF DEATH OF A SHAREHOLDER IN A JOINT ACCOUNT

If the share certificate has also been forwarded to the company it should be annotated similarly.

Any new share certificate in respect of the holding will be in the sole name(s) of the surviving shareholder(s).

Transmission

Registration of a grant of probate or letters of administration is only evidence of the identity of those entitled to act in the place of the deceased. It does not make the personal representatives shareholders in the company. This is effected by transmission of the shareholding.

Table A, regs 29–31 The personal representative can elect either to be registered as the shareholder or to have some other person nominated by him registered. In the former case the personal representative must give notice in writing requesting registration.

See Precedent 5B.9 (p 97) LETTER OF REQUEST FOR TRANSMISSION

If the personal representative elects to have some other person registered he should execute a stock transfer form in the usual way, signing as personal representative of the deceased shareholder. See Precedent 5B.1 for a stock transfer form.

Table A, reg 30 It should be noted that all the articles relating to a transfer of shares apply equally to a request for registration or a stock transfer executed by a personal representative. This includes any restrictions on transfer, and may cause problems for the personal representatives, especially if the articles give the directors an absolute discretion to refuse. Some articles include a provision which permits the directors to penalise personal representatives who do not either request to be registered or execute a stock transfer form, by withholding dividends and other financial benefits. It should be noted that such a provision is contained in the 1948 version of Table A (which many companies still have) but is not in the 1985 version.

No stamp duty is payable either on the request by the personal representatives to be registered as members or on a transfer of shares executed by personal representatives on behalf of the deceased. If the personal representatives elect to have the shares registered in their names, any subsequent transfer will bear stamp duty until such time as the duty is abolished (see p 81 above).

See p 82 above for restrictions on transfers.

Renunciation of shares

The directors may decide to give a right of renunciation to shareholders receiving an entitlement to shares under a rights or bonus issue. The following precedents deal with the procedures for the renunciation of shares in a private company.

FSA 1986, s 170 1. A private company is prohibited from offering its shares or debentures to the public. If shareholders are given the right to renounce their shares, this right may, unless restricted, result in a breach of this prohibition.

The definition of 'offers to the public' includes offering securities to the public at large and 'to any section of the public' (see *Gore-Browne on Companies*, at § 10.9). This is a very wide provision, but the offer is to be deemed to be the domestic concern of the maker and the recipient, if it is made to a member, employee or debenture holder of the company or their families, unless it is proved to the contrary.

Extreme care should be taken not to breach these provisions, otherwise both the company and its officers are guilty of a serious offence.

2. Any restriction on the transfer of shares should also be specifically attached to a right of renunciation.

3. Renunciations will be subject to stamp duty (or stamp duty reserve tax) as appropriate, until such duty on the transfer of shares is abolished (see note above).

The minutes of the directors' meeting following the shareholders' resolutions giving effect to the share issue will provide for the issue of renounceable letters of allotment.

See Precedent 5B.10 (p 98) DIRECTORS' MINUTES TO ISSUE RENOUNCEABLE LETTERS OF ALLOTMENT

This resolution must carefully state the last date upon which renunciation may be made and in the case of a rights issue whether renunciation can be made of shares prior to payment for them (nil paid) or only when fully paid. In a private company with a relatively small number of shareholders it is simpler to restrict the right to renounce to nil paid shares, which will probably be the most convenient for shareholders. Bonus shares require no payment and will always be renounced fully paid.

See Precedent 5B.11 (p 99) LETTER OF ALLOTMENT AND FORMS OF RENUNCIATION AND REGISTRATION FOR BONUS ISSUE

FA 1986, s 86 Stamp duty reserve tax is payable by renouncees on any renounced letter of allotment at the same rate and subject to the same exemptions as share transfer tax. The secretary should ensure renunciations are duly stamped prior to registration.

At the end of the renunciation period the directors will proceed to approve renunciations and make allotment as in a rights or bonus issue (Precedent 5A.9 and Precedent 5A.10) but the minutes will be amended to cover renunciation.

See Precedent 5B.12 (p 100) DIRECTORS' MINUTE APPROVING RENUNCIATIONS

Renunciations will be recorded in the Register of Allotments as an allotment to the renouncees. Form G 88(2) (Precedent 5A.10) is usually completed with the names and entitlement of the renouncees rather than those of the original allottees.

The above precedents provide for the acquisition, or renunciation, of provisional allotments in whole. They can be amended to cover part only (see Precedent 5B.11).

Precedent 5B.1

Stock Transfer Form

STOCK TRANSFER FORM

J30

(Above this line for Registrars only)

Consideration Money £ 10,000*	Certificate lodged with the Registrar **(For completion by the Registrar/Stock Exchange)**

Full name of Undertaking.	*[Name of the company]*	
Full description of Security.	ORDINARY SHARES	
Number or amount of Shares, Stock or other security and, in figures column only, number and denomination of units, if any.	Words FIVE THOUSAND	Figures (5,000 units of £1)
Name(s) of registered holder(s) should be given in full; the address should be given where there is only one holder. If the transfer is not made by the registered holder(s) insert also the name(s) and capacity (e.g., Executor(s)) of the person(s) making the transfer.	In the name(s) of *[name and address of A]*	Account Designation (if any)

I/We hereby transfer the above security out of the name(s) aforesaid to the person(s) named below *or to the several persons named in Parts 2 of Brokers Transfer Forms relating to the above security:* **Delete words in italics except for stock exchange transactions.** Signature(s) of transferor(s) 1. *[signature of A]* 2. .... 3. .... 4. .... **Bodies corporate should execute under their common seal.**	**Stamp of Selling Broker(s) or, for transactions which are not stock exchange transactions, of Agent(s), if any, acting for the Transferor(s).** *Date* ....

PLEASE SIGN HERE

Full name(s) and full postal address(es) (including County or, if applicable, Postal District number) of the person(s) to whom the security is transferred.

Please state title, if any, or whether Mr., Mrs. or Miss.

Please complete in typewriting or in Block Capitals.

[name and address of B]

Account Designation (if any)

I/We request that such entries be made in the register as are necessary to give effect to this transfer.

Stamp of Buying Broker(s) (if any)	**Stamp or name and address of person lodging this form (if other than the Buying Broker(s))**

EDITOR'S NOTE

* Sale price = £2 per share.

FORM of CERTIFICATE REQUIRED WHERE TRANSFER IS NOT LIABLE TO STAMP DUTY
Pursuant to the Stamp Duty (Exempt Instruments) Regulations 1987

(1) Delete as appropriate
(2) Insert "A", "B" or appropriate category

(1) I/We hereby certify that this instrument falls within category(2) __________ in the schedule to the Stamp Duty (Exempt Instruments) Regulations 1987, set out below.

*Signature(s)

*Description: "Transferor", "Solicitor", or state capacity of other person duly authorised to sign and giving the certificate from his known knowledge of the transaction.

Date ____________________ 19 ______

*NOTE — The above certificate should be signed by (i) the transferor(s) or (ii) a solicitor or other person (e.g. bank acting as trustee or executor) having a full knowledge of the facts. Such other person must state the capacity in which he signs, that he is authorised so to sign and gives the certificate from his own knowledge of the transaction.

SCHEDULE

A. The vesting of property subject to a trust in the trustees of the trust on the appointment of a new trustee, or in the continuing trustees on the retirement of a trustee.
B. The conveyance or transfer of property the subject of a specific devise or legacy to the beneficiary named in the will (or his nominee).
C. The conveyance or transfer of property which forms part of an intestate's estate to the person entitled on intestacy (or his nominee).
D. The appropriation of property within section 84(4) of the Finance Act 1985 (death: appropriation in satisfaction of a general legacy of money) or section 84(5) or (7) of that Act (death: appropriation in satisfaction of any interest of surviving spouse and in Scotland also of any interest of issue).
E. The conveyance or transfer of property which forms part of the residuary estate of a testator to a beneficiary (or his nominee) entitled solely by virtue of his entitlement under the will.
F. The conveyance or transfer of property out of a settlement in or towards satisfaction of a beneficiary's interest, not being an interest acquired for money or money's worth, being a conveyance or transfer constituting a distribution of property in accordance with the provisions of the settlement.
G. The conveyance or transfer of property on and in consideration only of marriage to a party to the marriage (or his nominee) or to trustees to be held on the terms of a settlement made in consideration only of the marriage .
H. The conveyance or transfer of property within section 83(1) of the Finance Act 1985 (transfers in connection with divorce etc.).
I. The conveyance or transfer by the liquidator of property which formed part of the assets of the company in liquidation to a shareholder of that company (or his nominee) in or towards satisfaction of the shareholder's rights on a winding-up.
J. The grant in fee simple of an easement in or over land for no consideration in money or money's worth.
K. The grant of a servitude for no consideration in money or money's worth.
L. The conveyance or transfer of property operating as a voluntary disposition *inter vivos* for no consideration in money or money's worth nor any consideration referred to in section 57 of the Stamp Act 1891 (conveyance in consideration of a debt etc.).
M The conveyance or transfer of property by an instrument within section 84(1) of the Finance Act 1985 (death:varying disposition).

Instructional Notes

1. In order to obtain exemption from Stamp Duty on transactions described in the above schedule the Certificate must be completed and may then be lodged for registration or otherwise acted upon. Adjudication by the Stamp Office is not required.
2. This form does not apply to transactions falling within categories (a) and (b) in the form of certificate required where the transfer is not liable to ad valorem stamp duty set out below. In these cases the form of certificate printed below should be used. Transactions within either of those categories require submission of the form to the Stamp Office and remain liable to 50p duty.

FORM OF CERTIFICATE REQUIRED WHERE TRANSFER IS NOT LIABLE TO *AD VALOREM* STAMP DUTY

Instruments of transfer are liable to a fixed duty of 50p when the transaction falls within one of the following categories:-

a Transfer by way of security for a loan or re-transfer to the original transferor on repayment of a loan.
b Transfer, not on sale and not arising under any contract of sale and where no beneficial interest in the property passes: (i) to a person who is a mere nominee of, and is nominated only by, the transferor; (ii) from a mere nominee who has at all times, held the property on behalf of the transferee, (iii) from one nominee to another nominee of the same beneficial owner where the first nominee has at all times held the property on behalf of that beneficial owner. (NOTE — This category does not include a transfer made in any of the following circumstances: (i) by a holder of stock, etc., following the grant of an option to purchase the stock, to the person entitled to the option or his nominee; (ii) to a nominee in contemplation of a contract for the sale of the stock, etc., then about to be entered into; (iii) from the nominee of a vendor, who has instructed the nominee orally or by some unstamped writing to hold stock, etc., in trust for a purchaser, to such a purchaser.)

(1) "I" or "We".
(2) Insert "(a)"or "(b)"
(3) Here set out concisely the facts explaining the transaction Adjudication may be required.

(1) hereby certify that the transaction in respect of which this transfer is made is one which falls within the category (2) above.

(3) ____________________

**Signature(s)*

**Description ("Transferor", "Solicitor", etc.)*

Date ____________________ *19* ______

*NOTE — The above certificate should be signed by (1) the transferor(s) or (2) a member of a stock exchange or a solicitor or an accredited representative of a bank acting for the transferor(s); in cases falling within (a) where the bank or its official nominee is a party to the transfer, a certificate, instead of setting out the facts, may be to the effect that "the transfer is excepted from Section 74 of the Finance (1909-10) Act 1910". A certificate in other cases should be signed by a solicitor or other person (e.g. a bank acting as trustee or executor) having a full knowledge of the facts.

Precedent 5B.2

A. Register of Transfers

Transfer No	Date of Registration	Transferee					Transferor				
		Name	No of Shares acquired	Price or Consideration	No of Share Certificate	Sealing Register Reference	Name	No of Shares for which certificate surrendered	Balance Certificate		Sealing Register Reference
									No of Shares	Certificate No	
6	*[date]*	B	5,000	10,000	15	33	A	5,000	N/A	N/A	N/A

B. Register of Members and Share Ledger (a) Transferor

Name A
Address ______ Dividends to ______
Class of Share ORDINARY
Denomination £1
Date of entry as member [*date 1*]
Date of cessation of membership [*date 2*]

Date of Allotment OR Entry of Transfer	References in Register		No of Share Certificate	Amount paid or agreed to be considered as paid	Acquisitions	Disposals	Balance	Remarks
	Allotments	Transfers						
[*date 1*]	3		3	£5,000	5,000		5,000	
[*date 2*]		6				5,000	nil	

C. Register of Members and Share Ledger (b) Transferee

Name B

Address

Dividends to

Class of Share ORDINARY

Denomination £1

Date of entry as member [*date 1*]

Date of cessation of membership

Date of Allotment OR Entry of Transfer	References in Register		No. of Share Certificate	Amount paid or agreed to be considered as paid	Acquisitions	Disposals	Balance	Remarks
	Allotments	Transfers						
[*date 2*]		6	15	£10,000	5,000	–	5,000	TRANSFERRED FROM A

Precedent 5B.3

(1) Resolution of the Board to Decline to Register a Share Transfer

That, in accordance with the power conferred by clause of the articles of association of the company, the directors decline to register the transfer of [*number*] of £ [*class*] shares in the company lodged by [*name A*] in favour of [*name B*].

(2) Letter to Shareholder Declining Registration of Transfer

Dear Sir,

In exercise of their powers under the articles of association the directors have resolved to refuse registration of the transfer of shares from [*name*] to yourself.

The transfer form and covering share certificate lodged by you are returned herewith.

Yours faithfully

Secretary

Precedent 5B.4

Notice to Server of a Stop Notice

To

Dear Sirs,

HOLDING OF ORDINARY SHARES REGISTERED IN THE NAME OF .

We refer to the Stop Notice dated [*date*] which you have served on this company in respect of the above shareholding.

We hereby inform you that a final dividend for the year ended [31 December 1989] of [5p] per share has been declared payable on [30 June 1990] in respect of the ordinary share capital.

In accordance with the provisions of the Companies Act we shall [pay the dividend to the registered holder] [register the transfer] unless an injunction to prevent us so doing is served on us within the next 15 days.

Yours faithfully

Secretary

Precedent 5B.5

Record in Share Register of Grant of Probate

DECEASED: 15/3/90 Personal Representatives: SAMUEL CAMPERDOWN: JOHN MOUNCER
PROBATE: 20/6/90 C/O CAMPERDOWNS
15 SQUARE BUILDINGS, LINCOLNS INN, LONDON

Name JOHN MORTON
Address BRAGDON HALL
DILSBOROUGH

Dividends to PERSONAL REPRESENTATIVES

Class of Share ORDINARY
Denomination £1
Date of entry as member 10/2/75
Date of cessation of membership

Date of Allotment OR Entry of Transfer	References in Register		No of Share Certificate	Amount paid or agreed to be considered as paid	Acquisitions	Disposals	Balance	Remarks
	Allotments	Transfers						
10/2/75			1	£100	100		100	

Precedent 5B.6

Statutory Declaration by Next of Kin in a Small Estate

I, [*name*], of [*address*], do solemnly and sincerely declare that:

1. I am the [*relationship*] of [*name of deceased*] ('the deceased'), a copy of whose death certificate is exhibited herewith.
2. The deceased died intestate on [*date*] and I am the only person entitled to the estate of the deceased.
3. The total value of the estate of the deceased in the United Kingdom, which includes shares of each, fully paid, in Limited, does not exceed £ .
4. No inheritance tax is payable in respect of the estate of the deceased.
5. I do not intend nor, to the best of my knowledge, does any other person intend to apply for a grant of administration of the estate of the deceased.

And I make this solemn declaration conscientiously believing the same to be true and by virtue of the provisions of the Statutory Declarations Act 1835.

Declared at [*place*] the day of
one thousand nine hundred and
before me

* A Commissioner for Oaths

EDITOR'S NOTES

* Or notary public, Justice of the Peace or solicitor having the powers conferred on a Commissioner for Oaths.
Paragraph 4 may be omitted if a letter from the Capital Taxes Office is produced.

Precedent 5B.7

Indemnity by Next of Kin in a Small Estate

The Directors
(* Limited) (* Plc)

In consideration of your company recognising me as the sole administrator of the estate of [*name*] deceased ('the deceased') without the production to the company of a grant of administration of the estate of the deceased, I hereby agree to indemnify you and the company from and against all claims, demands, losses, damages, costs, charges and expenses which you or the company in consequence thereof may sustain, incur or be liable for, and I undertake to complete at the request of the company, such document or documents as may be necessary to transfer into my name shares of each, fully paid, in the company which are registered in the name of the deceased. I further undertake to obtain and produce to the company a grant of administration of the estate of the deceased if so required by the company.

Dated this day of 19

Signature:

Address:

EDITOR'S NOTES

1. * Delete as appropriate.
2. This precedent should be used in conjunction with Precedent 5B.6.
3. A guarantee from the bank of the next of kin may, in some circumstances, be thought advisable, in which case the Indemnity should be endorsed as follows:

WE [*name*]
OF [*address*]

hereby join in the above indemnity.

Signed

On behalf of .*

*Bank, insurance company or guarantee society.

Precedent 5B.8

Record in Share Register of Death of a Shareholder in a Joint Account

DECEASED: 15/3/90   Death Certificate Exhibited 10/6/90

PROBATE: 20/5/90

Name ~~RODNEY BLACK AND~~ JAMES FAIRHILL   Class of Share ORDINARY

Address ~~10 ALEXIS CRESCENT~~ ~~LONDON~~   Dividends to JAMES FAIRHILL   Denomination £1

Date of entry as member 25/9/50

Date of cessation of membership

Date of Allotment OR Entry of Transfer	References in Register		No. of Share Certificate	Amount paid or agreed to be considered as paid	Acquisitions	Disposals	Balance	Remarks
	Allotments	Transfers						
[date]			27	£50,000	50,000		50,000	ALLOTMENT

Precedent 5B.9

Letter of Request for Transmission

LETTER OF REQUEST

J18

(above this line for Registrar's use only)

Request by executors or administrators of a deceased holder to be placed on the register as holders in their own right.

Full name and address of Undertaking.	To the directors of ....
*Full description of Security (see note below)	
Number or amount of Shares, Stock or other Security and, in figures column only, number and denomination of units if any.	Words | Figures (units of)
Full name of Deceased.	.... Deceased late of ....

I/We, the undersigned, being the personal representative(s) of the above-named deceased, hereby request you to register me/us in the books of the Company as the holder(s) of the above-mentioned Stock/Shares now registered in the name of the said deceased.

DATED this .... day of .... 19 ....

Signature(s) of Personal Representative(s)

....

....

....

Full name(s) and addresses of the Personal Representative(s) in the order in which they are to be registered (TYPEWRITTEN OR IN BLOCK CAPITALS)	....

IF AN ACCOUNT ALREADY EXISTS IN THE ABOVE NAME(S) THE ABOVE MENTIONED HOLDING WILL BE ADDED TO THAT ACCOUNT, UNLESS INSTRUCTIONS ARE GIVEN TO THE CONTRARY.

The Certificate(s) in the name of the deceased if not already with the Company's Registrars must accompany this form. * A separate Letter of Request should be used for each class of security. No stamp duty is payable on this form in the case of a Company registered in England: in the case of a Company registered in Scotland stamp duty may be payable.	Stamp or name and address of person lodging this form.

Precedent 5B.10

Directors' Minutes to Issue Renounceable Letters of Allotment

It was resolved that shareholders be given the opportunity to renounce their entitlement to the issue in whole or in part subject to approval of the renouncee by the directors within the terms of the restrictions on the transfer of shares in the articles of association of the company and the final dates for renunciation be [*dates*].

* [It was further resolved that entitlement to shares be available for renunciation only if the subscription due thereon be unpaid/fully paid**.]

The secretary was instructed to make arrangements accordingly.

EDITOR'S NOTE

* Include and adjust** as appropriate in circumstances of a rights issue. Unnecessary in a bonus issue.

Precedent 5B.11

Letter of Allotment and Forms of Renunciation and Registration for Bonus Issue

[*address*] [*date*]

FULLY PAID LETTER OF ALLOTMENT

Dear Shareholder,

In accordance with the resolution passed by the directors on 19 , you have been allotted shares of £1 each, such shares being fully paid pursuant to a resolution for the capitalisation of reserves passed by the company at an extraordinary meeting also held on 19 .

The shares comprised in this letter of allotment will rank for all future dividends and in all other respects pari pasu with the other existing shares of the company.

If you wish to keep all the shares now allotted you need do nothing.

Should you wish to renounce your right to the whole or part of such allotment in favour of some other person, you must sign the letter of renunciation. The registration application form overleaf, must be signed by the person(s) in whose favour the shares have been renounced, and this form returned to the registered office of the company on or before the close of business on . The directors reserve the right to decline to approve within the provisions of the articles of association of the company any renouncee, in which case the renouncement shall be void.

Unless this allotment letter is returned, duly renounced, on or before the close of business on , the certificate for the shares will be automatically issued in your name and will be delivered as soon as possible.

Yours faithfully,

[FORM OF RENUNCIATION

To the Directors of Ltd

I/We being entitled to an allotment of shares of each, fully paid, in the above-named company, renounce my/our right to of such shares in favour of the persons signing the Registration Application Form below.

.... [*signature*]
.... [*signature*]

*[*date*]

REGISTRATION APPLICATION FORM

To the Directors of Ltd

I/We accept the shares of each in the above-named company, renounced by the above written Letter of Renunciation, subject to the memorandum and articles of association of the company, and I/We request that such shares be registered in my/our name(s) [**and in the amounts indicated below]. I/We authorise you to send the share certificates to me/us at the address given below by post at my/our risk.

Shares .... [*signature*]
.... [*name in full*]
.... [*address*]
....
.... [*description*]

Shares .... [*signature*]
.... [*name in full*]
.... [*address*]
....
.... [*description*]

[*date*]

EDITOR'S NOTES

*The date of renunciation should align with that included in Precedent 5B.9.

**Delete as appropriate.

Precedent 5B.12

Directors' Minute Approving Renunciations

With the exception of the persons named in Minute 2 below all shareholders indicated that they had no wish to renounce their entitlement to the fully paid bonus shares allotted to them.

The following indicated their wish to renounce:

... to ...
... to ...
... to ...
... to ...

It was resolved to approve these renunciation(s).

Accordingly the secretary was instructed to issue the following share certificates:

NAMES NUMBER OF SHARES

5C Register of Members and Share Certificates

Register of Members

Every company must keep a register of its members showing their names and addresses
and the date of becoming, and ceasing to be, a member. If the company has a share
capital the Register must also contain a statement of the shares held by each member,
showing the share numbers (if any), classes of shares and amounts paid on them.
s 352 Equivalent information must be shown if the company has stock. If the company has
bearer shares, the fact of the issue of a warrant must appear on the Register of Members,
s 353 with details of the number and class of shares it covers, but with no personal details of
the holder.

The Register of Members is prima facie evidence of the matters directed or authorised by
s 361 the Companies Act 1985 to be inserted in it. As it is a public record of who owns the
shares and the extent to which they are paid up, entries on the Register, or deletions or
s 359 alterations, may be made only in accordance with proper procedures (eg on an allotment
or transfer of shares, or when payment is made). Any other entry (eg because an error has
been discovered) should be made only with the consent of the court granted on an
application for rectification of the Register.

Although comments relevant to the administration of the Register (eg 'subscriber's share')
s 360 may be made in the Register against individual entries, generally only the statutory
information should be shown and, in particular, no notice of any trust or beneficial
interest should appear. Designations such as 'A PLC' or 'B PLC' may properly be
accepted to create separate accounts for the same shareholder(s) and are not regarded as
implying a trust (see p 103).

See Precedent 5C.1 (p 104) SPECIMEN PAGE OF REGISTER OF MEMBERS AND SHARE LEDGER

See Precedent 5B.2 for entries on transfer of shares.

On the allotment or transfer of shares it may also be necessary to make entries in the Registers of Allotments, Register of Transfers, Register of Directors' Interests and in the case of a public company, Register of Directors' Dealings. (See Chapter 13 for Statutory Registers.)

Documents lodged for registration

The company secretary may receive a wide range of documents for registration in relation to the Share Register.

It is of course important, before registering any such document, to be satisfied that:

(a) it is right to so register it; and
(b) the document is an original or is a copy duly certified as such by a responsible person such as a solicitor.

In other than the smallest companies it is usual to maintain a register of these documents which will be numbered serially and copies filed. The originals will be returned to the sender.

See Precedent 5C.2 (p 105) REGISTER OF DOCUMENTS

See *Jordans Secretarial Administration*, at § 3.25, for a description of the principal types of document and action to be taken on them. It is usual to endorse the document with a note that it has been registered with the company.

See Precedent 5C.3 (p 105) FORM OF ENDORSEMENT ON DOCUMENTS REGISTERED

The more common types of document are as follows.

Change of address. The company secretary must insist that it is in writing.

See Precedent 5C.4 (p 106) NOTIFICATION OF CHANGE OF ADDRESS

Marriage. The marriage certificate will usually be exhibited. Such event may also occasion a change of address. Sometimes a marriage certificate may not be available, especially if contracted overseas, and in such cases a statutory declaration may be accepted.

See Precedent 5C.5 (p 107) STATUTORY DECLARATION ON MARRIAGE

Change of name. The deed poll will be exhibited in whatever form drawn, but it is essentially a statutory declaration. Change of name resulting from assumption of a title may be evidenced by extract from the *London Gazette* or similar authority.

See Precedent 5C.6 (p 108) STATUTORY DECLARATION ON CHANGE OF NAME

It is usual for share certificates to be sent to the company if the name of the shareholder changes. The company will note the new name on these and return them to the shareholder.

Power of attorney. The power may be either a general power or a special [restricted] power, amounting, perhaps, to a general proxy.

See Precedent 5C.7 (p 109) (1) GENERAL POWER OF ATTORNEY
(2) SPECIFIC BUT FORMING A GENERAL PROXY

An 'enduring power of attorney' under the Enduring Powers of Attorney Act 1985 may be lodged. If the grantor becomes incapable such power continues to be valid if duly registered at the Court of Protection. *Enduring Powers of Attorney – a practitioner's guide* (Jordans, 1991) or the company's solicitor should be consulted if such a document is lodged.

If a power of attorney (other than an 'enduring power' duly registered) is lodged, a 'protective notice' should be given by the company to the grantor before it is acted upon.

See Precedent 5C.8 (p 110) PROTECTIVE NOTICE BY COMPANY ON RECEIPT OF POWER OF ATTORNEY

In some circumstances, confusion can arise as to the identity of a shareholder. In some cases a 'declaration of identity' should be obtained before any instruction or action by the purported shareholder is recognised.

See Precedent 5C.9 (p 111) DECLARATION OF IDENTITY

Designated holdings

Sometimes shareholders request that for their convenience holdings in their name or joint names be split into separate designated holdings. The company may accede to this upon written instructions and without a transfer deed.

See Precedent 5C.10 (p 112) REQUEST FOR DESIGNATED SHAREHOLDINGS

Share certificates

s 186 A shareholding of a member of a company is prima facie evidenced by a 'share certificate'. It is usual for a separate certificate to be issued for each class of shares (if there is more than one class in issue) and in practice certificates are printed in different colours to identify each class.

See Precedent 5C.11 (p 113) SHARE CERTIFICATE (FULLY PAID SHARES)

The certificate should state whether the share is fully paid or, if partly paid, the amount paid up. When calls are paid on partly paid shares the certificate will be endorsed with details.

See Precedent 5C.12 (p 114) SHARE CERTIFICATE (PARTLY PAID SHARES)

The name(s) and details of shareholder(s) on the certificate must conform exactly with those recorded in the Register of Members.

Table A, reg 6; CA 1989, s 130 Share certificates have in the past always been issued under the company's seal, and Table A still provides for this. The Companies Act 1989 dispenses with the need for a company seal (see Chapter 12).

s 185 Share certificates should be issued within two months of the allotment or transfer of shares.

s 186 Not infrequently a shareholder loses his or her share certificate or the certificate gets destroyed. Since the certificate is prima facie title to the shares it is essential that an indemnity, endorsed by a bank, be obtained before a replacement certificate is issued.

See Precedent 5C.13 (p 115) INDEMNITY FOR LOST CERTIFICATE

Precedent 5C.1

Specimen Page of Register of Members and Share Ledger

Name ____________________

Address ____________________ Dividends to ____________________

Class of Share ORDINARY

Denomination £1

Date of entry as member 24/7/90

Date of cessation of membership ____________________

Date of Allotment OR Entry of Transfer	References in Register		No of Share Certificate	Amount paid or agreed to be considered as paid	Acquisitions	Disposals	Balance	Remarks
	Allotments	Transfers						
24/7/90	3		3	£50	50	–	50	

Precedent 5C.2

Register of Documents

[REGISTER OF DOCUMENTS]

Ref no	Date received	Shareholder	Shareholder ref	Nature of document	Remarks

EDITOR'S NOTE

The document should be endorsed, as in Precedent 5C.3, before return to the presentor.

Precedent 5C.3

Form of Endorsement on Documents Registered

Exhibited [*date*] EITHER (1) name of company and signature of secretary;
OR (2) rubber stamped with name of company and initialled by secretary as registrar.

XYZ Ltd Exhibited Date .... Ref no ....

Precedent 5C.4

Notification of Change of Address

To: The Registrar/Secretary

[insert name and address of company]

Date .... 19 .....

Please alter my address in the company's registers

From

....
....
....
....
....

To

Please complete in BLOCK CAPITALS

* Full Name ....

New Address ....

....
....
....

†Signature(s) ....
....
....
....

* If you are not the first holder or if you are an executor or administrator, please state name in which the holding is registered.

†If one address alone is given for a holding in a joint account, all joint holders must sign.

Precedent 5C.5

Statutory Declaration on Marriage

TO ALL WHOM IT MAY CONCERN

I, [*single name – spinster, bachelor, widow, widower, or as the case may be*], of [*former registered address*], do solemnly and sincerely declare that on [*date*] at [*church, register office, or as the case may be*], I married [*name of wife, husband*] and that my address is now [*address*].

And I make this solemn declaration conscientiously believing the same to be true and by virtue of the Statutory Declarations Act 1835.

Declared at	[*place*]	....
this 19		[*new signature*]
before me		
....		....
*A Commissioner for Oaths		[*old signature*]

* Or notary public, Justice of the Peace or solicitor having the powers conferred on a Commissioner for Oaths.

EDITOR'S NOTE

* This form may be used if a marriage certificate is not available for exhibition and may be appropriate when the ceremony has taken place outside the UK.

Precedent 5C.6

Statutory Declaration on Change of Name

To all whom it may concern

I, [*new name*], heretofore called and known by the name of [*former name*], [*occupation and address*], do solemnly and sincerely declare that on the day of 19 I did formally and wholly renounce, relinquish and abandon the use of my said surname of and then assumed and adopted and determined thenceforth on all occasions whatsoever to use and subscribe the name of instead of the said name of so as to be at all times hereafter to be called, known and described by the name of exclusively.

And I make this solemn declaration conscientiously believing the same to be true and by virtue of the Statutory Declarations Act 1835.

Declared at [*place*] ....
this 19 [*new signature*]
before me

formerly known as

....
*A Commissioner for Oaths [*old signature*]

* Or notary public, Justice of the Peace or solicitor having the powers conferred on a Commissioner for Oaths.

Precedent 5C.7

(1) General Power of Attorney

THIS GENERAL POWER OF ATTORNEY is made the day of 19 by [*name*], of [*address*].

I appoint [*name*] and ([*name*], of [*address*], jointly and severally)* to be my attorney(s)* in accordance with s 10 of the Powers of Attorney Act 1971.

IN WITNESS whereof I have hereunto set my hand and seal the day and year first above written.

SIGNED SEALED AND DELIVERED
by the said [*name*] .... [*signature*]

in the presence of .... [*signature*]
.... [*address*]

EDITOR'S NOTE

* Designed for joint attorneys. Delete if only one person appointed.

(2) Specific but Forming a General Proxy

BY THIS POWER OF ATTORNEY, I, [*name*], hereby appoint [*name*], of [*address*], (such appointment to be irrevocable for one year from the date hereof) in my name and on my behalf and in respect of all the shares in Limited of which I may for the time being be the registered holder to vote at all or any meetings of the members or of any particular class of members of Limited and at all or any adjournments of such meetings and at every poll that may be taken in consequence thereof and whenever he shall deem it expedient to do so to demand a poll and also to appoint from time to time any one or more proxies for any of the above purposes and for such one or more meetings as the said [*name*] shall think fit, and also from time to time to revoke any such appointment of a proxy or proxies.

Signed, sealed and delivered
by the above-named [*name*] .... [*signature*]

in the presence of .... [*signature*]
.... [*address*]

EDITOR'S NOTE

* As from 19 March 1985 no stamp duty is payable on powers of attorney or general proxies.

Precedent 5C.8

Protective Notice by Company on Receipt of Power of Attorney

LIMITED

Telephone: ....
Fax:

[*date*]

To: [*name*]
[*address*]

Dear Sir or Madam

You are hereby notified that the undermentioned power of attorney/general proxy purporting to have been given by you has been lodged at this office, and unless you advise me to the contrary by return of post, such power will be assumed to be in order and will be registered in respect of your shareholding in the company.

Yours faithfully

....
Secretary

Date of power	In favour of

Precedent 5C.9

Declaration of Identity

To the directors of

I, [*name*], of [*address*], hereby declare that I am one and the same person as of the same address who is registered in the books of your company as the holder of shares represented by certificate(s) nos and further I request and authorise you to enter my full and correct name, *viz*:
on your company's registers in respect of the above-mentioned shares.

Signature:
Date:

SUPPORTING DECLARATION

*I, [*name*],of [*address*], hereby declare that I have known the above-named for years and verify that (s)he is one and the same person as who signs the above declaration.

Signature: ....
Description: ....
Date: ....

For company's use only

EDITOR'S NOTES

Share certificate(s) must be lodged at the company's office with this request.
* The declarant should be a person holding a position such as Justice of the Peace, minister of religion, solicitor, chartered accountant, bank manager or doctor of medicine.

Precedent 5C.10

Request for Designated Shareholdings

The Secretary,
Ltd

Dear Sir,

I hereby request you to register 2,500 ordinary shares in the capital of the company registered in my name with the designation *'A' Account* and 2,500 with the designation *'B' Account.*

I enclose a certificate covering 5,000 ordinary shares and would be obliged if you would issue me with a new certificate for the designated holdings.

I also enclose a dividend payment request* in respect of each designated holding.

Yours faithfully

....

EDITOR'S NOTE

* The dividend payment request will be completed in the name of the shareholder's 'A' Account and 'B' Account respectively.

Precedent 5C.11

Share Certificate (Fully Paid Shares)

Certificate No. 1

Number of Shares 1,000

Barchester Biscuits
Limited

This is to Certify *that* Horace Grantly *of* 25 The Close Barchester

is/are the Registered holder(s) of one thousand *Shares of £* 1.00 *each* FULLY *paid in the above-named Company, subject to the Memorandum and Articles of Association of the Company.*

The Common Seal of the Company was hereto affixed in the presence of:

Directors [*name*]

[*name*]

Secretary

on 25 JULY 19

Barchester
Biscuits
Limited

NO TRANSFER OF ANY OF THE ABOVE MENTIONED SHARES CAN BE REGISTERED UNTIL THIS CERTIFICATE HAS BEEN DEPOSITED AT THE REGISTERED OFFICE OF THE COMPANY

Precedent 5C.12

Share Certificate (Partly Paid Shares)

[*Name of company*]

Certificate no Number of shares

This is to certify that [*name of shareholder*], of [*address*], is the registered holder of shares of £ each, paid up to the extent endorsed hereon and numbered to inclusive in the above-named company subject to the memorandum and articles of association of the company.

[Given under the common seal of the company] [Executed by the company] on 19 .

(Director)

(Secretary)

No transfer of any of the above-mentioned shares can be registered until this certificate has been deposited at the office of the company.

Amount paid up on share(s) is:		
Date	Amount per share	Initialled

Precedent 5C.13

Indemnity for Lost Certificate

J16a

(above this line for Registrar's use only)

To the Directors of ....

The original certificate(s) of title relating to the undermentioned securities of the above-named company has/have been lost or destroyed.

Neither the securities nor the certificate(s) of title thereto have been transferred, charged, lent or deposited or dealt with in any manner affecting the absolute title thereto and the person(s) named in the said certificate(s) is/are the person(s) entitled to be on the register in respect of such securities.

I/We request you to issue a duplicate certificate(s) of title for such securities and in consideration of your doing so, undertake (jointly and severally) to indemnify you and the company against all claims and demands (and any expenses thereof) which may be made against you or the company in consequence of your complying with this request and of the company permitting at any time hereafter a transfer of the said securities, or any part thereof, without the production of the said original certificate(s)..

I/We undertake to deliver to the company for cancellation the said original certificate(s) should the same ever be recovered.

Particulars of certificate(s) lost or destroyed

Particulars of Certificate	Amount and Class of Securities	In favour of

Dated this .... day of ....19......

SIGNATURE(S) ....

....

* We ....
of ....
hereby join in the above indemnity and undertaking.
Signed ....
On behalf of * ....
* Bank, Insurance Company or Guarantee Society

5D Redemption and Buy Back

Redemption or purchase by a company of its own shares

Introduction

ss 162, et seq These precedents deal with the purchase or redemption by a private company of its own shares out of (1) distributable profits as defined in the Companies Act 1985 and (2) capital. Additionally a company may use the proceeds of a fresh issue of shares for such purposes.

s 143 The purchase or redemption by a company of its own shares is unlawful unless it falls within the specific exemptions of the Companies Act 1985, described below.

A company must have adequate power in its memorandum and articles for such transactions (see Precedent 5D.1(2)).

These precedents are confined to the statutory procedures, but before commencing such transactions the company should take careful professional advice on accountancy, taxation and other aspects, as indeed should the vendor shareholder(s).

The votes attached to the shares which it is proposed should be bought back by the company must not be exercised in favour of the special resolution. If these votes are so exercised the resolution will not be deemed to have been passed if their vote was necessary to reach the required majority.

Details of any purchase or redemption of its shares by the company must be included in the directors' report attached to the accounts covering the accounting reference period in which the transaction took place.

If there are only two members in the company it is not possible for the whole of the shareholding of one of the members to be purchased or reduced so as to reduce the membership to only one person, unless a transfer or allotment is made to a new second shareholder within six months of the repurchase.

ss 171, 172 Repurchases which involve the issue of additional share capital, usually of a different class, require additional procedures relating to the issue of new shares, but the scheme will be similar to a purchase out of distributable profits.

Purchases out of distributable profits

The purchase by a company of its own shares must be made pursuant to a contract, the terms of which, or a memorandum the terms of which, are approved by special resolution of the company, subject to the company having relevant powers under its memorandum and articles to do so. If not, these must be changed first. The precedents assume the company needs to amend its articles to include the necessary powers but that the memorandum contains adequate objects and powers. (Table A, reg 35)

See Precedent 5D.1(1) (p 120) BOARD MINUTES TO CONVENE EGM TO AUTHORISE PURCHASE OF OWN SHARES

See Precedent 5D.1(2) (p 121) SPECIAL RESOLUTIONS TO AUTHORISE PURCHASE OF OWN SHARES

Resolution 1 of Precedent 5D.1(2) assumes that the company is using articles which incorporate Table A to the Companies Act 1948 or earlier acts. Adequate power is contained in the 1985 Table A and if articles are based on it then this resolution is unnecessary.

See Precedent 5D.1(3) (p 123) DRAFT CONTRACT FOR PURCHASE OF OWN SHARES

s 159(3) The purchase must be for cash, to be paid in full on completion; other consideration is not lawful.

s 164 The proposed contract must be available for inspection by members at the company's registered office for 15 days before the general meeting. The short notice procedure for general meetings should, therefore, not be used to reduce the notice period to less than 15 days.

s 114 CA 1989, Sch 15A If the transaction is completed by written resolution under statutory procedures the documents which would have been available at a meeting and exhibited prior to it must be circulated with the written resolution.

It is important that the voting rights on the shares to be purchased by the company are not exercised to vote in favour of the special resolution.

See Precedent 5D.1(4) (p 125) BOARD MINUTES FOLLOWING EGM APPROVING CONTRACT

See Precedent 5D.1(5) (p 126) FORM G 169 RETURN BY A COMPANY PURCHASING ITS OWN SHARES

Stamp duty (until abolished) is paid as if it is a transfer of shares on filing Form G 169, which must be lodged with the Registrar of Companies within 28 days of the repurchase.

ICTA 1988, s 129 If Inland Revenue clearance has not been obtained that the matter be treated as a capital transaction the vendor shareholder will be issued with a tax credit certificate treating the purchase as a distribution of profits and the credit will be accounted to advanced corporation tax on the next form CT/61 lodged by the company with the Revenue. (See Chapter 8.)

In some circumstances this may be an acceptable course to the company and the vendor shareholder. The taxation treatment of the transaction may be covered in the contract (see Precedent 5D(1)(3), Editor's Note 2).

See Precedent 5D.1(6) (p 127) NARRATIVE FOR TAX CREDIT CERTIFICATE

Appropriate entries must be made in the Register of Members.

See Precedent 5D.1(7) (p 128) ENTRIES IN THE REGISTER OF MEMBERS ON REPURCHASE OF SHARES

Repurchase or redemption of shares out of capital

ss 171–173 A private limited company may repurchase or redeem shares out of capital to the extent that available distributable profits or new shares issued for the purpose are insufficient. A public company may not do so. The amount so calculated is termed the 'permissible capital payment' (see *Jordans Secretarial Administration*, at § 2.53, for a fuller discussion of the background).

Procedures are as for payments out of distributable profits, but in addition:

1. The directors must make a statutory declaration in the prescribed form as to the amount of permissible capital payment, and the solvency of the company.

See Precedent 5D.2(1) (p 129) (a) FORM G 173 DECLARATION IN RELATION TO THE REDEMPTION OR PURCHASE OF SHARES OUT OF CAPITAL
(p 131) (b) DIRECTORS' MINUTES IN RELATION TO REPURCHASE OR REDEMPTION OF SHARES OUT OF CAPITAL

s 173 2. There must be annexed to this statutory declaration a report by the auditors to the directors covering the matters set out in the following precedent.

See Precedent 5D.2(2) (p 131) AUDITORS' REPORT IN ACCORDANCE WITH SECTION 173(5) OF THE COMPANIES ACT 1985

3. The proposed payment out of capital must be approved by special resolution passed within a week of the aforesaid statutory declaration and auditors' report. This will be an additional resolution to that required for a purchase out of distributable profits (see Precedent 5D.1(2)) but passed at the same meeting or by the same written resolution. If a written resolution is used it must be carefully timed to meet the limits set out above.

See Precedent 5D.2(3) (p 132) SPECIAL RESOLUTION GIVING APPROVAL FOR PRIVATE COMPANY TO PURCHASE OR REDEEM SHARES OUT OF CAPITAL

4. Within one week of the passing of the special resolution the company must give public notice of the payment out of capital.

This notice must appear in the *London Gazette* and either in a national newspaper or circulated to all creditors.

See Precedent 5D.2(4) (p 132) NOTICE IN *LONDON GAZETTE* AND EITHER IN NEWSPAPER OR TO ALL CREDITORS

5. Form G 173 and the auditors' report must be delivered to the Registrar of Companies not later than the date on which the public notice (Precedent 5D.2(4)) is published, or notice given to creditors, whichever is earlier.

6. Any member of the company who did not vote in favour of the special resolution or any creditor of the company may apply to the court within five weeks of the passing of the resolution for an order cancelling the resolution.

The form of an application to the court is beyond the scope of this work and should be settled by the applicants' legal advisors. A copy must be served on the company, which is then responsible for filing Form G 176 with the Registrar of Companies.

See Precedent 5D.2(5) (p 133) FORM G 176 NOTICE OF APPLICATION TO THE COURT FOR THE CANCELLATION OF A RESOLUTION FOR THE REDEMPTION OR PURCHASE OF SHARES OUT OF CAPITAL

7. For a period of five weeks from the date of the public notice the statutory declaration and auditors' report must be kept at the registered office of the company and be available for inspection by members or creditors.

8. Payment for the repurchase may be made six weeks after the date on which the special resolution was passed if there have been no objections (ie five weeks after the notice and one week after the special resolution was passed) but must be made before the expiry of seven weeks from the date of the special resolution.

Redemption of share capital

s 159

Table A, Art 3

A company can issue shares which can be redeemed at the option of the company or at the option of the shareholder so long as the company (1) has in issue at that time shares which are not redeemable and (2) there is power in the articles of association to issue redeemable shares. See *Jordans Secretarial Administration*, at § 2.53, for further discussion.

See Precedent 5D.3(1) (p 134) DRAFT ARTICLE FOR REDEEMABLE ORDINARY SHARES

The following precedents assume that shares are to be redeemed at par (provision can be made in the terms of issue to redeem at a premium either stated or on a formula) and that redemption will be made out of distributable profits or a new issue of shares. The additional procedures for a private company wishing to redeem shares out of capital are similar to repurchases out of capital, described above.

See Precedent 5D.3(2) (p 135) (a) RESOLUTION OF THE DIRECTORS TO REDEEM SHARES
(b) NOTICE TO SHAREHOLDERS

This precedent assumes the shares may be redeemed at the option of the company but the shareholders may be given the option instead of, or in addition to, the company.

It will be noted that issued shares are cancelled by redemption, but this does not affect the company's authorised capital.

Notice of every redemption must be given to the Registrar of Companies within one month on Form G 122.

See Precedent 5D.3(3) (p 136) FORM G 122 NOTICE OF CONSOLIDATION, DIVISION, SUB-DIVISION, REDEMPTION OR CANCELLATION OF SHARES, OR CONVERSION, RE-CONVERSION OF STOCK INTO SHARES

See Precedent 5D.3(4) (p 137) ENTRIES IN REGISTER OF MEMBERS ON REDEMPTION OF SHARES

Precedent 5D.1(1)

Board Minutes to Convene EGM to Authorise Purchase of Own Shares

1. It was noted that [*name*], desired [to sell his ordinary] [to retire from membership of the company and had offered to sell his] shares in the capital of the company to the company, under the provisions of the Companies Act 1985.

* 2. It was noted that the Inland Revenue had, by letters dated the day of 19 and the day of 19 given its approval to the scheme as a capital transaction.

3. It was resolved that it was in the best interests of the company for the company to purchase the shares.

4. A notice convening an extraordinary general meeting of the company for 10.30am on 19 was produced to the meeting. The extraordinary general meeting is to be convened to pass special resolutions for the following purposes.

   (i) To alter the company's articles to give an appropriate authority for the company to purchase its own shares [and, if necessary, to alter its memorandum to remove any prohibition].*
   (ii) To approve a contract of purchase between [*name*] and the company.
   (iii) To waive the pre-emption rights in the company's articles of association.*

   It was resolved that the notice of meeting be approved, signed by the secretary and served on the members, [the directors] and the company's auditors and that the members be requested to agree to the holding of the meeting at short notice.

5. It was resolved that the secretary be instructed to take all steps necessary to convene the extraordinary general meeting in accordance with Resolution 4.

EDITOR'S NOTE

* Adjust to circumstances (see Precedent 5D.1(2)). If the articles, or any resolution in force, give(s) shareholders the right to purchase shares offered for sale, this right must be waived if the purchaser is the company.

Precedent 5D.1(2)

Special Resolutions to Authorise Purchase of Own Shares

1. The company's articles of association be altered by the addition of the following new article, numbered [ ]*.

   'Subject to the provisions of Part V of the Companies Act 1985 the company may:

   ss 155, 159, 162, 171

   (a) pursuant to s 159 of that Act issue shares which are to be redeemed or are liable to be redeemed at the option of the company or the shareholder on such terms and in such manner as shall be provided by the articles of the company;

   (b) pursuant to s 162 of that Act purchase its own shares (including any redeemable shares);

   (c) pursuant to s 171 of that Act make a payment out of capital in respect of the redemption or purchase;

   (d) pursuant to s 155 of that Act give financial assistance for the purchase of its own shares or those of its holding company.'

   [Regulations 3 and 10 of Table A shall not apply to the company.]*

2. That the terms of the contract proposed to be made between (1) [*name*] and (2) the company for the purchase of [1,000 shares of £1 each] in the capital of the company, which terms are set out in the copy of the proposed contract produced to this meeting and for the purpose of identification signed by the chairman hereof, be and are hereby authorised.

3. That if and in so far as article 29 of the company's articles would (but for this resolution) have to be complied with before the terms of the proposed contract authorised by Resolution 1 above may be properly fulfilled, the said article shall be waived.

EDITOR'S NOTES

(*Resolution 1*)

(i) *[ ] Check with existing articles and delete if not necessary.

(ii) This Resolution is not necessary if the company's articles are based on the Companies Act 1985, Table A (see Table A, regs 3 and 35).

(iii) Article 10 was repealed by the Companies Act 1981. Therefore, companies formed after this Act came into force do not need to disapply this article.

[*Editor's Notes continue on next page*]

(*Resolution 3*)

This relates to any articles giving pre-emption rights to other members on a transfer of shares.

Although resolutions in this form are frequently used, there is an element of doubt whether such rights under the articles can be waived by a resolution in general meeting for the purpose of a specific transaction, as opposed to an alteration of the articles. If a member objected the matter could be contentious, so that a separate waiver signed by each shareholder, if practical, would be a more cautious approach.

Precedent 5D.1(3)

Draft Contract for Purchase of Own Shares

THIS AGREEMENT is made the day of 19 between

1. [*name*], of [*address*] (hereinafter called 'the vendor'); and

2. [*name*], whose registered office is situate at [*address*] (hereinafter called 'the purchaser').

WHEREAS

A. The purchaser was incorporated in England on 1 April 1986 under the Companies Act 1985 and has at the date hereof an authorised share capital of £ , of which all shares are issued as fully paid.

B. This agreement is made by the purchaser pursuant to the powers contained in Chapter VII of Part V of the Companies Act 1985 and by the articles of association of the company to purchase its own shares [and make permissible capital payment] and pursuant to a special resolution passed at an extraordinary general meeting of the purchaser held on [*date*].

NOW IT IS AGREED as follows.

1. The vendor shall sell and the purchaser shall purchase, free from all liens, charges and encumbrances [1,000 shares of £1 each] in the capital of the purchaser.*
2. The purchase price of each share of [£1] shall be £ in cash.
3. Completion of the sale and purchase of shares hereunder shall take place at the registered office of the purchaser at on [*date*] whereupon:
   (a) the vendor shall deliver to the purchaser the share certificate(s) in respect of the number of shares to be sold by the vendor hereunder or in the case of a lost certificate such indemnity as the purchaser shall reasonably require; and
   (b) the purchaser will deliver to the vendor a cheque for the consideration due to the vendor.
4. Time shall be of the essence for this agreement.
5. The purchaser warrants and represents to the vendor that all requirements of Chapter VII of the Companies Act 1985 relating to an 'off-market purchase' by a company of its own shares have been complied with.
6. (a) This agreement shall be binding upon the personal representatives or successors of the vendor, but shall not be assignable.
   (b) This agreement constitutes the whole agreement between the

parties hereto and no variation hereof shall be effective unless made in writing.

(c) This agreement shall be governed by the law of England.

AS WITNESS this agreement has been signed by or on behalf of the parties hereto the day and year first before written.

SIGNED by the said ....

in the presence of ....

SIGNED by ....

for and on behalf of ....

in the presence of ....

EDITOR'S NOTES

1. *Here add, if necessary, arrangements as to dividends due, eg 'and such shares are to be sold at the dividend declared on [*date*] of pence per share'.
2. If desired, the proposed tax treatment may be specified, in which case clause 5 should be renumbered 5(a) and the following subclauses added:

   '(b) the purchase is made out of distributable profits of the purchaser as defined in the Companies Act 1985 ('the Act') and in accordance with s 162(2) of the Act'.

   [*OR*]

   '(b) subject to appropriate clearance by the Inland Revenue the purchase of its own shares by the purchaser will be treated as a distribution by the purchaser and in no circumstances will the provisions of s 219 of the Income and Corporation Taxes Act 1988 apply to the transaction'.

Precedent 5D.1(4)

Board Minutes Following EGM Approving Contract

1. The secretary reported that at an extraordinary general meeting of the company held immediately before this meeting the following special resolutions had been passed.

[*as Precedent 5D.1(2).*]

2. [*Name*] was authorised to execute this contract on behalf of the company with [*name*].

3. The secretary was instructed to file the resolutions with the Registrar of Companies within 15 days of the meeting and to file Form G 169 [and stamp duty]* within 28 days of completion of the purchase.

4. The secretary was also instructed to notify the Board of Inland Revenue of the purchase immediately after the execution of the contract and to retain the contract with the records of the company for a period of 10 years from the date of execution.

. . . .
Chairman

EDITOR'S NOTE

* This will not apply when stamp duty on share transfers is abolished.

Precedent 5D.1(5)

Return by a company purchasing its own shares

169

Pursuant to section 169 of the Companies Act 1985

Please do not write in this margin

Please complete legibly, preferably in black type, or bold block lettering

* insert full name of company

Note
This return must be delivered to the Registrar within a period of 28 days beginning with the first date on which shares to which it relates were delivered to the company

§ A private company is not required to give this information

‡ Insert Director, Secretary, Receiver, Administrator, Administrative Receiver or Receiver (Scotland) as appropriate

Please do not write in the space below. For Inland Revenue use only.

To the Registrar of Companies

For official use

Company number 9 236 452

Name of company

*BILLBROOK ENTERPRISES LTD

Shares were purchased by the company under section 162 of the above Act as follows:

Class of shares	ORDINARY		
Number of shares purchased	1,000		
Nominal value of each share	£1		
Date(s) on which the shares were delivered to the company	20/6/90		
Maximum prices paid § for each share			
Minimum prices paid § for each share			

The aggregate amount paid by the company for the shares to which this return relates was:	£ 10,000
Stamp duty payable pursuant to section 66 of the Finance Act 1986 on the aggregate amount at 50p per £100 or part of £100	£ 50

Signed J. F. Runciman Designation‡ Director Date 2/7/90

Presentor's name address and reference (if any):

For official Use

General Section | Post room

Precedent 5D.1(6)

Narrative for Tax Credit Certificate

Purchase by the company of its shares out of distributable profits	£10,000*
Tax credit	£ 3,333**

EDITOR'S NOTES

The tax credit attaches only to payments out of distributable profits and unless the Inland Revenue has approved the purchase, so that it is not to be treated as a distribution. No tax credit will be given in respect of *permissible capital payments* (as defined) (see p 118).

* This figure will be the amount by which the contract price exceeds the nominal value of the shares sold.

** Standard rate tax credit (25p standard rate is used in this example).

Precedent 5D.1(7)

Entries in the Register of Members on Repurchase of Shares

Name MARY MORTON

Address ______________________ Dividends to ______________________

Class of Share ORDINARY

Denomination £1

Date of entry as member 20/9/81

Date of cessation of membership ______________

Date of Allotment OR Entry of Transfer	References in Register		No. of Share Certificate	Amount paid or agreed to be considered as paid	Acquisitions	Disposals	Balance	Remarks
	Allotments	Transfers						
[*date*]	5,000					1,000	4,000	1,000 Shares repurchased
								pursuant to special resolution dated [*date*]

Precedent 5D.2(1)(a)

Declaration in relation to the redemption or purchase of shares out of capital

173

Please do not write in this margin

Pursuant to section 173 of the Companies Act 1985

Please complete legibly, preferably in black type,or bold block lettering

To the Registrar of Companies

For official use

Company number

Name of company

* insert full name of company

*

Note
Please read the notes on page 2 before completing this form.

ø insert name(s) and address(es) of all the directors

I/We ø ______________________________

† delete as appropriate

~~[the sole director]~~[all the directors]† of the above company do solemnly and sincerely declare that:

§ delete whichever is inappropriate

The business of the company is:

~~(a) that of a [recognised bank][licensed institution]† within the meaning of the Banking Act 1979§~~

~~(b) that of a person authorised under section 3 or 4 of the Insurance Companies Act 1982 to carry on insurance business in the United Kingdom§~~

(c) that of something other than the above§

The company is proposing to make a payment out of capital for the redemption or purchase of its own shares

The amount of the permissible capital payment for the shares in question is £______________ (note 1)

Continued overleaf

Presentor's name address and reference (if any):

For official Use General Section	Post room

I/We have made full enquiry into the affairs and prospects of the company, and I/we have formed the opinion:

Please do not write in this margin

Please complete legibly, preferably in black type, or bold block lettering

(a) as regards its initial situation immediately following the date on which the payment out of capital is proposed to be made, that there will be no grounds on which the company could then be found unable to pay its debts (note 2), and

(b) as regards its prospects for the year immediately following that date, that, having regard to my/our intentions with respect to the management of the company's business during that year and to the amount and character of the financial resources which will in my/our view be available during that year, the company will be able to continue to carry on business as a going concern (and will accordingly be able to pay its debts as they fall due) throughout that year.(note 2)

And I/we make this solemn declaration conscientiously believing the same to be true and by virtue of the provisions of the Statutory Declarations Act 1835.

Declared at ______________________________ Declarant(s) to sign below

____

____

the __________ day of ______________________

one thousand nine hundred and ______________

____

before me ______________________________

A Commissioner for Oaths, or Notary Public, or Justice of the Peace, or Solicitor having the powers conferred on a Commissioner for Oaths.

Notes

1 'Permissible capital payment' means an amount which, taken together with
(i) any available profits of the company; and
(ii) the proceeds of any fresh issue of shares made for the purposes of the redemption or purchase;
is equal to the price of redemption or purchase.
'Available profits' means the company's profits which are available for distribution (within the meaning of section 172 and 263 of the Companies Act 1985).
The question whether the company has any profits so available and the amount of any such profits is to be determined in accordance with section 172 of the Companies Act 1985.

2 Contingent and prospective liabilities of the company must be taken into account, see sections 173(4) & 517 of the Companies Act 1985.

3 A copy of this declaration together with a copy of the auditors report required by section 173 of the Companies Act 1985, must be delivered to the Registrar of Companies not later than the day on which the company publishes the notice required by section 175(1) of the Companies Act 1985, or first publishes or gives the notice required by section 175(2), whichever is the earlier.

Precedent 5D.2(1)(b)

Directors' Minutes in Relation to Repurchase or Redemption of Shares out of Capital

[*The minutes of the directors will follow the form of Precedent 5D.1(1) with the following amendments.*]

[*Para 4 insert sub clause*:]

(iv) To approve payment of part of the consideration out of the capital of the company.

[*add additional para*:]

6. A draft statutory declaration (Form G 173) as required by s 173 of the Companies Act 1985 in relation to a payment out of capital was tabled together with a draft confirmatory report of the auditors as required by s 174. The contents of the statutory declaration were agreed to be in all respects complete and correct and it was approved for declaration by all directors.

   A draft notice for publication required by s 175 was also tabled and appended and any one director or the secretary were authorised to sign and publish it upon the matters therein stated being completed.

Precedent 5D.2(2)

Auditors' Report in Accordance with Section 173(5) of the Companies Act 1985

We have inquired into the company's affairs and report that in our opinion the permissible capital payment specified in the directors' statutory declaration is, in our view, properly determined in accordance with ss 171 and 172 of the 1985 Act. We are not aware of anything to indicate that the opinion expressed by the directors in their statutory declaration is unreasonable in all the circumstances.

. . . . 19 . . .   . Chartered Accountants

Precedent 5D.2(3)

Special Resolution Giving Approval for Private Company to Purchase or Redeem Shares out of Capital

SPECIAL RESOLUTION

That the payment by the company of £ out of capital as defined in ss 171 to 173 (inclusive) of the Companies Act 1985 in respect of *[redemption at a price of £ per share of [*number*] of the company's [*describe redeemable shares*] under ss 159–161 (inclusive) of the said Act] *[the purchase by the company at a price of £ per share of [*number*] of the company's [*describe shares*] under s 162 of the said Act] be and it is hereby authorised.

EDITOR'S NOTE

* Delete alternative which does not apply (redemption/repurchase) and complete appropriately.

Precedent 5D.2(4)

Notice in *London Gazette* and Either in Newspaper or To All Creditors

[*Name of company*]

s 175 TO WHOM IT MAY CONCERN. Notice is hereby given pursuant to s 175 of the Companies Act 1985 that:

(1) the above named company has approved a payment out of capital for the purpose of acquiring its own shares by [redemption/purchase];

(2) the amount of the permissible capital payment for the shares in question is [£] and the resolution approving such payment out of capital was passed on [*date*];

(3) the statutory declaration of the directors' and the auditors' report required by ss 173 and 174 of the said Act are available for inspection at the company's registered office at [*address of registered office*];

(4) any creditor of the company may at any time within the five weeks immediately following [*date of resolution*] apply to the court under ss 176 and 177 of the Act for an order prohibiting the payment.

.... [*signature of director or secretary or of solicitors or other agent on behalf of the company*]

Precedent 5D.2(5)

Notice of application to the Court for the cancellation of a resolution for the redemption or purchase of shares out of capital

176

Please do not write in this margin

Pursuant to section 176 of the Companies Act 1985

Please complete legibly, preferably in black type, or bold block lettering

To the Registrar of Companies

For official use

Company number

Name of company

* insert full name of company

* DILSBOROUGH PROJECTS

gives notice that an application has been made to the Court for the cancellation of the special resolution dated 5 JULY 1989 approving payment out of capital for the redemption or purchase of some of the company's shares.

‡ Insert Director, Secretary, Administrator, Administrative Receiver or Receiver (Scotland) as appropriate

Signed [signature] Designation‡ DIRECTOR Date 17 JULY 1989

Presentor's name address and reference (if any):

For official Use
General Section | Post room

Precedent 5D.3(1)

Draft Article for Redeemable Ordinary Shares*

1. The redeemable ordinary shares of each shall, save as to the provisions for redemption hereinafter contained, rank pari passu with the ordinary shares in the capital of the company.

2.(a) The company may, subject to the provisions of the Companies Act 1985, at any time redeem the whole [or any part] of the redeemable ordinary shares upon giving to the shareholders, whose shares are to be redeemed, not less than three months' notice in writing expiring on 30 September in any year** before the date fixed for redemption. The company shall not be entitled to redeem any redeemable ordinary share unless it is a fully paid share.

(b) In the case of a partial redemption the redeemable ordinary shares to be redeemed shall be selected by drawings to be made at such place and in such manner as the directors in their absolute discretion shall determine.

(c) The company shall redeem the whole of the redeemable ordinary shares then outstanding on 19 , or so soon thereafter as the company shall be able to comply with the statutory provisions for the time being affecting such redemption. Not less than three months' previous notice in writing shall be given to the holders of such shares specifying the date upon which the same will be redeemed.

(d) Any notice of redemption shall specify the particular shares to be redeemed, the date fixed for redemption and the place at which the certificates for such shares are to be presented for redemption. At the time and place so fixed, each holder thereof shall be bound to surrender to the company for cancellation the certificates for his shares which are to be redeemed for cancellation [together with a receipt for the moneys payable to him upon the redemption of such shares]. Upon such surrender the company shall pay to him the amount due upon redemption. If any certificate so surrendered to the company shall include any redeemable ordinary shares not then to be redeemed, a fresh certificate for those shares shall be issued without charge.

(e) There shall be paid on each redeemable ordinary share redeemed [*the amount paid up thereon*].***

EDITOR'S NOTES

* This precedent provides for redemption at the option of the company with a requirement to redeem on or after a fixed date. It can be re-drafted to provide for redemption at the option of shareholders (if so desired). Any drafting should be done by the company's professional advisers.

** The dates for redemption need careful definition and professional advice should be taken.

*** Redemption terms may be provided as suited to circumstances. An alternative would be to provide a formula which must be precise and readily quantifiable. This precedent confines repayment to par value.

Precedent 5D.3(2)

(a) Resolution of the Directors to Redeem Shares

It was resolved that pursuant to the articles of association the whole of the class of 10 per cent redeemable preference shares in the capital of the company consisting of 10,000 £1 shares fully paid be redeemed on [*date*] [at par]* [and the dividend on these shares for the six months ending on [*same date*] be and is hereby declared payable on that date].

The secretary was asked to advise the shareholders and make all necessary administrative arrangements.

EDITOR'S NOTE

* Here enter redemption price if other than par value.

(b) Notice to Shareholders

As empowered by the articles of association of the company the directors have resolved that the company redeem the whole of its class of 10,000 £1 10 per cent redeemable preference shares in its capital at a price of £1 per share on [*date*] [and have declared a dividend on these shares for the six months ending on that date].

You are hereby given notice of the proposed redemption in respect of the 1,000 shares held by you.

You are asked to complete the attached form and forward it together with your share certificate(s) to the secretary of the company at [*address*] to arrive on or before [*date, a week before redemption*].

By order of the Board

Secretary

Redemption of 10 per cent preference shares of £1 each

NAME:

NO OF SHARES HELD:

PAYMENT DATE:

PROCEEDS: £

Payment will be made by cheque to the shareholder at the registered address unless the box below is completed.

Please pay redemption proceeds to: .... Name .... Address

[*Signature*] [*date*]

Precedent 5D.3(3)

Notice of consolidation, division, sub-division, redemption or cancellation of shares, or conversion, re-conversion of stock into shares

122

Please do not write in this margin

Pursuant to section 122 of the Companies Act 1985

Please complete legibly, preferably in black type, or bold block lettering

To the Registrar of Companies

For official use

Company number

Name of company

* insert full name of company

*

gives notice that:

10,000 ORDINARY SHARES OF £1 EACH IN THE CAPITAL OF THE COMPANY WERE REDEEMED ON [*date*]

‡ Insert Director, Secretary, Administrator, Administrative Receiver or Receiver (Scotland) as appropriate

Signed | Designation‡ | Date

Presentor's name address and reference (if any):

For official Use

General Section | Post room

Precedent 5D.3(4)

Entries in Register of Members on Redemption of Shares

Name ____________________ Class of Share ____________________

Address ____________________ Dividends to ____________________ Denomination ____________________

____________________ ____________________ Date of entry as member ____________________

____________________ ____________________ Date of cessation of membership ____________________

Date of Allotment OR Entry of Transfer	References in Register		No of Share Certificate	Amount paid or agreed to be considered as paid	Acquisitions	Disposals	Balance	Remarks
	Allotments	Transfers						
b/forward							1,000	
[*date*]						1,000		REDEEMED PURSUANT TO A MINUTE OF THE DIRECTORS DATED [*date*].

5E Financial Assistance by a Private Company for the Acquisition of Its Own Shares

Introduction

ss 151–154 There are strict prohibitions on companies providing financial assistance (widely defined) to an individual or other company to acquire their shares (or those of their holding company) (see *Gore-Browne on Companies*, at § 13.9; *Jordans Secretarial Administration*, at § 2.5.4).

s 155 Private companies are exempt from these prohibitions if (a) the net assets are not reduced by an amount that is greater than the distributable profits and (b) the procedures outlined below are followed.

A private company can also give assistance towards purchase of the shares in its holding company so long as the holding company and any ultimate holding company is also a private company.

1948 Table A, reg 10 These exemptions were brought in by the Companies Act 1981 and companies incorporated before that date usually have in their articles (as in the 1948 Table A before amendment by the 1981 Act) a prohibition on all forms of financial assistance. It is necessary, therefore, to check the articles and if necessary amend them before proceeding with any proposal to give financial assistance (see Precedent 5D.1(2), Resolution 1). It may also be necessary to amend the memorandum to ensure there are adequate powers and no prohibitions.

This section deals only with procedures and careful reference should be made to *Gore-Browne on Companies* and *Jordans Secretarial Administration* (as above) to ensure that any proposed transaction falls within the exemptions. A breach of the exemptions is a criminal offence by the recipient of the assistance and by the directors of the company. It should be noted that there are restrictions on companies giving loans to their directors (see p 269) which remain effective even if the procedures below are followed.

Procedures

s 155 A statutory declaration in the prescribed form must be made by the directors of the company proposing to give the financial assistance.

s 156 Annexed to the statutory declaration must be a report by the auditors confirming that they are not aware of anything to indicate that the opinion expressed by the directors in the declaration is unreasonable.

It will be noted that in making the statement in the statutory declaration as to the solvency of this company, the directors must take account of contingent and prospective liabilities.

See Precedent 5E.1 (p 141) MINUTES OF DIRECTORS RESOLVING TO GIVE FINANCIAL ASSISTANCE

See Precedent 5E.2 (p 142) FORM G 155(6)a DECLARATION IN RELATION TO ASSISTANCE FOR THE ACQUISITION OF SHARES

See Precedent 5E.3 (p 145) REPORT BY THE AUDITORS UNDER SECTION 156(4) OF THE COMPANIES ACT 1985

Unless it is a wholly owned subsidiary proposing to provide assistance, the proposed assistance must be approved by a special resolution of the company passed within seven days of the date of the statutory declaration of the directors. If passed at a general meeting the statutory declaration and auditors' report must be available at the meeting or circulated with the written resolution. If passed by written resolution, copies of such documents must be sent to the members before or at the same time as the written resolution.

Sch 15A CA 1989, s 114

See Precedent 5E.4 (p 145) SPECIAL RESOLUTION TO APPROVE FINANCIAL ASSISTANCE FOR PURCHASE OF SHARES IN COMPANY GIVING THE ASSISTANCE

If the financial assistance is being given by a subsidiary for the acquisition of shares in its holding company, a special resolution approving the assistance must be passed by the holding company and any intermediate holding company, unless any such company is a wholly owned subsidiary.

See Precedent 5E.5 (p 145) MINUTE OF THE DIRECTORS OF THE HOLDING COMPANY WHEN FINANCIAL ASSISTANCE FOR ACQUISITION OF SHARES IN IT IS PROVIDED BY A SUBSIDIARY

See Precedent 5E.6 (p 146) FORM G 155(6)b DECLARATION BY THE DIRECTORS OF A HOLDING COMPANY IN RELATION TO ASSISTANCE FOR THE ACQUISITION OF SHARES

See Precedent 5E.7 (p 149) SPECIAL RESOLUTION OF HOLDING COMPANY TO APPROVE GIVING OF FINANCIAL ASSISTANCE BY SUBSIDIARY FOR PURCHASE OF SHARES IN HOLDING COMPANY

The statutory declaration, the auditors' report and the special resolution must be filed with the Registrar of Companies within 15 days of the passing of the special resolution.

s 157 Within 28 days of the passing of such special resolution any members who did not vote in favour of it and who together hold not less than 10 per cent in nominal value of the company's share capital or any class thereof may apply to the court for cancellation of the resolution.

The form of an application to the court is outside the scope of this work and should be settled by the applicant's legal advisers.

Upon notification of such an application the company must forthwith file Form G 157 with the Registrar of Companies.

See Precedent 5E.8 (p 150) FORM G 157 NOTICE OF APPLICATION MADE TO THE COURT FOR THE CANCELLATION OF A SPECIAL RESOLUTION REGARDING FINANCIAL ASSISTANCE FOR THE ACQUISITION OF SHARES

Subsequently, any court order confirming or cancelling the special resolution must be filed with the Registrar of Companies within 15 days or such longer period as the court may direct.

Payment of the financial assistance cannot be made until the expiry of 28 days from the passing of the resolution, during which period objection may be made unless:

(a) all shareholders voted in person or by proxy in favour of the special resolution; or
(b) the statutory written resolution procedures (see ss 381A, 381B, 381C and Sch 15A, para 4, of the Companies Act 1985) is used. In which case copies of the statutory declaration and auditors' report should be circulated with the resolution.

Any payment must be made within eight weeks of the passing of the statutory declaration.

Precedent 5E.1

Minutes of Directors Resolving to Give Financial Assistance

1. It was proposed that the company give financial assistance towards the purchase of its own shares as follows.

Loan to [*name*] of [£50,000] for the acquisition of [50,000 'A' ordinary] shares of [£1] each at [par].

2. It was reported that it would only be possible to enter into the foregoing documents if the conditions of ss 155 to 158 of the Companies Act 1985 had been duly satisfied.

The directors accordingly studied the appropriate statutory declaration required by s 155(6) of the said Act and it was reported that they had received from the company's auditors a report in the form prescribed by s 156(4) of the said Act.

3. Each of the directors present indicated that they were satisfied that the declaration could be made, having taken into consideration the debts and contingent and prospective liabilities of the company for the purposes of s 156(3) of the Companies Act 1985.

4. [*It was resolved that an extraordinary general meeting of the company should be called for [*date*] at which a special resolution approving the transaction would be proposed.] **[Since the company would be at the relevant time a wholly owned subsidiary of   Ltd there existed no requirement for a special resolution to approve the giving of financial assistance.]

5. Accordingly, it was resolved that ***[subject to the special resolution referred to above having been passed] any two directors and the secretary be authorised to carry out all such acts as may be requisite for the completion of any formalities to which the company is a party in respect of the transaction.

There being no further business the meeting was declared closed.

.... Chairman

EDITOR'S NOTE

*, **, *** } Delete whichever is inapplicable.

Precedent 5E.2

Declaration in relation to assistance for the acquisition of shares.

Please do not write in this margin

Pursuant to section 155(6) of the Companies Act 1985

Please complete legibly, preferably in black type, or bold block lettering

Note
Please read the notes on page 3 before completing this form.

* insert full name of company

ø insert name(s) and address(es) of all the directors

To the Registrar of Companies

For official use

Company number

Name of company

* DILSBOROUGH PROJECTS LIMITED

I/We ø [*A*]

[*B*]

[*C*]

[*D*]

[*Note: all directors must join in this declaration*]

† delete as appropriate

§ delete whichever is inappropriate

[~~the sole director~~][all the directors]† of the above company do solemnly and sincerely declare that:

The business of the company is:

~~(a) that of a [recognised bank][licensed institution]† within the meaning of the Banking Act 1979§~~

~~(b) that of a person authorised under section 3 or 4 of the Insurance Companies Act 1982 to carry on insurance business in the United Kingdom§~~

(c) something other than the above§

The company is proposing to give financial assistance in connection with the acquisition of shares in the [company] ~~[company's holding company~~ ______________________________ Limited]†

The assistance is for the purpose of [that acquisition][~~reducing or discharging a liability incurred for the purpose of that acquisition~~].†

The number and class of the shares acquired or to be acquired is: 50,000 'A' ORDINARY SHARES OF £1 EACH

Presentor's name address and reference (if any):

For official Use
General Section | Post room

The assistance is to be given to: (note 2) THE ACQUIROR
REGINALD MORTON (SEE BELOW)

Please do not write in this margin

Please complete legibly, preferably in black type, or bold block lettering

The assistance will take the form of:

* [A LOAN FROM THE COMPANY OF £50,000]
TO REGINALD MORTON FOR THE PURPOSE
OF ACQUIRING 50,000 'A' ORDINARY
SHARES OF £1 EACH IN THE CAPITAL OF
THE COMPANY

The person who ~~[has acquired]~~[will acquire]† the shares is:
REGINALD MORTON, HOPPETT HALL, DILSBOROUGH

† delete as appropriate

The principal terms on which the assistance will be given are:

* [THE LOAN WILL BEAR INTEREST AT ONE PER CENT
OVER THE BASE RATE OF MELMOTTE'S BANK PLC
AND BE REPAYABLE IN FULL ON 31 MARCH 1995]

The amount of cash to be transferred to the person assisted is £ *50,000 **NIL

The value of any asset to be transferred to the person assisted is £ NIL

The date on which the assistance is to be given is*** ______ 19 ____

Please do not write in this margin

Please complete legibly, preferably in black type, or bold block lettering

* delete either (a) or (b) as appropriate

I/We have formed the opinion, as regards the company's initial situation immediately following the date on which the assistance is proposed to be given, that there will be no ground on which it could then be found to be unable to pay its debts.(note 3)

(a)[I/We have formed the opinion that the company will be able to pay its debts as they fall due during the year immediately following that date]*(note 3)

~~(b)[It is intended to commence the winding-up of the company within 12 months of that date, and I/we have formed the opinion that the company will be able to pay its debts in full within 12 months of the commencement of the winding up.]*(note 3)~~

And I/we make this solemn declaration conscientiously believing the same to be true and by virtue of the provisions of the Statutory Declarations Act 1835.

Declared at ______________________

____

____

the__________ day of ______________

one thousand nine hundred and ______________

____

before me ______________________

A Commissioner for Oaths or Notary Public of Justice of the Peace or a Solicitor having the powers conferred on A Commissioner for Oaths.

Declarants to sign below

NOTES

1 For the meaning of "a person incurring a liability" and "reducing or discharging a liability" see section 152(3) of the Companies Act 1985.

2 Insert full name(s) and address(es) of the person(s) to whom assistance is to be given; if a recipient is a company the registered office address should be shown.

3 Contingent and prospective liabilities of the company are to be taken into account - see section 156(3) of the Companies Act 1985.

4 The auditors' report required by section 156(4) of the Companies Act 1985 must be annexed to this form.

EDITOR'S NOTE

* } Specimen narratives for different types of transactions.
** }

*** A date after the expiry of 28 days from the date of the special resolution approving the transaction.

Precedent 5E.3

*Report by the Auditors under Section 156(4) of the Companies Act 1985

We have enquired into the state of affairs of Ltd as at [*date*]** and we are not aware of anything to indicate that the opinion expressed by the directors in the foregoing declaration is unreasonable in all the circumstances.

EDITOR'S NOTES

*The report will be addressed to the directors and must be annexed to Form G 155(6)a when filed with the Registrar of Companies.
**This will be the latest practical date prior to the statutory declaration.

Precedent 5E.4

Special Resolution to Approve Financial Assistance for Purchase of Shares in Company Giving the Assistance

That the provision by the company of financial assistance to [*name*] for the purpose of acquiring [5,000 'A'] shares [of £1 each] in the capital of the company be and is hereby approved.

Precedent 5E.5

Minute of the Directors of the Holding Company when Financial Assistance for Acquisition of Shares in It is Provided by a Subsidiary

IT WAS REPORTED that it would only be possible for the company, and its relevant subsidiaries to enter into the foregoing documents if the conditions of ss 155 to 158 of the Companies Act 1985 had been duly satisfied. In that connection it was reported that the directors [and the directors of the company's subsidiaries] had made the appropriate statutory declarations required by s 155(6) of the said Act, and that such directors had received reports from the company's auditors in the form prescribed by s 156(4) of the said Act.

Accordingly, IT WAS RESOLVED that the documents referred to above be and are hereby approved and be executed or otherwise entered into in a manner prescribed by the articles of association.

Precedent 5E.6

Declaration by the directors of a holding company in relation to assistance for the acquisition of shares

Please do not write in this margin

Pursuant to section 155(6) of the Companies Act 1985

Please complete legibly, preferably in black type, or bold block lettering

To the Registrar of Companies

For official use

Company number

Note
Please read the notes on page 3 before completing this form.

Name of company

* BILLBROOK ENTERPRISES LTD

* insert full name of company

ø insert name(s) and address(es) of all the directors

I/We ø [*A*]

[*B*]

[*C*]

[*D*]

† delete as appropriate

[the sole director][all the directors]† of the above company (hereinafter called 'this company') do solemnly and sincerely declare that:

§ delete whichever is inappropriate

The business of this company is:

~~(a) that of a [recognised bank][licensed institution]† within the meaning of the Banking Act 1979§~~

~~(b) that of a person authorised under section 3 or 4 of the Insurance Companies Act 1982 to carry on insurance business in the United Kingdom§~~

(c) something other than the above§

This company is [the][a] holding company of* DILSBOROUGH PROJECTS LIMITED ______ which is proposing to give financial assistance in connection with the acquisition of shares in [this company][______ ~~the holding company of this company.]†~~

Presentor's name address and reference (if any):

For official Use

General Section

Post room

The assistance is for the purpose of [that acquisition][reducing or discharging a liability incurred for the purpose of that acquisition].† (note 1)

Please do not write in this margin

Please complete legibly, preferably in black type, or bold block lettering

The number and class of the shares acquired or to be acquired is: ______________________

____

The assistance is to be given to: (note 2) ______________________

____

____

____

The assistance will take the form of:

The person who [has acquired][will acquire]† the shares is:

† delete as appropriate

____

____

The principal terms on which the assistance will be given are:

The amount (if any) by which the net assets of the company which is giving the assistance will be reduced by giving it is ______________________

The amount of cash to be transferred to the person assisted is £______________________

The value of any asset to be transferred to the person assisted is £______________________

Please do not write in this margin

Please complete legibly, preferably in black type, or bold block lettering

The date on which the assistance is to be given is__________________ 19 ________

I/We have formed the opinion, as regards this company's initial situation immediately following the date on which the assistance is proposed to be given, that there will be no ground on which it could then be found to be unable to pay its debts.(note 3)

* delete either (a) or (b) as appropriate

(a)[I/We have formed the opinion that this company will be able to pay it's debts as they fall due during the year immediately following that date]*(note 3)

(b)[It is intended to commence the winding-up of this company within 12 months of that date, and I/we have formed the opinion that this company will be able to pay its debts in full within 12 months of the commencement of the winding up.]*(note 3)

And I/we make this solemn declaration conscientiously believing the same to be true and by virtue of the provisions of the Statutory Declarations Act 1835.

Declared at __________________ Declarants to sign below

____

____

the________ day of ____________

one thousand nine hundred and ____________

____

before me __________________

A Commissioner for Oaths or Notary Public of Justice of the Peace or a Solicitor having the powers conferred on A Commissioner for Oaths.

NOTES

1 For the meaning of "a person incurring a liability" and "reducing or discharging a liability" see section 152(3) of the Companies Act 1985.

2 Insert full name(s) and address(es) of the person(s) to whom assistance is to be given; if a recipient is a company the registered office address should be shown.

3 Contingent and prospective liabilities of the company are to be taken into account - see section 156(3) of the Companies Act 1985.

4 The auditors' report required by section 156(4) of the Companies Act 1985 must be annexed to this form.

EDITOR'S NOTE

This form will be completed in a manner similar to Precedent 5E.2, except as indicated.

Precedent 5E.7

Special Resolution of Holding Company to Approve Giving of Financial Assistance by Subsidiary for Purchase of Shares in Holding Company

That the provision by [*X Ltd*], a subsidiary company of the company, of financial assistance to [*name of intending purchaser*] for the purpose of acquiring [*number*] [*class*] shares in the capital of the company be and is hereby approved.

Precedent 5E.8

Notice of application made to the Court for the cancellation of a special resolution regarding financial assistance for the acquisition of shares

157

Please do not write in this margin

Pursuant to section 157(3) of the Companies Act 1985

Please complete legibly, preferably in black type, or bold block lettering

To the Registrar of Companies

For official use

Company number

Name of company

* DILSBOROUGH PROJECTS LIMITED

* insert full name of company

gives notice that an application has been made to the Court on 15 JULY 1989

for the cancellation of the special resolution passed by the company on 5 JULY 1989

approving the giving of financial assistance by

† delete as appropriate

[the company]†

ø insert full name of the subsidiary company proposing to give the financial assistance

~~[the company's subsidiary ø~~ ______________________

______________________]†

for the purchase of shares :—

(a) [in the company]†

§ insert full name of the holding company in relation to the acquisition of whose shares financial assistance is proposed to be given

~~(b) [in §~~ ______________________

______________________ ~~, the company's holding company].†~~

‡ Insert Director, Secretary, Administrator, Administrative Receiver or Receiver (Scotland) as appropriate

Signed G Botsey   Designation‡ Director   Date 17 JULY 1989

Presentor's name address and reference (if any):

For official Use
General Section | Post room

Chapter 6

BORROWING AND DEBENTURES

General

Power to borrow and charge the assets of the company as security, and the exercise of such power, depends on the terms of the memorandum and articles of association. This section assumes that such power exists and may be exercised without limitation by the directors.

See Appendix 2 for specimen memorandum clause covering borrowing powers and specimen article empowering directors to exercise this power.

The most usual form of borrowing and charge on the assets of a company is a bank overdraft supported by an 'all monies' debenture giving a fixed and floating charge as security.

See *Jordans Secretarial Administration*, at § 2.68, for further discussion.

The following precedents cover the position in England and Wales. Law and procedures in Scotland are different.

See Precedent 6.1 (p 154) DIRECTORS' RESOLUTION TO ENTER INTO AN 'ALL MONIES' DEBENTURE

See Precedent 6.2 (p 155) SPECIMEN BANK 'ALL MONIES' DEBENTURE GIVING A FIXED AND FLOATING CHARGE

s 407 All charges given on the assets of a company must be entered in the Register of Charges
s 408 kept by the company and a copy of every instrument creating a charge must be kept at the registered office.

This Register must contain details of all charges on the company's property whether or not registrable with the Registrar of Companies. These will include both legal charges on assets, including floating charges, and equitable charges (eg deposit of deeds of a property with an undertaking to charge at a later date if so required).

See Chapter 13 for statutory registers generally.

See Precedent 6.3 (p 161) REGISTER OF MORTGAGES AND CHARGES

s 395 Charges of the specific types listed in the Companies Act must be filed with the Registrar of Companies. Such filing, complete in all details, must be made within 21 days of the date of creation of the charge otherwise the charge becomes void against other creditors or a liquidator and any borrowing it is purported to secure becomes immediately repayable. See *Jordans Secretarial Administration*, at § 2.69.

The Companies Act 1989 makes substantial changes in the registration procedures and the relevant sections are expected to come into force in late 1991. The following precedents deal with existing procedures and the new procedures are summarised at the end of this section.

The company must complete and deliver to the Registrar of Companies Form M 395 together with the original charge document and a copy certified by, for example, a solicitor, as a true copy of the original. This is sometimes done by the lender, but responsibility lies with the company.

See Precedent 6.4 (p 162) FORM M 395 PARTICULARS OF A MORTGAGE OR CHARGE

This form must be completed correctly and in adequate detail to provide a clear description of:

(a) the document creating the charge;
(b) the amount due or secured under the charge;
(c) the property charged.

If the completion of this form is deficient it will be returned by the Registrar unfiled and valuable time for registration will be lost.

s 402 When Form M 395 has been registered the Registrar of Companies will issue a Certificate of Registration which is conclusive evidence of registration and the date thereof.

See Precedent 6.5 (p 164) CERTIFICATE OF REGISTRATION OF A MORTGAGE OR CHARGE

s 402 A copy of this certificate must be endorsed on every document by which a registered charge is secured, eg on the debenture deed.

It should be noted also that charges on land will in most cases be registrable under the Land Charges Act 1972 or the Land Registration Act 1925 and should be so registered at the Land Charges Registry or the Land Registry if the charge is to be fully protected. This is the responsibility of the lenders and will usually be undertaken by their solicitors.

If a company acquires property which is subject to an existing charge, which if created by
s 400 the company would have been registrable, it must file particulars of the charges on Form M 400 within 21 days of acquisition.

See Precedent 6.6 (p 165) FORM M 400 PARTICULARS OF A CHARGE SUBJECT TO WHICH PROPERTY HAS BEEN ACQUIRED

A debenture or other charge document will be released on repayment of the borrowing by completion of a form of discharge usually printed on the reverse.

See Precedent 6.7 (p 166) FORM OF DISCHARGE OF A DEBENTURE

An entry in the company's Register of Charges will be needed to record the discharge. See Precedent 6.3.

s 403 The borrower may (and indeed, should) file a declaration of satisfaction. This form needs to be sworn as a statutory declaration.

See Precedent 6.8 (p 167) FORM M 403a DECLARATION OF SATISFACTION IN FULL OR IN PART OF MORTGAGE OR CHARGE

Upon receipt of such document the Registrar of Companies will appropriately endorse his Register of Charges and place the declaration on the company's file.

Revised Procedures under Companies Act 1989

CA 1989, ss 92–104 Revised procedures are expected to come into force in 1991 or 1992 and additional notes (including the prescribed particulars that are to be registered) and revised prescribed forms will be issued by the Registrar of Companies upon the making of the relevant statutory instrument.

The filing time limit for a registrable charge will remain at 21 days and there are redefinitions of what is registrable.

The company or anyone interested in the charge may file the Form M 395 (under the old procedure the company alone is responsible – although the chargee often acts for it).

The new system will alter the position on late delivery of particulars. At the present time the registration particulars must be filed complete before the expiry of the 21 day limit. If not, a court order is necessary for late registration to be effected. The new procedure CA 1989, s 95 makes it possible to perfect the charge by allowing the delivery of the correct particulars after expiry of the 21 day limit, without recourse to the courts, but until those particulars are delivered the charge will be void against an administrator, liquidator or anyone acquiring an interest in the property, such as a purchaser or a subsequent chargee.

If a memorandum of satisfaction is filed on discharge of a charge it will need to be signed both by the company and the chargee releasing the charge. At present only a statutory declaration by an officer of the company is required.

Precedent 6.1

Directors' Resolution to Enter Into an 'All Monies' Debenture

There was produced to the meeting an all monies debenture in favour of Melmotte's Bank plc, in the standard form, creating a fixed and floating charge on the assets of the company.

It was resolved that the terms and conditions of the debenture be and are approved and accepted and that this debenture document be entered into as a deed* [under the seal of the company] **[and any two directors be authorised to execute it].

EDITOR'S NOTES

* If the company uses a seal.
** If the company has discontinued the use of the seal.

Precedent 6.2

Specimen Bank 'All Monies' Debenture Giving a Fixed and Floating Charge

Debenture

Insert company's name as registered

1. THE BUSH HOTEL (DILSBOROUGH) LTD
(hereinafter called 'the Company') whose registered office is at

10 MARKET PLACE
DILSBOROUGH
RUFFORDSHIRE
RV15 3AB

will on demand in writing made to the Company pay or discharge to Melmotte's Bank PLC (hereinafter called 'the Bank') all moneys and liabilities which shall for the time being (and whether on or at any time after such demand) be due owing or incurred to the Bank by the Company whether actually or contingently and whether solely or jointly with any other person and whether as principal or surety and including interest discount commission or other lawful charges and expenses which the Bank may in the course of its business charge in respect of any of the matters aforesaid or for keeping the Company's account and so that interest shall be computed and compounded according to the usual mode of the bank as well after as before any demand made or judgement obtained hereunder.

2. A demand for payment or any other demand or notice under this Debenture may be made or given by any manager or officer of the Bank or of any branch thereof by letter addressed to the Company and sent by post to or left at the registered office of the Company or its last known place of business and if sent by post shall be deemed to have been made or given at noon on the day following the day the letter was posted.

3. The Company as beneficial owner hereby charges with the payment or discharge of all moneys and liabilities hereby covenanted to be paid or discharged by the Company:

(*a*) by way of legal mortgage all the freehold and leasehold property of the Company the title to which is registered at HM Land Registry and which is described in the Schedule hereto together with all buildings fixtures (including trade fixtures) and fixed plant and machinery from time to time thereon;
(*b*) by way of legal mortgage all other freehold and leasehold property of the Company now vested in it (whether or not registered at HM Land Registry) together with all buildings fixtures (including trade fixtures) and fixed plant and machinery from time to time thereon;
(*c*) by way of first fixed charge all future freehold and leasehold property of the Company together with all buildings fixtures (including trade fixtures) and fixed plant and machinery from time to time thereon and all the goodwill and uncalled capital for the time being of the Company;

(*d*) by way of first fixed charge all book debts and other debts now and from time to time due or owing to the Company;
(*e*) by way of a first floating charge all other the undertaking and assets of the Company whatsoever and wheresoever both present and future but so that the Company is not to be at liberty to create any mortgage or charge upon and so that no lien shall in any case or in any manner arise on or affect any part of the said premises either in priority to or *pari passu* with the charge hereby created and further that the Company shall have no power without the consent of the Bank to part with or dispose of any part of such premises except by way of sale in the ordinary course of its business.

Any debentures mortgages or charges hereafter created by the Company (otherwise than in favour of the Bank) shall be expressed to be subject to this Debenture. The Company shall subject to the rights of any prior mortgagee deposit with the Bank and the Bank during the continuance of this security shall be entitled to hold all deeds and documents of title relating to the Company's freehold and leasehold property for the time being and the Company shall on demand in writing made to the Company by the Bank at the cost of the Company execute a valid legal mortgage of any freehold and leasehold properties acquired by it after the date hereof and the fixed plant and machinery thereon to secure the payment or discharge to the Bank of the moneys and liabilities hereby secured such legal mortgage to be in such form as the Bank may require.

4. This security shall be a continuing security to the Bank notwithstanding any settlement of account or other matter or thing whatsoever and shall be without prejudice and in addition to any other security whether by way of mortgage equitable charge or otherwise howsoever which the Bank may now or any time hereafter hold on the property of the Company or any part thereof for or in respect of the moneys hereby secured or any of them or any part thereof respectively.

5. During the continuance of this security the Company:—

(*a*) shall furnish to the Bank copies of the trading and profit and loss account and audited balance sheet in respect of each financial year of the Company and of every subsidiary thereof forthwith upon the same becoming available and not in any event later than the expiration of three months from the end of such financial year and also from time to time such other financial statements and information respecting the assets and liabilities of the Company as the Bank may reasonably require;
(*b*) shall maintain the aggregate value of the Company's book debts (excluding debts owing by any subsidiary of the Company) and cash in hand as appearing in the Company's books and of its stock according to the best estimate that can be formed without it being necessary to take stock for the purpose at a sum to be fixed by the Bank from time to time and whenever required by the Bank obtain from the Managing Director of the Company for the time being or if there shall be no Managing Director then from one of the Directors of the Company and furnish to the Bank a certificate showing the said aggregate value;
(*c*) shall pay into the Company's account with the Bank all moneys which

it may receive in respect of the book debts and other debts hereby charged and shall not without the prior consent of the Bank in writing purport to charge or assign the same in favour of any other person and shall if called upon to do so by the Bank execute a legal assignment of such book debts and other debts to the Bank;
(*d*) shall insure and keep insured with an insurance office or underwriters to be approved by the Bank in writing from time to time and if so required by the Bank in the joint names of the Company and the Bank such of its property as is insurable against loss or damage by fire and such other risks as the Bank may from time to time require to the full replacement value thereof and shall maintain such other insurances as are normally maintained by prudent companies carrying on similar businesses and will duly pay all premiums and other moneys necessary for effecting and keeping up such insurances within one week of the same becoming due and will on demand produce to the Bank the policies of such insurance and the receipts for such payments and if default shall at any time be made by the Company in effecting or keeping up such insurance as aforesaid or in producing any such policy or receipt to the Bank on demand the Bank may take out or renew such insurances in any sum which the Bank may think expedient and all moneys expended by the Bank under this provision shall be deemed to be properly paid by the Bank;
(*e*) shall keep all buildings and all plant machinery fixtures fittings and other effects in or upon the same and every part thereof in good repair and in good working order and condition.

6. (*a*) At any time after the Bank shall have demanded payment of any moneys hereby secured or if a petition shall be presented to the Court under section 9 of the Insolvency Act 1986 for the making of an administration order in respect of the Company or if requested by the Company the Bank may appoint by writing any person or persons (whether an officer of the Bank or not) to be a receiver and manager or receivers and managers (hereinafter called 'the Receiver' which expression shall where the context so admits include the plural and any substituted receiver and manager or receivers and managers) of all or any part of the property hereby charged.
(*b*) The Bank may from time to time determine the remuneration of the Receiver and may remove the Receiver and appoint another in his place.
(*c*) The Receiver shall be the agent of the Company (which subject to the provisions of the Companies Act 1985 shall alone be personally liable for his acts defaults and remuneration) and shall have and be entitled to exercise all powers conferred by the Law of Property Act 1925 in the same way as if the Receiver had been duly appointed thereunder and in particular by way of addition to but without hereby limiting any general powers hereinbefore referred to (and without prejudice to the Bank's power of sale) the Receiver shall have power to do the following things namely:

(i) to take possession of collect and get in all or any part of the property hereby charged and for that purpose to take any proceedings in the name of the Company or otherwise as he shall think fit;
(ii) to carry on or concur in carrying on the business of the

Company and to raise money from the Bank or others on the security of any property hereby charged;

(iii) to sell or concur in selling let or concur in letting and to terminate or to accept surrenders of leases or tenancies of any of the property hereby charged in such manner and generally on such terms and conditions as he shall think fit and to carry any such transactions into effect in the name of and on behalf of the Company;

(iv) to make any arrangement or compromise which the Bank or he shall think fit;

(v) to make and effect all repairs improvements and insurances;

(vi) to appoint managers officers and agents for the aforesaid purposes at such salaries as he may determine;

(vii) to call up all or any portion of the uncalled capital of the Company;

(viii) to do all such other acts and things as may be considered to be incidental or conducive to any of the matters or powers aforesaid and which he lawfully may or can do.

7. The Company hereby irrevocably appoints the Bank and the Receiver jointly and also severally the Attorney and Attorneys of the Company for the Company and in its name and on its behalf and as its act and deed or otherwise to seal and deliver and otherwise perfect any deed assurance agreement instrument or act which may be required or may be deemed proper for any of the purposes aforesaid and the Company hereby declares that as and when the security hereby created shall become enforceable the Company will hold all the property hereby charged (subject to the Company's right of redemption) Upon Trust to convey assign or otherwise deal with the same in such manner and to such person as the Bank shall direct and declares that it shall be lawful for the Bank by an instrument under its Common Seal to appoint a new trustee or new trustees of the said property and in particular at any time or times to appoint a new trustee or new trustees thereof in place of the Company as if the Company desired to be discharged from the trust or in place of any trustee or trustees appointed under this power as if he or they were dead.

8. Any moneys received under the powers hereby conferred shall subject to the repayment of any claims having priority to this Debenture be paid or applied in the following order of priority:

(*a*) in satisfaction of all costs charges and expenses properly incurred and payments properly made by the Bank or the Receiver and of the remuneration of the Receiver;
(*b*) in or towards satisfaction of the moneys outstanding and secured by this Debenture;
(*c*) as to the surplus (if any) to the person or persons entitled thereto.

9. During the continuance of this security no statutory or other power of granting or agreeing to grant or of accepting or agreeing to accept surrenders of leases or tenancies of the freehold and leasehold property hereby charged or any part thereof shall be capable of being exercised by the Company without the previous consent in writing of the Bank nor shall

section 93 of the Law of Property Act 1925 dealing with the consolidation of mortgages apply to this security.

10. Section 103 of the said Act shall not apply to this security but the statutory power of sale shall as between the Bank and a purchaser from the Bank arise on and be exercisable at any time after the execution of this security provided that the Bank shall not exercise the said power of sale until payment of the moneys hereby secured has been demanded or the Receiver has been appointed but this proviso shall not affect a purchaser or put him upon inquiry whether such demand or appointment has been made.

11. All costs charges and expenses incurred hereunder by the Bank and all other moneys paid by the Bank or by the Receiver in perfecting or otherwise in connection with this security or in respect of the property hereby charged including (without prejudice to the generality of the forego- ing) all moneys expended by the Bank under clause 5 hereof and all costs of the Bank or of the Receiver of all proceedings for the enforcement of the security hereby constituted or for obtaining payment of the moneys hereby secured or arising out of or in connection with the acts authorised by clause 6 hereof (and so that any taxation of the Bank costs charges and expenses shall be on the basis of solicitor and own client) shall be recoverable from the Company as a debt and may be debited to any account of the Company and shall bear interest accordingly and shall be charged on the premises comprised herein and the charge hereby conferred shall be in addition and without prejudice to any and every other remedy lien or security which the Bank may or but for the said charge would have for the moneys hereby secured or any part thereof.

12. In respect of any freehold or leasehold property hereby charged the title to which is registered at HM Land Registry it is hereby certified that the charge created by this Debenture does not contravene any of the provisions of the Memorandum and Articles of Association of the Company.

13. In this Debenture where the context so admits the expression 'the Bank' shall include persons deriving title under the Bank and any reference herein to any statute or any section of any statute shall be deemed to include reference to any statutory modification or re-enactment thereof for the time being in force.

Given under the Common Seal of the Company this 12 day of DECEMBER 1986.

The Schedule above referred to

Details of registered land

County/London Borough	Title No	Address of Property
RUFFORDSHIRE	12394T	THE BUSH HOTEL 10 MARKET PLACE DILSBOROUGH

The Common Seal of the Company was hereunto affixed in pursuance of a Resolution of the Board of Directors in the presence of

J. F. Runciman Director

J J Joyce Secretary

Company's Registered Number 4 527 326

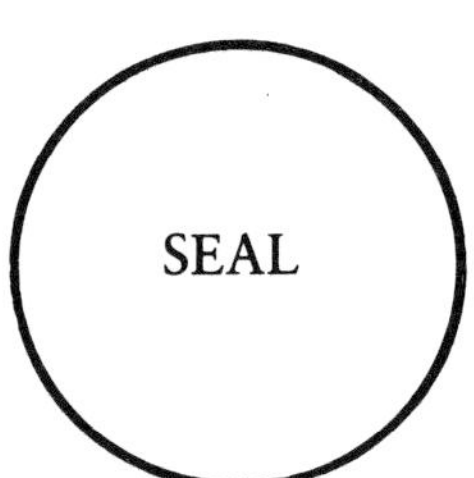

The address for service of the Bank in the case of any registered land is:—

[*We are indebted to Barclays Bank plc for permission to use this precedent which is their standard form of 'all monies' debenture giving fixed and floating charges.*]

Precedent 6.3

Register of Mortgages and Charges

Entry No.	Particulars of Charges			Rate of Interest	Description of Property Charged	Name and Address of Persons entitled to Charge	Date of discharge of Charge	Remarks
	Date	Description of Instrument Creating Charge	Amount of Charge					
1	12/12/86	ALL MONIES, FIXED AND FLOATING	*[amount due to chargee]*	VARIABLE	BUSH HOTEL,	MELMOTTE'S BANK PLC	5/3/90	
		CHARGES			DILSBOROUGH. ALL	LOMBARD ST, LONDON		
					ASSETS FOR THE	EC2		
					TIME BEING OWNED			
					BY THE COMPANY			

Precedent 6.4

M

Particulars of a mortgage or charge

Please do not write in this margin

Pursuant to section 395 of the Companies Act 1985

Please complete legibly, preferably in black type, or bold block lettering

To the Registrar of Companies

For official use

Company number: 4 527 326

Name of company

* THE BUSH HOTEL (DILSBOROUGH) LTD

* insert full name of company

Date of creation of the charge

12 DECEMBER 1986

Description of the instrument (if any) creating or evidencing the charge (note 2)

DEBENTURE

Amount secured by the mortgage or charge

ALL MONIES AND LIABILITIES WHICH SHALL FOR THE TIME BEING BE DUE OWING OR INCURRED TO THE BANK BY THE COMPANY WHETHER ACTUALLY OR CONTINGENTLY INCLUDING INTEREST, DISCOUNT, COMMISSION OR OTHER LAWFUL CHARGES AND EXPENSES

Names and addresses of the mortgagees or persons entitled to the charge

MELMOTTE'S BANK PLC
LOMBARD ST LONDON

Postcode EC2M 32X

Presentor's name address and reference (if any):

For official Use

Mortgage Section

Post room

Time critical reference

Short particulars of all the property mortgaged or charged

1. THE BUSH HOTEL, DILSBOROUGH, RUFFORDSHIRE TOGETHER WITH ALL BUILDINGS, FIXTURES (INCLUDING TRADE FIXTURES) AND FIXED PLANT AND MACHINERY FROM TIME TO TIME, BY WAY OF LEGAL MORTGAGE.
2. ALL OTHER FREEHOLD/LEASEHOLD PROPERTY NOW VESTED IN THE COMPANY (WHETHER OR NOT REGISTERED AT HM LAND REGISTRY) WITH ALL BUILDINGS, FIXTURES (INCLUDING TRADE FIXTURES) AND FIXED PLANT AND MACHINERY FROM TIME TO TIME BY WAY OF LEGAL MORTGAGE.
3. BY WAY OF FIRST FIXED CHARGE, ALL FUTURE FREEHOLD/LEASEHOLD PROPERTY, TOGETHER WITH ALL BUILDINGS, FIXTURES (INCLUDING TRADE FIXTURES) FIXED PLANT AND MACHINERY FROM TIME TO TIME THEREON, ALL GOODWILL AND UNCALLED CAPITAL.
4. BY WAY OF FIRST FIXED CHARGE ALL BOOK DEBTS AND OTHER DEBTS NOW AND FROM TIME TO TIME DUE OR OWING.
5. BY WAY OF FIRST FIXED CHARGE ALL OTHER UNDERTAKING AND ASSETS OF THE COMPANY WHATSOEVER OR WHERESOEVER BOTH PRESENT AND FUTURE SO THAT THE COMPANY MAY NOT CREATE ANY MORTGAGE OR CHARGE THEREON AND SO NO LIEN SHALL ARISE ON OR AFFECT ANY PART OF THE SAID PREMISES IN PRIORITY TO OR PARI PASSU WITH THE CHARGE HEREBY CREATED AND THE COMPANY SHALL HAVE NO POWER WITHOUT CONSENT TO PART WITH OR DISPOSE OF ANY PART OF SUCH PREMISES EXCEPT BY SALE IN THE ORDINARY COURSE OF BUSINESS. ANY DEBENTURES, MORTGAGES OR CHARGES HEREAFTER SHALL BE EXPRESSED TO BE SUBJECT TO THE DEBENTURE.

Please do not write in this margin

Please complete legibly, preferably in black type, or bold block lettering

Particulars as to commission allowance or discount (note 3)

NONE

Signed G M Sharp Date 14 DECEMBER 1986

On behalf of ~~[company]~~[mortgagee/chargee]†[Secretary]

† delete as appropriate

Notes

1 The original instrument (if any) creating or evidencing the charge, together with these prescribed particulars correctly completed must be delivered to the Registrar of Companies within 21 days after the date of creation of the charge (section 395). If the property is situated and the charge was created outside the United Kingdom delivery to the Registrar must be effected within 21 days after the date on which the instrument could in due course of post, and if dispatched with due diligence, have been received in the United Kingdom (section 398). A copy of the instrument creating the charge will be accepted where the property charged is situated and the charge was created outside the United Kingdom (section 398) and in such cases the copy must be verified to be a correct copy either by the company or by the person who has delivered or sent the copy to the registrar. The verification must be signed by or on behalf of the person giving the verification and where this is given by a body corporate it must be signed by an officer of that body. A verified copy will also be accepted where section 398(4) applies (property situate in Scotland or Northern Ireland and Form No 398 is submitted.

2 A description of the instrument, eg "Trust Deed", "Debenture", "Mortgage" or "Legal charge", etc, as the case may be, should be given.

3 In this section there should be inserted the amount or rate per cent. of the commission, allowance or discount (if any) paid or made either directly or indirectly by the company to any person in consideration of his;
(a) subscribing or agreeing to subscribe, whether absolutely or conditionally, or
(b) procuring or agreeing to procure subscriptions, whether absolute or conditional,
for any of the debentures included in this return. The rate of interest payable under the terms of the debentures should not be entered.

4 If any of the spaces in this form provide insufficient space the particulars must be entered on the prescribed continuation sheet.

Precedent 6.5

Certificate of Registration of a Mortgage or Charge

I hereby certify that a mortgage or charge dated 12 December 1986 and created by The Bush Hotel (Dilsborough) Ltd for securing all moneys now due or hereafter to become due or from time to time accruing due from the Company to Melmotte's Bank Plc on any account whatsoever was registered pursuant to s 395 of the Companies Act 1985 on 14 December 1986.

Given under my hand at Cardiff on 15 December 1986.

....
Assistant Registrar of Companies

EDITOR'S NOTE

The above Registrar's Certificate, when completed, should itself be attached to the debenture (Precedent 6.2).

Precedent 6.6

Particulars of a charge subject to which property has been acquired

Please do not write in this margin

Pursuant to section 400 of the Companies Act 1985

Please complete legibly, preferably in black type, or bold block lettering

To the Registrar of Companies

For official use

Company number 4 527 326

Name of company

* insert full name of company

* THE BUSH HOTEL (DILSBOROUGH) LTD

Date and description of the instrument (if any) creating or evidencing the charge (note 1)

10 JUNE 1985 MORTGAGE

Amount secured by the charge £20,000

Names and addresses of the persons entitled to the charge

THE STAR INSURANCE CO PLC
CORNHILL, LONDON EC2

Short particulars of the property charged

THE SUN INN
CHURCH STREET
RUFFORD
RUFFORDSHIRE

Continue overleaf as necessary

Date of the acquisition of the property 5 SEPTEMBER 1988

Signed J. F. Runciman Designation‡ DIRECTOR Date 5/9/88

Precedent 6.7

Form of Discharge of a Debenture

RECEIPT PURSUANT TO SECTION 115 OF THE LAW OF PROPERTY ACT 1925

MELMOTTE'S BANK PLC hereby acknowledges this 5th day of March 1990 that it has received the balance of the moneys (including interest and costs) secured by the within written Deed, the payment having been made by The Bush Hotel, Dilsborough Ltd.

For and on behalf of **Melmotte's Bank PLC.**

H Catchpenny

(REGIONAL GENERAL MANAGER)

Precedent 6.8

M

Declaration of satisfaction in full or in part of mortgage or charge

Please do not write in this margin

Pursuant to section 403(1) of the Companies Act 1985

To the Registrar of Companies

For official use

Company number: 4 527 326

Please complete legibly, preferably in black type or, bold block lettering

Name of company

* THE BUSH HOTEL (DILSBOROUGH) LTD

* insert full name of company

I, J F RUNCIMAN

of THE BUSH HOTEL, DILSBOROUGH

† delete as appropriate

[a director][the secretary][the administrator][the administrative receiver]† of the above company, do solemnly and sincerely declare that the debt for which the charge described below was given has been paid or satisfied in [full][ ]†

‡ insert a description of the instrument(s) creating or evidencing the charge, eg 'Mortgage', 'Charge', 'Debenture' etc.

Date and Description of charge‡ 12 DECEMBER 1986 LEGAL CHARGE

Date of Registrationø 14 DECEMBER 1986

ø the date of registration may be confirmed from the certificate

Name and address of [chargee][trustee for the debenture holders]

MELMOTTE'S BANK PLC, LOMBARD ST, LONDON EC 2

Short particulars of property charged§

THE BUSH HOTEL, DILSBOROUGH, RUFFORDSHIRE AND ALL MONIES

§ insert brief details of property

And I make this solemn declaration conscientiously believing the same to be true and by virtue of the provisions of the Statutory Declarations Act 1835.

Declared at 75 HIGH STREET
DILSBOROUGH

Declarant to sign below

J. F. Runciman

the 5 day of MARCH

one thousand nine hundred and NINETY

before me Gregory Marlows

A Commissioner for Oaths or Notary Public or Justice of the Peace or Solicitor having the powers conferred on a Commissioner for Oaths

Presentor's name address and reference (if any):

For official Use

Mortgage Section | Post room

Chapter 7

ANNUAL REPORT, ACCOUNTS, AND AUDITORS

7A Annual Report and Accounts

Introduction

The detailed form and contents of company accounts and annual reports are outside the scope of this book and the following section is confined to secretarial aspects and some of the legal requirements which are more commonly encountered.

The statutory provisions were substantially altered by the Companies Act 1989, which substituted new sections in Part VII of the 1985 Act and replaced Schs 4 to 10 of that Act with new Schedules.

ns 221 Every company must keep accounting records sufficient to show and explain the company's transactions and to disclose at any time, with reasonable accuracy, the financial
ns 226 position of the company. The directors must prepare a balance sheet and profit and loss
ns 241 account for each accounting reference period which gives a true and fair view, and,
together with the reports of the directors and of the auditors, these must be laid before
the company in general meeting, and delivered to the Registrar of Companies for filing,
ns 252 unless the company has passed an elective resolution to dispense with this requirement.
(Subject in both cases to permitted exceptions.) See Chapter 14C for elective resolutions.

Accounting reference date

nss 223–225 If no notice is given to the Registrar of Companies the company's accounting reference date will be the last day of the month in which the anniversary of its incorporation falls and the annual report and accounts for the preceding year must be prepared at that date.

The directors may resolve (within nine months of the date of incorporation of the company) on a different accounting reference date and give notice of that date to the Registrar on Form G 224. A company's first accounting reference date must be not less than six months, or more than 18 months, after its date of incorporation.

There is a leeway of seven days on either side of the accounting reference date for the actual date to which the accounts are made up; to accommodate, for example, an exact 52 week year if this is more convenient for the company.

See Precedent 7A.1 (p 173) DIRECTORS' RESOLUTION TO FIX ACCOUNTING REFERENCE DATE

See Precedent 7A.2 (p 173) FORM G 224 NOTICE OF ACCOUNTING REFERENCE DATE

A company may change its accounting reference date either from the date fixed by the Registrar of Companies or from the date of its choice, by a resolution of the directors and by giving notice to the Registrar on Form G 225(1) or Form G 225(2).

nss 224–226 Apart from shortening the accounting reference period, or re-aligning it so that those of subsidiary and holding companies are the same, the restrictions on changes to the accounting reference date means that an accounting period cannot exceed 18 months, or be extended beyond 12 months, more than once every five years.

See Precedent 7A.3 (p 174) DIRECTORS' RESOLUTION TO CHANGE ACCOUNTING REFERENCE DATE

See Precedent 7A.4 NOTICES OF NEW ACCOUNTING REFERENCE DATE
(p 175) (1) G 225(1) GIVEN DURING THE COURSE OF AN ACCOUNTING REFERENCE PERIOD

(p 176) (2) G 225(2) GIVEN AFTER THE END OF AN ACCOUNTING REFERENCE PERIOD BY A PARENT OR SUBSIDIARY UNDERTAKING OR BY A COMPANY SUBJECT TO AN ADMINISTRATION ORDER

Approval, signing and registration of report and accounts

nss 233–234 The directors' report and accounts of the company must be prepared in accordance with statutory requirements and be approved by the Board of directors. The directors' report must then be signed by either one director or the secretary of the company and the accounts signed by one director.

See Precedent 7A.5 (p 177) MINUTES OF THE DIRECTORS APPROVING DIRECTORS' REPORT AND ACCOUNTS

nss 235–236 The report and accounts duly signed will then be submitted to the auditors for completion of their report. The auditors' report must be signed by the auditors or, if a partnership, in the partnership's name, by a person authorised by it to sign.

ns 242 The name of the signatories to the report and accounts and the name of the auditors must be stated on the documents laid before the general meeting and circulated. These documents are also required to be delivered to the Registrar of Companies and the above mentioned signatories must be in manuscript on the copies so filed.

Contravention of accounting reference period

If accounts happen to be laid before shareholders and filed with the Registrar of Companies made up to a date which contravenes the accounting reference period rules, an addendum to the directors' report should be filed with the Registrar of Companies in the form of the following precedent adjusted to the circumstance.

See Precedent 7A.6 (p 178) CONTRAVENTION OF ACCOUNTING REFERENCE PERIOD: ADDENDUM TO DIRECTORS' REPORT TO BE FILED WITH THE REGISTRAR OF COMPANIES

A minute of the Board of directors should first approve the addendum.

See Precedent 7A.7 (p 178) MINUTE OF DIRECTORS APPROVING THE ADDENDUM TO THE DIRECTORS' REPORT

ns 245 Annual accounts of a company, laid before a general meeting and filed with the Registrar of Companies, and any directors' reports which do not comply with Companies Acts, may be revised either voluntarily by the directors or on an application to the court by the Secretary of State or a person authorised by him.

The following precedent deals only with voluntary revisions, which must be confined to correction of aspects in which the requirements of the Act were not met and consequential alterations.

See Precedent 7A.8 (p 179) REVISION OF ANNUAL ACCOUNTS AND DIRECTORS' REPORT – DIRECTORS' MINUTES

Exemptions from delivery of accounts and other documents

This section does not include exemptions arising from elective resolutions – for which see Chapter 14C.

Small and medium-sized companies

nss 246–249 A small or medium-sized private company which is not otherwise ineligible may file modified accounts instead of full statutory accounts. See *Jordans Secretarial Administration*, at § 14.19.8, for definitions and criteria.

If a company qualifies for exemption in respect of its previous financial year it may also use the exemption in the current year even if the criteria are not met in that year.

See Precedent 7A.9 (p 180) DIRECTORS' RESOLUTION TO FILE MODIFIED ACCOUNTS

See Precedent 7A.10 (p 180) STATEMENT TO APPEAR ON BALANCE SHEET WHEN MODIFIED ACCOUNTS PREPARED

See Precedent 7A.11 (p 180) AUDIT REPORT WHEN MODIFIED ACCOUNTS PREPARED

It must be noted that these exemptions do not alter the requirement that unmodified accounts be prepared and (unless the company has passed an elective resolution to dispense with this requirement) laid before members.

Dormant companies

See *Jordans Secretarial Administration*, at § 4.19.12, for definition of a dormant company.

ns 250 A dormant company may resolve, by special resolution, to make itself exempt from the provisions of the Companies Act 1985 relating to the audit of accounts and is entitled to the same exemptions from filing accounts which attach to a small company.

The special resolution will be proposed at the general meeting at which the previous accounts were laid, or in the case of a new company at a general meeting, before any accounts are laid. The resolution may also be passed by written resolution in lieu of a general meeting (see p 314).

See Precedent 7A.12 (p 181) SPECIAL RESOLUTION OF DORMANT COMPANY TO EXEMPT ITSELF FROM PROVISIONS RELATING TO THE AUDIT OF ACCOUNTS

The balance sheet of a dormant company must bear a certificate by the directors confirming that it was dormant throughout the financial year if it is to take advantage of the above exemptions.

See Precedent 7A.13 (p 181) CERTIFICATE TO APPEAR ON BALANCE SHEET OF A DORMANT COMPANY

Time limits for laying and delivering accounts

s 242 Accounts must, unless the company has passed an elective resolution to dispense with this requirement, be laid before the general meeting and delivered to the Registrar of Companies within seven months of the end of the accounting reference period, if a public company, and within 10 months, if a private company.

An extension of three months to these timescales can be claimed by a company with overseas business interests, as defined on Form G 244, which must then be delivered to the Registrar of Companies to obtain this extension.

See Precedent 7A.14 (p 181) MINUTES OF DIRECTORS CLAIMING EXTENSION OF THE TIME FOR LAYING AND DELIVERING ACCOUNTS IF COMPANY HAS OVERSEAS BUSINESS AND INTERESTS

See Precedent 7A.15 (p 182) FORM G 244 NOTICE OF CLAIM TO EXTENSION OF PERIOD ALLOWED FOR LAYING AND DELIVERING ACCOUNTS – OVERSEA BUSINESS OR INTERESTS

The annual return

CA 1989, ss 139(1) 363–365 SIs 1990, Nos 1707, 1766 Every company is required to file an annual return with the Registrar of Companies. The format, content and timing of the annual return is altered by the Companies Act 1989 of which the relevant sections came into effect on 1 October 1990. Although there are transitional provisions for unfiled 1990 returns, all returns due after 1 October 1990 may be filed in the new format, which becomes compulsory for all 1991 returns. This section sets out the 1989 Act requirements.

Under the new procedures companies will make up their annual return on either:

(a) the anniversary of the company's incorporation; or
(b) if an annual return has been filed at a different date, the anniversary of that date (ie this will apply to most existing companies at the commencement date of this legislation).

Alternatively, a company may choose as its return date a date that is within 12 months of the relevant anniversary stated above and many may regard it convenient to align this return date with the accounting date. Once decided upon this date must be kept.

The annual return must be filed within 28 days of its return date and signed by a director or secretary of the company.

The new prescribed format of the annual return omits much of the detail about share capital structure and does not require notification of indebtedness. It does, however, introduce a classification of a company's activities by reference to VAT codes, and the date of birth of directors in all companies must be included.

SI 1991/1259 *See* Precedent 7A.16 (p 183 *et seq*) FORMS 363a, 363b AND 363s ANNUAL RETURN (1991 EDITIONS)

A fee (see Introduction) is charged on filing the return. Cheques should be made payable to 'Companies House'.

Form 363 in its revised version is prescribed for use as from 1 October 1990. Initially this will be in the version 363a which requires detailed completion by the company to provide the material for input into the computerised system at Companies House.

Subsequently, Forms 363b and 363s will be used. The Registrar of Companies will supply these forms with the reminder he sends out prior to the due date of the return.

Form 363s, the final version, is a 'shuttle document' which will reflect the current entries on the register held by the Registrar of Companies. Its completion will be confined to checking its contents and entering amendments.

Once introduced it will be possible to use Forms 363b and 363s to notify a change in registered office not already notified on Form G 287, or the resignation of directors or secretary and changes in particulars relating to them not already notified on Form 288. Form 288 must, however, be used to notify any *new* appointment of a director or secretary and contain the written consent of the appointee.

The annual return requires the company to state its principal business activities.

See Precedent 7A.17 (p 197) TRADE CLASSIFICATIONS FOR ANNUAL RETURN

Precedent 7A.1

Directors' Resolution to Fix Accounting Reference Date

It was resolved that the accounting reference date of the company be [30 June] and notice thereof be filed with the Registrar of Companies.

Precedent 7A.2

Notice of accounting reference date (to be delivered within 9 months of incorporation)

224

Please do not write in this margin

Pursuant to section 224 of the Companies Act 1985
as inserted by section 3 of the Companies Act 1989

Please complete legibly, preferably in black type, or bold block lettering

To the Registrar of Companies
(Address overleaf)

Company number: 9 874 563

Name of company

* insert full name of company

* DILSBOROUGH ASSOCIATES LTD

gives notice that the date on which the company's accounting reference period is to be treated as coming to an end in each successive year is as shown below:

Important
The accounting reference date to be entered alongside should be completed as in the following examples:

Day		Month	
3	0	0	6

5 April

Day		Month	
0	5	0	4

30 June

Day		Month	
3	0	0	6

31 December

Day		Month	
3	1	1	2

‡ Insert Director, Secretary, Admininstrator, Administrative Receiver or Receiver (Scotland) as appropriate

Signed J. F. Runciman Designation‡ DIRECTOR Date 31 JANUARY 1990

Precedent 7A.3

Directors' Resolution to Change Accounting Reference Date

Resolved that the accounting reference date of the company be changed from [30 June] to [30 September] *[and accounts be made up for the 15 months ending 30 September 19] **[and accounts be made up for the three months ending 30 September to align with the accounting reference date of the holding company] and notice thereof be filed with the Registrar of Companies.

EDITOR'S NOTES

* Change made before end of existing accounting reference period: use Form G 225(1).

**Change made after end of existing accounting reference period to align with holding company: use Form G 225(2).

Precedent 7A.4(1)

Notice of new accounting reference date given during the course of an accounting reference period

Please do not write in this margin

Pursuant to section 225(1) of the Companies Act 1985 as inserted by section 3 of the Companies Act 1989

Please complete legibly, preferably in black type, or bold block lettering

1. To the Registrar of Companies
(Address overleaf - Note 6)

Company number: 9 874 563

Name of company

* insert full name of company

* DILSBOROUGH ASSOCIATES LTD

Note
Details of day and month in 2, 3 and 4 should be the same.
Please read notes 1 to 5 overleaf before completing this form.

2. gives notice that the company's new accounting reference date on which the current accounting reference period and each subsequent accounting reference period of the company is to be treated as coming, or as having come, to an end is

Day		Month	
3	0	0	9

3. The current accounting reference period of the company is to be treated as ~~[shortened]~~[extended]† and ~~[is to be treated as having come to an end]~~[will come to an end]† on

Day		Month		Year			
3	0	0	9	**1**	**9**	9	0

† delete as appropriate

4. If this notice states that the current accounting reference period of the company is to be extended, and reliance is being placed on the exception in paragraph (a) in the second part of section 225(4) of the Companies Act 1985, the following statement should be completed:

The company is a [subsidiary]~~[parent]~~† undertaking of
BILLBROOK ENTERPRISES LTD
, company number 9 236 452
the accounting reference date of which is 30 SEPTEMBER

5. If this notice is being given by a company which is subject to an administration order and this notice states that the current accounting reference period of the company is to be extended AND it is to be extended beyond 18 months OR reliance is not being placed on the second part of section 225(4) of the Companies Act 1985, the following statement should be completed:

An administration order was made in relation to the company on ______________
and it is still in force.

‡ Insert Director, Secretary, Receiver, Admininstrator, Administrative Receiver or Receiver (Scotland) as appropriate

6. Signed J. F. Runciman   Designation‡ DIRECTOR   Date 20 JUNE 1990

Presentor's name address telephone number and reference (if any):

For official use D.E.B.	Post room

Precedent 7A.4(2)

225(2)

Notice of new accounting reference date given after the end of an accounting reference period by a parent or subsidiary undertaking or by a company subject to an administration order

Please do not write in this margin

Pursuant to section 225(2) of the Companies Act 1985 as inserted by section 3 of the Companies Act 1989

Please complete legibly, preferably in black type, or bold block lettering

1. To the Registrar of Companies
(Address overleaf - Note 7)

Company number: 9 874 563

Name of company

* insert full name of company

* DILSBOROUGH ASSOCIATES LTD

Note
Details of day and month in 2, 3 and 4 should be the same.
Please read notes 1 to 6 overleaf before completing this form.

† delete as appropriate

2. gives notice that the company's new accounting reference date on which the previous accounting reference period and each subsequent accounting reference period of the company is to be treated as coming, or as having come, to an end is

Day		Month	
3	0	0	9

3. The previous accounting reference period of the company is to be treated as ~~[shortened]~~[extended]† and [is to be treated as having come to an end]~~[will come to an end]~~† on

Day		Month		Year			
3	0	0	9	**1**	**9**		

If neither of these statements can be completed, the notice cannot be given.

4. If this notice is given by a company which is a subsidiary or parent undertaking but which is not subject to an administration order, the following statement should be completed:

The company is a [subsidiary][parent]† undertaking of BILLBROOK ENTERPRISES LTD

, company number 9 236 452

the accounting reference date of which is 30 SEPTEMBER

5. ~~If this notice is given by a company which is subject to an administration order, the following statement should be completed:~~

~~An administration order was made in relation to the company on ______ and it is still in force.~~

‡ Insert Director, Secretary, Receiver, Admininstrator, Administrative Receiver or Receiver (Scotland) as appropriate

6. Signed J. F. Runciman Designation‡ DIRECTOR Date 20 OCTOBER 1990

Presentor's name address telephone number and reference (if any):

For official use D.E.B.	Post room

Precedent 7A.5

Minutes of the Directors Approving Directors' Report and Accounts

IT WAS RESOLVED:

THAT the directors' report and accounts for the year ended [31 March 1990] have been prepared in accordance with the Companies Act 1985 and are hereby approved and that [*name*] be authorised to sign on behalf of the Board of directors the directors' report and the balance sheet of the company as at the [31 March 1990], having all documents and accounts attached thereto as required by the Companies Act 1985.

IT WAS ALSO RESOLVED:

THAT the secretary be instructed to convene an annual general meeting of the company to be held on [24 June 1990].

EDITOR'S NOTE

For use in respect of accounts for periods beginning on or after 23 December 1989 to which new signature rules apply, ie the Board of directors must approve the annual accounts and the directors' report, one director must sign the balance sheet on their behalf and one director or the secretary must sign the directors' report on behalf of the directors.

Precedent 7A.6

Contravention of Accounting Reference Period: Addendum to Directors' Report to be Filed with the Registrar of Companies

Company Name.............

Company Number...........

The attached accounts, which do not comply with the provisions of ss 224, 225 and 227 of the Companies Act 1985, were prepared for the period to for the following reason(s):

[*here specify reasons.*]

We undertake that the next and future accounts have been and/or will be prepared for each accounting reference period in compliance with the Companies Act 1985.

Signed ....Director (on behalf of the Board)

Precedent 7A.7

Minute of Directors Approving the Addendum to the Directors' Report

A draft addendum to the directors' report for the period ended , explaining why such period contravenes the statutory provisions as to accounting reference dates, was tabled.

The document was approved for filing with the Registrar of Companies and [*name*] was authorised to sign it on behalf of the Board.

Precedent 7A.8

Revision of Annual Accounts and Directors' Report – Directors' Minutes

[(*Name*) representing the auditors joined the meeting.]

The Board was advised that the accounts and directors' report in respect of the year ending [30 June 1990], laid before the annual general meeting of the company on [15 November 1990] and subsequently filed with the Registrar of Companies, failed to comply with the requirements of the Companies Act in the following respects:

[(a) a capital commitment entered into on [30 May 1990] for the purchase of equipment totalling £125,000, was not included in the notes to the accounts – Note 10];

[(b) the shareholding of [*name*] had inadvertently been omitted from the schedule of directors' shareholdings in the capital of the company – Note 5].

[*or as the case may be*].

It was resolved that revised copies of the accounts be prepared and, after audit, laid before a general meeting of the company convened for the purpose and such revised accounts be subsequently filed with the Registrar of Companies under the provisions of s 245 of the Companies Act 1985.

[*Name*] was authorised to sign the revised accounts on behalf of the Board.

EDITOR'S NOTE

The following may be suitable as a letter to the Registrar of Companies forwarding the revised account.

> 'We enclose accounts and directors' report for the year ended [30 June 1990] revised under the provisions of s 245 of the Companies Act 1985 and laid before a general meeting of the Company on [15 July 1990]. Please substitute the accounts for those filed with you on [20 December 1990] in respect of the same accounting period.'

Precedent 7A.9

Directors' Resolution to File Modified Accounts

Resolved that since the company met the criteria for a [small] [medium-sized] company entitling modified accounts to be filed, this exemption should be used, modified accounts be prepared and filed accordingly, and any one director be authorised to sign the requisite statement on the balance sheet.

Precedent 7A.10

Statement to Appear on Balance Sheet when Modified Accounts Prepared

In preparing these modified accounts we have relied upon the exemptions for individual accounts in ns 246 of the Companies Act 1985 on the basis that the company is entitled to the benefit of those exemptions as a [small] [medium-sized] company.

.... Director *[date]*

Precedent 7A.11

Audit Report when Modified Accounts Prepared

In our opinion, the directors are entitled by ss 246 to 249 of the Companies Act 1985 to deliver modified financial statements for the financial year as claimed in the directors' statement and, in particular, the modified financial statements have been properly prepared in accordance with Sch 8 of the Act. We are not required to express an audit opinion on the truth and fairness of these modified financial statements.

We reported, as auditors of   Limited, to the members on   19   , on the company's financial statements prepared under the Companies Acts for the year ended   19   , and our audit opinion was as follows:

'We have audited the financial statements on pages...........

[insert full text audit opinion]

.... and comply with the Companies Acts'.

Precedent 7A.12

Special Resolution of Dormant Company to Exempt Itself from Provisions Relating to Audit of Accounts

[EITHER]

The company having been dormant from the time of its formation and no accounts having been laid before it in general meeting, the company resolves to make itself exempt from the provisions of Part VII of the Companies Act 1985 relating to the audit of accounts.

[OR]

The accounts of the company for the financial year ending 19 having been laid before the company in general meeting, and the company having qualified as small in that year and having been dormant since the end of it and is not required to prepare group accounts for that year, the company resolves to make itself exempt from the provisions of Part VII of the Companies Act 1985 relating to the audit of accounts.

Precedent 7A.13

Certificate to Appear on Balance Sheet of a Dormant Company

The company was dormant (within the meaning of s 250 of the Companies Act 1985) throughout the accounting period ending at the date of this balance sheet.

Director

Precedent 7A.14

Minutes of Directors Claiming Extension of the Time for Laying and Delivering Accounts if Company has Overseas Business and Interests

Resolved that in accordance with the provisions of s 244 of the Companies Act 1985 the company shall claim an extension of up to three months of the period allowed for laying accounts before its members and in delivering such accounts to the Registrar of Companies in view of its overseas business and interests.

Precedent 7A.15

Notice of claim to extension of period allowed for laying and delivering accounts - oversea business or interests

244

Please do not write in this margin

Pursuant to section 244 of the Companies Act 1985
as inserted by section 11 of the Companies Act 1989

Please complete legibly, preferably in black type, or bold block lettering

To the Registrar of Companies
(Address overleaf)

Company number

Name of company

* insert full name of company

*

The directors of this company give notice that the company is carrying on business, or has interests, outside the United Kingdom, the Channel Islands and the Isle of Man and claim an extension of three months to the period allowed under this section for laying and delivering accounts in relation to the financial year of the company [ending][which ended on]†

† delete as appropriate

Day		Month		Year			
				1	9		

‡ Insert Director, Secretary, Administrator, Administrative Receiver or Receiver (Scotland) as appropriate

Signed Designation‡ Date

Notes

1. A company which carries on business or has interests outside the United Kingdom, the Channel Islands and the Isle of Man may, by giving notice in the prescribed form to the Registrar of Companies under section 244(3) of the Act, claim an extension of three months to the period which otherwise would be allowed for the laying and delivery of accounts under section 244(1).

2. Notice must be given before the expiry of the period which would otherwise be allowed under section 244(1).

3. A separate notice will be required for each period for which the claim is made.

4. The date in the box on the form should be completed in the manner illustrated below.

0	5	0	4	1	9	8	5

Precedent 7A.16

363a
Annual Return

This form should be completed in black.

Company number	**CN** 4 527 326
Company name	BUSH HOTEL (DILSBOROUGH) LTD

Date of this return *(See note 1)*
The information in this return is made up to

Day Month Year
DA 3 0 0 9 9 0
Show date

Date of next return *(See note 2)*
If you wish to make your next return to a date earlier than the anniversary of this return please show the date here. Companies House will then send a form at the appropriate time.

DB 3 1 0 3 9 1

Registered Office *(See note 3)*
Show here the address **at the date of this return**.

Any change of registered office **must** be notified on form 287.

RO	10 MARKET PLACE
Post town	DILSBOROUGH
County/Region	RUFFORDSHIRE
Postcode	RU15 3AB

Principal business activities
(See note 4)
Show trade classification code number(s) for principal activity or activities.

PA 8 8 4 1

If the code number cannot be determined, give a brief description of principal activity.

Register of members
(See note 5)
If the register of members is not kept at the registered office, state here where it is kept.

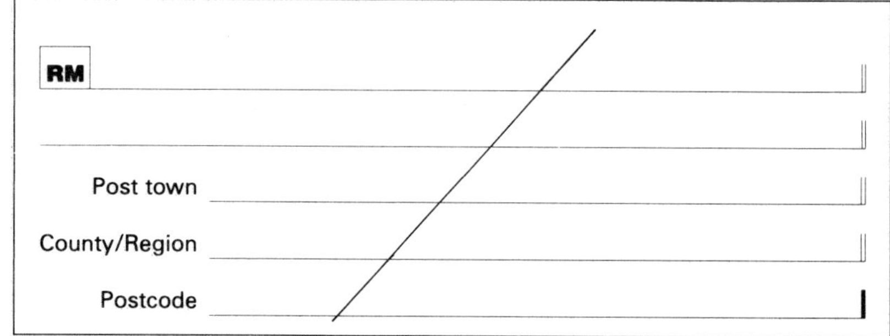
RM

Post town

County/Region

Postcode

Register of Debenture holders
(See note 6)
If there is a register of debenture holders and it is not kept at the registered office, state here where it is kept.

RD

Post town

County/Region

Postcode

Company type *(See note 7)*

Public limited company	T1	
Private company limited by shares	T2	✓
Private company limited by guarantee without share capital	T3	
Private company limited by shares exempt under section 30	T4	
Private company limited by guarantee exempt under section 30	T5	
Private unlimited company with share capital	T6	
Private unlimited company without share capital	T7	

Please mark the appropriate box.

Company Secretary *(See note 8)*
(Please photocopy this area to provide details of joint secretaries).

Details of a new company secretary **must** be notified on form 288.

Name

*Style/Title	CS MR
Forenames	JOHN JAMES
Surname	JOYCER
*Honours etc	FCA
Previous forenames	
Previous surname	

Address

Usual residential address must be given. In the case of a corporation, give the registered or principal office address.

AD THE HAVEN
ROOK LANE

Post town DILSBOROUGH

County/Region RUFFORDSHIRE

Postcode RU15 4CD Country UK

* Voluntary details

Directors (continued)

Name	*Style/Title	**CD** MR
	Forenames	JOHN FRANK
	Surname	RUNCIMAN
	*Honours etc	
	Previous forenames	
	Previous surname	
Address		**AD** THE BUSH HOTEL
Usual residential address must be given. In the case of a corporation, give the registered or principal office address.		
	Post town	DILSBOROUGH
	County/Region	RUFFORDSHIRE
	Postcode	RU15 3AD — Country UK
	Date of birth	**DO** 2 0 0 5 3 0 — Nationality **NA** BRITISH
	Business occupation	**OC** HOTELIER
	Other directorships	**OD** DILSBOROUGH VINTNERS LTD
		RUFFORDSHIRE TRAVEL LTD

Name	*Style/Title	**CD** MR
	Forenames	ELIAS MITCHELL
	Surname	GOTOBED
	*Honours etc	
	Previous forenames	
	Previous surname	
Address		**AD** 230 CHESTNUT STREET
Usual residential address must be given. In the case of a corporation, give the registered or principal office address.		
	Post town	MILAWUKA CITY
	County/Region	MILAWUKA
	Postcode	052 930 — Country USA
	Date of birth	**DO** — Nationality **NA** USA
	Business occupation	**OC** TRAVEL AGENT
	Other directorships	**OD**

* Voluntary details

Issued share capital *(See note 9)*
Enter details of all the shares in issue at the date of this return.

Class	Number	Aggregate Nominal Value
ORDINARY		
25p EACH	200,000	£50,000
Totals	200,000	£50,000

List of past and present members
(Use attached schedule where appropriate)

A full list is required if one was not included with either of the last two returns.
(See note 10)

Please mark the appropriate box(es)

There were no changes in the period ☐

	on paper	not on paper
A list of changes is enclosed	☐	☐
A full list of members is enclosed	☐	☐

Elective resolutions *(See note 11)*
(Private companies only)

If an election is in force at the date of this return to dispense with annual general meetings, *mark this box* ☐

If an election is in force at the date of this return to dispense with laying accounts in general meetings, *mark this box* ☐

Certificate
I certify that the information given in this return is true to the best of my knowledge and belief.

Signed J. F. Runciman ~~Secretary~~/Director*
*(*delete as appropriate)*

Date 23/8/90

This return includes NO continuation sheets.
(enter number)

To whom should Companies House direct any enquiries about the information shown in this return?

JOHN JAMES JOYCER FCA
10 MARKET PLACE
DILSBOROUGH
RUFFORDSHIRE
Postcode RU15 3AB
Telephone 0456-98910
Extension

When you have signed the return send it with the fee to the Registrar of Companies at

Companies House, Crown Way, Cardiff CF4 3UZ
for companies registered in England and Wales
or
Companies House, 100-102 George Street, Edinburgh EH2 3DJ
for companies registered in Scotland.

LIST OF PAST AND PRESENT MEMBERS **SCHEDULE TO FORM 363**

Company Number: 4 527 326

Company Name: BUSH HOTEL (DILSBOROUGH) LTD

Name	Address	Account of Shares			Remarks
		Number of shares or amount of stock held by existing members at date of this return.	Particulars of shares transferred since the date of the last return, or, in the case of the first return, since the incorporation of the company, by (a) persons who are still members, and (b) persons who have ceased to be members.		
			Number	Date of Registration of Transfer	
J F RUNCIMAN	BUSH HOTEL, DILSBOROUGH	55,000	5,000	30/12/89	To L A TWENTYMAN
L A TWENTYMAN	CHOWTON FARM, BRIGHTON	5,000		30/12/85	For J F RUNCIMAN

Continued overleaf

363b
Annual Return

of company number CN

company name

This form should be completed in black.

Date of this return
The information in this return should be made up to a date not later than

Day Month Year
DA

If you are making the return up to an earlier date please show the date here.

Date of next return
If you wish to make your next return to a date earlier than the anniversary of this return, please show the date here. Companies House will then send a form at the appropriate time.

DB

Registered Office

This is the address registered by Companies House as at

Use this space to notify a change of registered office address.

RO

Post town

County/Region

Postcode

Principal business activities

Show trade classification code number for principal activity or activities.

PA

If the code number cannot be determined give a brief description of principal activity.

Register of members

If the register of members is not kept at the registered office, state here where it is kept.

RM

Post town

County/Region

Postcode

Register of Debenture holders

If there is a register of debenture holders and it is not kept at the registered office, state here where it is kept.

RD

Post town

County/Region

Postcode

Company type

Public limited company	T1
Private company limited by shares	T2
Private company limited by guarantee without share capital	T3
Private company limited by shares exempt under section 30	T4
Private company limited by guarantee exempt under section 30	T5
Private unlimited company with share capital	T6
Private unlimited company without share capital	T7

Please mark the appropriate box.

Company Secretary

(Please photocopy this area to provide details of joint secretaries).

Details of a new company secretary **must** be notified on form 288.

Name *Style/Title — CS

Forenames

Surname

*Honours etc

Previous forenames

Previous surname

Address — AD

Usual residential address must be given. In the case of a corporation, give the registered or principal office address.

Post town

County/Region

Postcode Country

* Voluntary details

Directors
Please list directors in alphabetical order.

Details of new directors **must** be notified on form 288.

Name *Style/Title CD
Forenames
Surname
*Honours etc
Previous forenames
Previous surname

Address AD

Usual residential address must be given. In the case of a corporation, give the registered or principal office address.

Post town
County/Region
Postcode
Country

Date of birth DO
Nationality NA
Business occupation OC
Other directorships OD

Name *Style/Title CD
Forenames
Surname
*Honours etc
Previous forenames
Previous surname

Address AD

Usual residential address must be given. In the case of a corporation, give the registered or principal office address.

Post town
County/Region
Postcode
Country

Date of birth DO
Nationality NA
Business occupation OC
Other directorships OD

* Voluntary details

Issued share capital
Enter details of all the shares in issue at the date of this return.

Class	Number	Aggregate Nominal Value
Totals		

List of past and present members
(Use attached schedule where appropriate)

A full list is required if one was not included with either of the last two returns.

Please mark the appropriate box(es)

There were no changes in the period ☐

	on paper	not on paper
A list of changes is enclosed	☐	☐
A full list of members is enclosed	☐	☐

Elective resolutions
(Private companies only)

If an election is in force at the date of this return to dispense with annual general meetings, *mark this box* ☐

If an election is in force at the date of this return to dispense with laying accounts in general meetings, *mark this box* ☐

Certificate
I certify that the information given in this return is true to the best of my knowledge and belief.

Signed .... Secretary/Director*
*(*delete as appropriate)*

Date ....

This return includes .... continuation sheets.
(enter number)

To whom should Companies House direct any enquiries about the information shown in this return?

____

____

____

______________________________ Postcode ______________

Telephone ______________________________ Extension ______________

When you have signed the return send it with the fee to the Registrar of Companies at

Companies House, Crown Way, Cardiff CF4 3UZ
for companies registered in England and Wales
or
Companies House, 100-102 George Street, Edinburgh EH2 3DJ
for companies registered in Scotland.

LIST OF PAST AND PRESENT MEMBERS **SCHEDULE TO FORM 363**

Company Number:

Company Name:

Name	Address	Account of Shares: Number of shares or amount of stock held by existing members at date of this return.	Account of Shares: Particulars of shares transferred since the date of the last return, or, in the case of the first return, since the incorporation of the company, by (a) persons who are still members, and (b) persons who have ceased to be members. Number	Date of Registration of Transfer	Remarks

Continued overleaf

363s

Annual Return

of company number

company name

company type

This form should be completed in black.

The information printed below is taken from Companies House records as at

If this information requires amendment use the spaces opposite.

Date of this return

The information in this return should be made up to a date not later than

Day Month Year

If you are making the return up to an earlier date, show the date here.

Day Month Year

Date of next return

If you wish to make your next return to a date earlier than the anniversary of this return please show the date here. Companies House will then send a form at the appropriate time.

Day Month Year

Registered Office

This is the address registered by Companies House.

Principal business activities

Trade classification is

If the code number cannot be determined give a brief description of principal activity.

Register of members
The register is kept at

If the information shown needs amendment, give details below and, for secretary and director particulars, the date of any change.

Register of debenture holders
Any register of debenture holders (or a duplicate) is kept at

Company Secretary
Particulars of a new secretary **must** be notified on form 288.

Particulars

If this person has ceased to be secretary, please state when.

Day	Month	Year

Directors
Particulars of a new director **must** be notified on form 288.

Particulars

If this person has ceased to be a director, please state when.

Day	Month	Year

Other directorships.

Issued share capital

Enter details of all shares in issue at the date of this return.

Class	Number	Aggregate nominal value
Totals		

List of past and present members

(Use attached schedule where appropriate)

A full list is required if one was not included with either of the last two returns.

Please mark the appropriate box.

There were no changes in the period ☐

The last full members list was at

	on paper	not on paper
A list of changes is enclosed	☐	☐
A full list of members is enclosed	☐	☐

Elective resolutions

(Private companies only)

If an elective resolution is in force at the date of this return to dispense with annual general meetings, *mark this box.* ☐

If an elective resolution is in force at the date of this return to dispense with laying accounts in general meetings, *mark this box.* ☐

Certificate

I certify that the information given in this return is true to the best of my knowledge and belief.

Signed ....

Secretary/Director*
**(delete as appropriate)*

Date ....

This return includes .... continuation sheets.
(enter number)

To whom should Companies House direct any enquiries about the information shown in this return?

Postcode

Telephone Ext

LIST OF PAST AND PRESENT MEMBERS **SCHEDULE TO FORM 363**

Company Number:		Account of Shares			
Company Name:		Number of shares or amount of stock held by existing members at date of this return.	Particulars of shares transferred since the date of the last return, or, in the case of the first return, since the incorporation of the company, by (a) persons who are still members, and (b) persons who have ceased to be members.		Remarks
Name	Address		Number	Date of Registration of Transfer	

Continued overleaf

Precedent 7A.17

Trade Classifications for Annual Return

TRADE CLASSIFICATION

This classification is based on the VAT trade classification but there are some additional codes (numbered from 9500).

Trade Code	PRIMARY INDUSTRIES
	Group 01 – Agriculture, forestry and fishing
0011	Livestock farming (including pigs and poultry)
0012	Arable farming
0013	Dairying
0014	Mixed farming (no more than 50% in any of the above)
0015	Breeding of non-food producing animals (including horses)
0016	Agricultural contracting
0017	Market gardening and fruit farming
0018	Flower and seed growing
0020	Forestry
0030	Fishing
	Group 02 – Mining and quarrying
1010	Coal mining other than opencast (heading 5030)
1020	Stone and slate quarrying and mining
1030	Chalk, clay, sand and gravel extraction
1040	Petroleum and natural gas
1090	Other mining and quarrying
	MANUFACTURING INDUSTRIES
	Group 03 – Food, drink and tobacco
2110	Grain milling
2120	Bread and flour confectionery (including retailing wholly or mainly of own products) (see also code 8206)
2130	Biscuits
2140	Bacon-curing meat and fish products
2151	Milk and milk products (other than ice cream)
2152	Ice cream
2160	Sugar
2170	Cocoa, chocolate and sugar confectionery
2180	Fruit and vegetable products
2190	Animal and poultry foods
2210	Vegetable and animal oils and fats
2290	Food industries not elsewhere specified
2310	Brewing and malting

Trade Code	MANUFACTURING INDUSTRIES (cont)
2320	Soft drinks
2391	Spirit distilling and compounding
2392	British wines cider and perry
2400	Tobacco
	Group 04 – Coal and petroleum products
2610	Coke ovens and manufactured fuel
2620	Mineral oil refining
2630	Lubricating oils and greases
	Group 05 – Chemicals and allied industries
2710	General chemicals (manufacture of chemical elements organic and inorganic compounds (except pharmaceuticals, dyestuffs and pesticides))
2720	Pharmaceutical chemicals and preparations
2730	Toilet preparations
2740	Paint
2750	Soap and detergents
2760	Synthetic resins, plastics materials and synthetic rubber
2770	Dyestuffs and pigments
2780	Fertilizers
2790	Other chemical industries (polishes, adhesives, explosives and fireworks, pesticides, printing ink, surgical bandages etc, photographic chemical materials)
	Group 06 – Metal manufacture
3110	Iron and steel (general)
3120	Steel tubes
3130	Iron castings etc
3210	Aluminium and aluminium alloys
3220	Copper, brass and other copper alloys
3230	Other base metals
	Group 07 – Mechanical engineering
3310	Agricultural machinery (except tractors)
3320	Metal working machine tools
3330	Pumps, valves and compressors
3340	Industrial engines
3350	Textile machinery and accessories
3360	Construction and earth moving equipment
3370	Mechanical handling equipment
3380	Office machinery

Trade Code	MANUFACTURING INDUSTRIES (cont)
3390	Other machinery
3410	Industrial (including process) plant and steel work
3420	Ordnance and small arms
3490	Other mechanical engineering not elsewhere specified
	Group 08 – Instrument engineering
3510	Photographic and document copying equipment
3520	Watches and clocks
3530	Surgical instruments and appliances
3540	Scientific and industrial instruments and systems
	Group 09 – Electrical engineering
3610	Electrical machinery
3620	Insulated wires and cables
3630	Telegraph and telephone apparatus and equipment
3640	Radio and electronic components
3651	Gramophone records and tape recordings
3659	Other broadcast receiving and sound reproducing equipment
3660	Electronic computers
3670	Radio, radar and electronic capital goods
3680	Electric appliances primarily for domestic use
3690	Other electrical goods
	Group 10 – Shipbuilding, boatbuilding and marine engineering
3700	Shipbuilding, boatbuilding and marine engineering
	Group 11 – Vehicles
3800	Wheeled tractor manufacturing
3811	Motor vehicle manufacturing
3812	Caravan manufacturing
3820	Motor cycle, tricycle and pedal cycle manufacturing
3830	Aerospace equipment manufacturing and repairing
3840	Locomotives and railway track equipment
3850	Railway carriages, wagons and trams
	Group 12 – Metal goods not elsewhere specified
3900	Engineers small tools and gauges
3910	Hand tools and implements
3920	Cutlery, spoons, forks, plated tableware etc
3930	Bolts, nuts, screws, rivets etc
3940	Wire and wire manufactures
3950	Cans and metal boxes
3961	Jewellery manufacturing
3962	Jewellery processing
3963	Precious metals and articles of precious metal (other than jewellery)

Trade Code	MANUFACTURING INDUSTRIES (cont)
3990	Metal industries not elsewhere specified
	Group 13 – Textiles
4110	Production of man-made fibres
4120	Spinning and doubling on the cotton and flax systems
4130	Weaving of cotton, linen and man-made fibres
4140	Woollen and worsted
4150	Jute
4160	Rope, twine and net
4170	Hosiery and other knitted goods
4180	Lace
4190	Carpets
4210	Narrow fabrics (not more than 30cm wide)
4220	Made up textiles
4230	Textile finishing
4290	Other textile industries
	Group 14 – Leather, leather goods and fur
4310	Leather (tanning and dressing) and fellmongery
4321	Handbags (including handbags of plastic and imitation leather)
4322	Travel goods (including goods of plastic and imitation leather)
4329	Other leather goods (including imitation leather)
4331	Fur processing
4339	Other fur
	Group 15 – Clothing and footwear
4410	Weatherproof outerwear
4420	Men's and boys' tailored outerwear
4430	Women's and girls' tailored outerwear
4440	Overalls and men's shirts, underwear etc
4450	Dresses, lingerie, infants' wear etc
4460	Hats, caps and millinery
4490	Dress industries not elsewhere specified
4500	Footwear
	Group 16 – Bricks, ceramics, glass, cement, etc
4610	Bricks, fireclay and refractory goods
4620	Ceramics
4630	Glass
4640	Cement
4690	Abrasives and building materials not elsewhere specified
	Group 17 – Timber, furniture etc
4710	Timber
4721	Upholstery
4722	Chair frames (other than of metal)
4729	Other furniture for home or office use
4730	Bedding etc

Trade Code	MANUFACTURING INDUSTRIES (cont)
4740	Shop and office fitting
4750	Wooden containers and baskets
4791	Garden furniture
4799	Other miscellaneous wood and cork manufacturing
	Group 18 – Paper, printing and publishing
4810	Paper and board
4820	Packaging products of paper, board and associated materials
4830	Manufactured stationery
4840	Manufactures of paper and board not elsewhere specified
4850	Printing and publishing of newspapers
4860	Printing and publishing of periodicals
4891	Publishing of books
4892	Greeting cards
4893	Prints and reproductions
4894	Bookbinding
4899	Other printing
	Group 19 – Other manufacturing industries
4910	Rubber
4920	Linoleum, plastics floor-coverings, leathercloth, etc
4930	Brushes and brooms
4940	Toys, games, children's carriages and sports equipment
4950	Miscellaneous stationers' goods
4960	Plastics products not elsewhere specified
4991	Musical instruments
4992	Imitation jewellery
4999	Other miscellaneous manufacturing industries

CONSTRUCTION

Group 20 – Construction

Trade Code	Description
5001	General builders
5002	Building and civil engineering contractors
5003	Civil engineering contractors
5004	Plumbers
5005	Joiners and carpenters
5006	Painters and decorators
5007	Roofing contractors
5008	Plastering contractors
5009	Glazing contractors
5011	Demolition contractors
5012	Scaffolding specialists
5013	Reinforced concrete specialists
5014	Heating and ventilating engineers
5015	Electrical contractors
5016	Asphalt and tar spraying contractors
5017	Plant hirers
5018	Flooring contractors
5019	Constructional engineers
5021	Insulating specialists
5022	Suspended ceiling specialists
5023	Wall and floor tiling specialists

Trade Code	CONSTRUCTION (cont)
5029	Specialists not elsewhere specified
5030	Opencast coal mining

UTILITIES

Group 21 – Gas, electricity and water

Trade Code	Description
6010	Gas
6020	Electricity
6030	Water

TRANSPORT AND COMMUNICATION

Group 22 – Transport and communication

Trade Code	Description
7010	Railways
7021	Omnibus and tramway services
7022	Taxis and private hire cars
7030	Road haulage contracting for general hire or reward
7040	Other road haulage
7050	Sea transport
7060	Port and inland water transport
7070	Air transport
7080	Postal services and telecommunications
7091	Shipping agents and forwarding agents
7092	Travel agents
7093	Driving instruction
7094	Operation of car parks, toll roads and toll bridges
7099	Other miscellaneous transport services and storage

DISTRIBUTIVE TRADES

Group 23 – Wholesale distribution

(NB Wholesaling of motor vehicles (new and second hand), including motor cycles and caravans is allocated to heading 8941 and not to the headings within this group).

Wholesale distribution of:

Trade Code	Description
8101	Fresh meat, fish, fruit and vegetables
8102	Alcoholic drink (including bottling)
8109	Other food and drink
8110	Petroleum products
8121	Chemists' sundries
8122	Clocks and watches
8123	Clothing
8124	Furs
8125	Textiles
8126	Footwear
8127	Electrical goods
8128	Radio, TV sets, tape recorders, tape recordings and gramophone records
8129	Jewellery
8131	Imitation jewellery
8132	Musical instruments

Trade Code	DISTRIBUTIVE TRADES (cont)
8133	Photographic goods
8134	Toys
8135	Travel and fancy goods (including shopping bags)
8136	Furniture and floor coverings
8137	China, glassware, hardware and ironmongery
8138	Paper and board products, including reading material
8139	Leasing and office furniture, vending machines, juke boxes and gaming machines
8149	Other goods

Group 24 – Retail distribution

(NB Retailing of motor vehicles (new and second hand), including motor cycles and caravans, is allocated to heading 8941 and not to the headings within this group).

8201	Grocers
8202	Dairymen
8204	Fishmongers and poulterers
8205	Greengrocers and fruiterers
8206	Bread and flour confectioners selling wholly or mainly bought in goods (see also code 2120)
8207	Off licences
8211	Department stores
8212	Variety and other general stores
8213	General mail order houses
8214	Confectioners, tobacconists and newsagents
8215	Footwear shops
8216	Men's and boys' wear shops
8217	Women's and girls' wear, household textiles and general clothing shops
8218	Retail furriers
8219	Domestic furniture shops, floor coverings shops, furniture and upholstery repairers
8221	Antique dealers, second hand furniture shops, art dealers, picture framers and dealers in stamps and coins
8222	Radio and electrical goods shops (excluding radio and TV rental and relay shops)
8223	Radio and TV rental shops
8224	Hardware, china, wallpaper and paint shops
8225	Cycle and perambulator shops
8226	Bookshops and stationers
8227	Chemists and photographic shops
8228	Opticians
8229	Jewellery, watch and clock retailers and repairers
8231	Leather goods, sports goods, toys and fancy goods shops
8232	Music shops (including gramophone records)
8233	Florists, nurserymen and garden shops

Trade Code	DISTRIBUTIVE TRADES (cont)
8234	Pet and pet food shops
8239	Other non-food shops

Group 25 – Dealers

(NB Dealing in motor vehicles (new and second hand), including motor cycles and caravans, is allocated to heading 8941 and not to the headings within this group).

8311	Coal and oil merchants (not including bulk oil distributors or petrol filling stations)
8312	Builders' merchants
8313	Corn, seed and agricultural merchants, dealers in livestock
8321	Dealing in industrial materials
8322	Dealing in scrap and other waste metals
8323	Dealing in industrial and agricultural machinery
8324	Leasing industrial and office machinery

SERVICES

Group 26 – Insurance, banking, finance and business services

8600	Insurance
8610	Banking and bill discounting
8621	Stockbrokers
8622	Unit and investment trusts
8629	Other financial institutions
8630	Property owning and managing (see also 9600)
8640	Advertising and market research
8651	Industrial and commercial valuers, auctioneers and transfer agents
8652	Chartered or company secretaries (firms acting as)
8653	Computer services
8654	Contract cleaning
8655	Management consultants
8656	Staff bureaux and employment agencies
8657	Duplicating, calculating and typewriting agencies
8659	Other business services

Group 27 – Professional and scientific services

8710	Accountancy services
8720	Educational services
8730	Legal services
8741	Hospital and consultant services
8742	Local authority health services
8743	General medical services
8744	Dental services
8749	Other medical services
8750	Religious organisations
8760	Research and development services
8791	Veterinary services
8792	Surveying (various kinds)
8793	Architects (private practice)
8794	Draughtsmen (private practice)

Trade Code	SERVICES (cont)
8795	Consultant engineers
8796	Research chemists, analytical chemists, assayers, non-medical bacteriologists, metallurgists and geologists (private practices)
8797	Professional and scientific representative bodies
8798	Artists, sculptors, designers, authors, journalists (free-lance) and composers
8799	Other professional and scientific services
	Group 28 – Miscellaneous services
8811	Cinemas
8812	Theatres, music halls etc, radio and television services (excluding relay services), film and recording studios etc
8813	Performers and performing groups (drama, music, variety etc)
8814	Radio and television relay services
8821	Dance halls and dancing schools
8822	Sport
8829	Other recreations
8830	Betting and gaming
8841	Hotels and other residential establishments
8842	Holiday camps, camping and holiday caravan sites
8851	Restaurants, cafes, snack bars etc, selling food for consumption on the premises only
8852	Fish and chip shops, sandwich and snack bars and other establishments selling food partly or wholly for consumption off the premises
8860	Public houses
8870	Clubs (excluding sports clubs and gaming clubs)

Trade Code	SERVICES (cont)
8880	Catering contractors
8891	Men's hairdressing and manicure
8892	Women's hairdressing and manicure
8921	Launderettes
8922	Laundries
8923	Hire of towels linen and industrial clothing
8930	Dry cleaning, job dyeing, carpet beating etc
8941	Distribution, repair and servicing of motor vehicles (including wholesaling, retailing and dealing in motor vehicles and caravans (new and second hand), tyres, motor accessories and spares)
8942	Petrol filling stations
8950	Repair of boots and shoes
8991	Funeral direction, cemeteries and crematoria
8992	Photography and photographic processing
8993	Welfare and charitable services
8994	Public museums, libraries and galleries
8995	Political parties and associations
8996	Service of Commonwealth and foreign governments
8997	Trade associations and unions
8999	Other services
	Group 29 – Public administration and defence
9010	National government service
9060	Local government service
	Other codes
9500	Holding company
9600	Residents' property management company
9999	Dormant company

7B Auditors

Introduction

CA 1989, ss 118–123 The Companies Act 1989 substantially alters the provisions relating to the appointment, rights, remuneration, removal and resignation of auditors, repealing ss 384–394 and substituting 18 new sections. These new sections came into force on 1 April 1990 and the following precedents are based on them. See *Jordans Secretarial Administration*, at § 4.35 *et seq*, for description of circumstances and detailed requirements to which the precedents relate.

See Precedent 7B.1 (p 205) RESOLUTION OF DIRECTORS TO APPOINT AUDITORS
(1) AS FIRST AUDITORS
(2) TO FILL A CASUAL VACANCY

ns 385(2) ns 385A At each general meeting at which accounts are laid the company must, unless it passed an elective resolution to dispense with this requirement, appoint auditors to hold office until the conclusion of the next such general meeting. The following precedents assume the retiring auditor is re-appointed. If the auditor is not to be re-appointed, see Precedent 7B.5 and following.

See Precedent 7B.2 (p 205) ORDINARY RESOLUTION TO RE-APPOINT AUDITORS

It is usual for the remuneration of the auditors to be left for the directors to fix.

See Precedent 7B.3 (p 205) RESOLUTION OF DIRECTORS APPROVING AUDITORS' REMUNERATION

ns 250 A dormant company (as defined) may, by special resolution, exclude the appointment of auditors while it remains dormant (see Precedent 7A.12).

ns 386 See Precedent 14C.6 for elective resolution to dispense with annual appointment of auditors. See Precedent 14C.10 for form of ordinary resolution to revoke such elective resolution.

If an auditor ceases to hold office for whatever reason a statement must be given to the company by the auditor setting out any circumstances relevant thereto which should be brought to the attention of members or creditors of the company or stating that there are none. If the statement is of circumstances which the auditor considers should be brought to the attention of the members or creditors of the company, the company must, within 14 days after its deposit, either send a copy of it to all those who are entitled to receive
ns 238 copies of the statutory accounts, or apply to the court for relief from such requirement. If such an application is made the auditor must be notified of this by the company within 21 days of deposit of the statement. In the absence of such notification the auditor must send a copy of the statement to the Registrar of Companies within seven days after the expiry of that period.

See Precedent 7B.4 (p 206) STATEMENT BY PERSON CEASING TO HOLD OFFICE AS AUDITOR

If a change is to be made in auditors and it is intended in general meeting to:

(a) appoint an auditor other than the retiring auditor;
(b) fill a casual vacancy in the office of auditor;
(c) re-appoint a retiring auditor appointed by the directors to fill a casual vacancy;
(d) remove an auditor before the expiration of term of office;

special notice (see Chapter 14) must be given for the requisite ordinary resolution.

The following are precedents for the Board resolutions and ordinary resolutions of the company in the different circumstances of change of auditor outlined above.

See Precedent 7B.5 (p 207) TO APPOINT AUDITOR OTHER THAN THE RETIRING AUDITOR

(1) DIRECTORS' RESOLUTION

(2) ORDINARY RESOLUTION

See Precedent 7B.6 (p 207) TO FILL A CASUAL VACANCY IN THE OFFICE OF AUDITOR

(1) DIRECTORS' RESOLUTION

(2) ORDINARY RESOLUTION

See Precedent 7B.7 (p 208) TO RE-APPOINT AN AUDITOR APPOINTED BY THE DIRECTORS TO FILL A CASUAL VACANCY

(1) DIRECTORS' RESOLUTION

(2) ORDINARY RESOLUTION

See Precedent 7B.8 (p 208) TO REMOVE AN AUDITOR BEFORE EXPIRATION OF TERM OF OFFICE

(1) DIRECTORS' RESOLUTION

(2) ORDINARY RESOLUTION

Subsequent to the passing of a resolution to remove an auditor before the expiration of term of office, notice thereof must be given to the Registrar of Companies on Form G 386.

See Precedent 7B.9 (p 209) FORM G 386 NOTICE OF PASSING OF RESOLUTION REMOVING AN AUDITOR

When using special notice procedure (for which see Precedent 14A.16) a copy of the proposed ordinary resolution must be sent to both the auditors proposed to be appointed and the auditor who has resigned or whom it is proposed be removed. The outgoing
ns 394 auditor has the right to require the directors to convene an extraordinary general meeting of the company to consider the circumstances of resignation (or removal) and the right to make written representations to the company and require their circulation to members
ns 238 and others who have a right to receive copies of accounts.

The company must circulate a copy of these representations to every person to whom notice of the meeting will be or has been sent, or if received too late for such circulation, the auditors can require that the representations are read to the meeting.

See Precedent 7B.10 (p 210) LETTERS TO AUDITORS ENCLOSING NOTICE OF RESOLUTION TO APPOINT DIFFERENT AUDITORS

(1) TO PROPOSED NEW AUDITORS

(2) TO THE RETIRING AUDITORS

See Precedent 7B.11 (p 211) LETTER TO MEMBERS ENCLOSING WRITTEN REPRESENTATIONS FROM OUTGOING AUDITORS

In addition to any direct contact with members in accordance with the above precedent, an auditor not being reappointed must complete and file a statement on retirement or removal (see Precedent 7B.4).

Precedent 7B.1

Resolution of Directors to Appoint Auditors

(1) As First Auditors

Resolved that Messrs be the auditors of this company to hold office until the conclusion of the first general meeting of the company at which accounts are laid.

(2) To Fill a Casual Vacancy

Reported that [*name*] had given notice [that he was retiring from practice on 31 March 1990 and] wished to relinquish his appointment as auditor of the company on that date. Resolved that Messrs be appointed auditors in succession to [*name*] to hold office from the date of his retirement until the conclusion of the next general meeting of the company, at which accounts are laid.

Precedent 7B.2

Ordinary Resolution to Re-appoint Auditors

Resolved that Messrs be re-appointed auditors of the company to hold office until the conclusion of the next general meeting at which accounts are laid and the directors be authorised to fix their remuneration.

Precedent 7B.3

Resolution of Directors Approving Auditors' Remuneration

Resolved that the remuneration of the auditors for the audit of the company's accounting period ended [*date*] be agreed at £ inclusive of expenses.

EDITOR'S NOTE

The figure stated is remuneration for the audit of the accounts. The auditors may have provided accounting and associated services and advice, which should be billed separately.

Precedent 7B.4

Statement by person ceasing to hold office as auditor

Pursuant to section 394 of the Companies Act 1985 as inserted by section 123 of the Companies Act 1989

Company Number

Name of Company ______________________________

____

Registered Office ______________________________

____

I/We* ______________________________

of ______________________________

____

____

hereby give notice in accordance with section 394 of the Companies Act 1985 that

(a) I/We confirm that in connection with my/our ceasing to hold office there are no circumstances which I/we consider should be brought to the notice of members or creditors of the company.

(b) I/We consider the following circumstances connected with my/our ceasing to hold office should be brought to the notice of the members or creditors of the company:-

Signed ______________________________

NOTES

* Delete as appropriate

1. A copy of this notice must be sent to the Registrar of Companies within 14 days of its receipt at the Registered Office of the company.

2. A copy of any circumstances stated at (b) above, must be sent to every person who under the Companies Act 1985 is entitled to be sent copies of the accounts.

Precedent 7B.5

To Appoint Auditor Other Than the Retiring Auditor

(1) Directors' Resolution

Resolved that a resolution be put at the next general meeting at which accounts are laid, to propose the appointment of Messrs in place of Messrs as auditors of the company and that the secretary attend to all the necessary statutory formalities.

(2) Ordinary Resolution

Resolved that Messrs be appointed auditors of the company in place of Messrs to hold office until the conclusion of the next general meeting at which accounts are laid and that the directors be authorised to fix their remuneration.

Precedent 7B.6

To Fill a Casual Vacancy in the Office of Auditor

(1) Directors' Resolution

Resolved that an extraordinary general meeting of the company be called to consider an ordinary resolution to appoint Messrs auditors of the company in place of [*name*] deceased.

(2) Ordinary Resolution

Resolved that Messrs be appointed auditors of the company in place of [*name*] deceased, to hold office until the conclusion of the next general meeting at which accounts are laid, and the directors be authorised to fix their remuneration.

Precedent 7B.7

To Re-appoint an Auditor Appointed by the Directors to Fill a Casual Vacancy

(1) Directors' Resolution

Resolved that a resolution be put to the general meeting at which accounts are laid of the company to reappoint Messrs as auditors of this company, they having been appointed* by the Board pursuant to s 388 of the Companies Act 1985 to fill this vacancy caused by the resignation of Messrs

(2) Ordinary Resolution

Resolved that Messrs **[who were appointed by the directors upon the resignation of [*name*] during the year, and offer themselves for re-appointment] be re-appointed as auditors of the company and the directors are authorised to fix their remuneration.

EDITOR'S NOTES

* The directors will have used Precedent 7B.2 to fill the casual vacancy.

** It may be convenient to incorporate the bracketed section in the directors' report and not include in the resolution itself.

Precedent 7B.8

To Remove an Auditor Before Expiration of Term of Office

(1) Directors' Resolution

Resolved that an extraordinary general meeting of the company be called to consider a resolution to remove Messrs from the office of auditor of the company and appoint Messrs in their place in view of [*here set out reason*].

The secretary was asked to deal with all necessary statutory formalities.

(2) Ordinary Resolution

Resolved that Messrs are hereby removed from the office of auditor of the company and Messrs appointed in their place, to hold office until the conclusion of the next general meeting at which accounts are laid and the directors are authorised to fix their remuneration.

Precedent 7B.9

G

Notice of passing of resolution removing an auditor

Please do not write in this margin

Pursuant to section 386 of the Companies Act 1985

Please complete legibly, preferably in black type, or bold block lettering

To the Registrar of Companies

For official use

Company number

Name of company

* insert full name of company

*

gives notice that by a resolution passed at a general meeting of the company

on ______________________ 19 ______

§ insert name and address of removed auditor(s)

§ ______________________

of ______________________

Postcode: ______________________

was removed as auditor before the expiration of his term of office, with effect from

ø delete or complete as appropriate

[the passing of the resolution]ø

[______________________ 19______]ø

‡ Insert Director, Secretary, Administrator, Administrative Receiver or Receiver (Scotland) as appropriate

Signed | Designation‡ | Date

Presentor's name address and reference (if any):

For official Use

General Section | Post room

Precedent 7B.10

Letters to Auditors Enclosing Notice of Resolution to Appoint Different Auditors

(1) To Proposed New Auditors

Dear Sirs,

We enclose in accordance with the provisions of s 388 of the Companies Act 1985, a copy of an ordinary resolution to be proposed under special notice at the [annual] [extraordinary] general meeting of the company to be called for [*date*]. You will observe that this resolution will (if passed) appoint you auditors of the company.

Yours faithfully,

for Ltd

Secretary

(2) To the Retiring Auditors

Dear Sirs,

We enclose in accordance with the provisions of s 388 of the Companies Act 1985, a copy of an ordinary resolution to be proposed under special notice at the [annual] [extraordinary] general meeting of the company to be called for [*date*]. You will observe that this resolution [will, if passed, result in your ceasing to be auditors of the company] [arises as a result of your resignation as auditor of the company]*.

You will be aware of your statutory rights and responsibilities in this respect.

**[If you wish to avail yourselves of the right to make written representations to members, we should be obliged to receive them for circulation not later than [*date*].]

Yours faithfully,

for Ltd

Secretary

EDITOR'S NOTES

* Complete as appropriate.

** Include if removal is a result of friction between auditor and client.

See alternative form in Precedent 14A.16.

Precedent 7B.11

Letter to Members Enclosing Written Representations from Outgoing Auditors

The following representations have been received from the auditors who are being replaced if the resolution to be proposed at the [extraordinary] [annual] general meeting of the company called for [*date*] is passed.

In accordance with s 388 of the Companies Act 1985, these representations are being circulated to all members of the company who are entitled to receive notice of this meeting.

Chapter 8

DIVIDENDS AND LOAN INTEREST

Dividends

Shareholders receive income from their shares by payment of a dividend by the company.

ss 263–281 Dividends may only be paid out of the profits available for distribution (for definition see *Jordans Secretarial Administration*, at §§ 3.29–3.31).

The dividend declared will be the amount of the cash payment by the company to the shareholder to which will attach a tax credit. The dividend, together with the tax credit, will constitute the gross income of the shareholder for taxation purposes and the tax credit will be equivalent to the standard rate of income tax currently in force on that gross amount.

EXAMPLE

Dividend of 7½% on 1,000 £1 shares	£ 75.00
Tax credit (standard rate 25% per cent)	£ 25.00
Gross Income	£100.00

The company is required to account to the Inland Revenue for tax credits, which are returned on Inland Revenue Form CT61(Z), and is assessed to advance corporation tax (ACT), which may be set off against mainstream corporation tax (see Part VI of the Income and Corporation Taxes Act 1988 – (Company Distributions and Tax Credits)).

The company will give the shareholder a tax credit certificate when paying the dividend.

See Precedent 8.1 (p 216) EXTRACT FROM INLAND REVENUE FORM CT61(Z) FOR RETURNING PARTICULARS

See Precedent 8.2 (p 217) DIVIDEND PAYMENT COUNTERFOIL INCORPORATING TAX CREDIT CERTIFICATE

Dividends may be classified as follows.

(1) Payments made on periodic dates at specific rates as provided in the articles of association, eg preference share dividends.

(2) Payments on classes of shares which carry no fixed entitlements, ie:
   (a) interim dividends;
   (b) final dividends.

A directors' resolution is necessary before any dividend is paid, as they must be satisfied that distributable profits are available to meet it.

Table A, reg 103 Preference and other periodic dividends and interim dividends are resolved upon by the directors.

See Precedent 8.3 (p 218) DIRECTORS' RESOLUTION TO PAY PREFERENCE DIVIDEND

See Precedent 8.4 (p 218) DIRECTORS' RESOLUTION TO PAY INTERIM ORDINARY DIVIDEND

A final dividend is declared by the company in general meeting (usually annual general meeting). It does not become a debt due until so declared.

Table A, reg 102 The shareholders in general meeting may not declare any dividend larger than that recommended to them by the directors but may reduce the dividend below that recommendation. In approving the annual report and accounts for presentation to shareholders, it is necessary to pass a directors' resolution recommending any final dividend, if it is intended that a dividend is to be declared by the shareholders.

It is possible, and often convenient, to pay a second or subsequent interim dividend on a directors' resolution and omit any final dividend declared by shareholders.

See Precedent 8.5 (p 218) DIRECTORS' RESOLUTION RECOMMENDING FINAL ORDINARY DIVIDEND

See Precedent 8.6 (p 218) SHAREHOLDERS' RESOLUTION DECLARING FINAL ORDINARY DIVIDEND

See Precedent 8.7 (p 219) WORDING FOR DIRECTORS' REPORT COVERING DIVIDEND PAYMENTS

(1) INTERIM AND NO FINAL DIVIDEND

(2) INTERIM AND FINAL DIVIDEND

See Precedent 8.8 (p 219) DIVIDEND AGENDA ITEM IN NOTICE OF AGM

It will be seen that in any resolution proposing or declaring a dividend it is necessary to determine and state:

(1) the date of payment;
(2) the date of record, ie the date at which the Register of Shareholders is ruled off for the purpose of preparing the dividend list;
(3) the rate of dividend (by which the cash payment is calculated);
(4) the accounting period to which it applies.

Subject to the articles of association, there is no restriction in company law on paying a dividend in excess of the distributable profits for the specific accounting period so long as there are adequate distributable profits brought forward from earlier years.

Many larger companies maintain separate dividend accounts at their bank – usually one for each class of shares. When the dividend is declared the total cash payment will be transferred to the dividend account and dividend cheques or warrants drawn on that account.

Table A, reg 106 Dividends will usually be paid direct to the shareholder at his registered address (or to the first named shareholder in a joint account). The shareholder may, however, give the company a mandate to pay the dividend direct to a bank account.

See Precedent 8.9 (p 220) LETTER TO SHAREHOLDER REGARDING DIVIDEND MANDATE

See Precedent 8.10 (p 221) REQUEST FOR PAYMENT OF INTEREST OR DIVIDENDS ('DIVIDEND MANDATE')

If the dividend is paid in this manner, it is usual to forward the tax credit certificate to the bank.

The box at the foot of the mandate should be completed to indicate the account at the bank to which the dividend is to be credited. This is, however, a matter between the bank and the shareholder and no concern of the company.

Should the shareholder change the branch of bank to which dividends are mandated, or change account number, a written instruction may be accepted to alter the mandate.

See Precedent 8.11 (p 222) NOTICE OF CHANGE OF BRANCH OR ACCOUNT TO WHICH DIVIDENDS MANDATED

Circumstances arise in which a shareholder may wish to waive his right to a dividend. To achieve this, a formal waiver must be lodged with the company before the dividend is declared and becomes a debt from the company due to the shareholders.

Any shareholder proposing to waive dividends should first take appropriate professional advice on the tax effect.

See Precedent 8.12 (p 223) WAIVER OF DIVIDEND

Sometimes dividend warrants get lost or destroyed prior to payment. In such circumstances, an indemnity should be obtained from the shareholder before a replacement is issued.

See Precedent 8.13 (p 224) INDEMNITY FOR LOST DIVIDEND WARRANT

Loan Interest

The terms and conditions as to interest payments will be part of a loan agreement or debenture deed. Thus, interest becomes payable on the due date without the need of any Board resolution.

Interest will be paid under deduction of tax at standard rate and tax so deducted will be accounted for in the company's Schedule F return to the Inland Revenue.

Interest on loans and debentures is a charge on the company's pre-tax profits and not a distribution of profits, so interest is calculated gross and tax deducted from the resultant amount, as opposed to dividends which are declared and paid net and have tax credit added to the net amount to reach the gross figure.

EXAMPLE

Interest on loan of £1,000 at 10% payable half yearly

Half yearly interest	£50.00
Less tax at standard rate	
(eg 25%)	£12.50
Net payment to loan holder	£37.50

The company will issue to the loan holder a certificate for the tax deducted from the interest. This will either be in the form of a counterfoil or remittance advice with the payment cheque or on the Revenue Form R185.

See Precedent 8.14 CERTIFICATE FOR TAX DEDUCTED FOR LOAN INTEREST
(p 225) (1) NOTICE OF INTEREST AND TAX VOUCHER
(p 226) (2) FORM R185

If loan interest is to be paid direct to a bank account a mandate form will be used (see Precedent 8.11).

Precedent 8.1

Extract from Inland Revenue Form CT61(Z) for Returning Particulars

Qualifying distributions
1 Return under Schedule 13 ICTA 1988

• *Payments made on different dates should be listed separately. If necessary attach a separate schedule.*

		Date distribution made		Amount of distribution (£)	+ Advance Corporation Tax payable (£)	= Amount of franked payment (£)
a	**Money payments** (other than dividends shown at **b** below) which are liable to advance corporation tax	31 10 90	02	7,500 : 00	2,500 : 00	10,000 : 00
b	**Dividends** for which advance corporation tax is accounted for in spite of an election under S247(1) ICTA 1988		04			

c	Total of franked payments for this return period		05	10,000 : 00
d	*Less* set-off of franked investment income (item **2h**) (Box 24)		06	
e	Franked payments on which advance corporation tax payable	(05 – 06)	▸	10,000 : 00
f	Advance corporation tax payable thereon		07	2,500 : 00
g	Additional amount paid to certain non-residents under Regulations SI 1973 No. 317 • *Attach form 251.B Divs/FD in duplicate*		09	
h	**Total advance corporation tax payable** • *Carry forward to payslip, box 1*	(07 – 09 if positive)	10	2,500 : 00
i	Reimbursements claimed where additional amounts paid to non-residents exceeds tax otherwise payable • *Carry forward to 6a Page 4*	(09 – 07 if positive)	11	

EDITOR'S NOTE

Part 1 of the form should be completed when a qualifying distribution is made which is a money payment and the company is liable to account for advance corporation tax on it, eg on payment of a dividend.

Precedent 8.2

Dividend Payment Counterfoil Incorporating Tax Credit Certificate

The Company Limited
Dividend on Ordinary £1 Shares

I certify that advance corporation tax of an amount equal to that shown as tax credit will be accounted for to the Collector of Taxes. This voucher should be kept. It will be accepted by the Inland Revenue as evidence of tax credit in respect of which you may be entitled to claim payment or relief.

J Stickatit
Secretary

PAYMENT	INTERIM OR FINAL	YEAR ENDING	RECORD DATE
10	Interim	30 September 1990	20/10/1990

HOLDING	PENCE PER SHARE
100	5p

TAX CREDIT	AMOUNT PAYABLE
1.66	5.00

DATE PAYABLE
31/7/1990

Shareholders

....
....
....
....

EDITOR'S NOTE

This dividend counterfoil is completed to reflect the dividend declared in Precedent 8.4, at a standard tax rate of 25 per cent.

Precedent 8.3

Directors' Resolution to Pay Preference Dividend

That the dividend due on the class of five per cent preference shares on 30 September 19 , for the half year ended on that date, be paid on that date to preference shareholders registered at the close of business on 20 September 19 .

Precedent 8.4

Directors' Resolution to Pay Interim Ordinary Dividend

That an interim dividend in respect of the year ending 30 September 19 , be paid at the rate of five pence per £1 ordinary share on the 31 July 19 , to ordinary shareholders registered at the close of business on 20 July 19 .

Precedent 8.5

Directors' Resolution Recommending Final Ordinary Dividend

That a final dividend of eight pence per £1 ordinary share in respect of the year ended 30 September 19 , be recommended for declaration on the ordinary shares and payable on 20 December 19 , to ordinary shareholders registered at the close of business on 10 December 19 .

Precedent 8.6

Shareholders' Resolution Declaring Final Ordinary Dividend

That a final dividend in respect of the year ended 30 September 19 , be declared payable at the rate of eight pence per ordinary share on 20 December 19 , to shareholders registered at the close of business on 10 December 19 .

Precedent 8.7

Wording for Directors' Report Covering Dividend Payments

(1) Interim and No Final Dividend

Dividends have been paid on the ordinary shares as set out in the profit and loss account on page .* The directors do not recommend the declaration of any dividend beyond those already paid.

Ordinary Dividend	1st Interim	5p per share	5,000
	2nd Interim	8p per share	8,000
			13,000

EDITOR'S NOTE

*The relevant page in the accounts.

(2) Interim and Final Dividend

An interim dividend of five pence per share has been paid and the directors recommend a final dividend of eight pence per share, in respect of the year ended 30 September 19 , making a total for the year of 13 pence per share. The proposed final dividend will, if approved by shareholders, be paid on 20 December 19 , to shareholders registered at the close of business on 10 December 19 .

Precedent 8.8

Dividend Agenda Item in Notice of AGM

To declare a dividend.

EDITOR'S NOTE

The description and note of dividend will have been covered in the directors' report, as above.

Precedent 8.9

Letter to Shareholder Regarding Dividend Mandate

Dear Shareholder

If you have not already given instructions to the company on payment of dividends may we point out the advantages of having them paid direct to your bank account. This not only ensures the prompt crediting of dividends to your bank account on the due date but also eliminates the risk of warrants being lost or mislaid, which can arise when a change of address has not been recorded with us or if you are ill or absent from home for any reason.

If you would like us to pay your dividends in this way please complete the mandate form on the reverse of this letter and pass it to your bank for the insertion of the bank's reference number. The bank will then send it to us for implementation. Future tax vouchers will be forwarded to you through your bankers.

Yours faithfully

Company Secretary

Precedent 8.10

Request for Payment of Interest or Dividends ('Dividend Mandate')

Above this line for Registrar's use only.

Name of Undertaking	
Please complete in typewriting or in block capitals. Full name and address of first named or sole holder. Full name(s) of joint holder(s) (if any). Any change of address should be notified by quoting former and present address.	Account Designation (if any)
Full name and address of the bank branch, firm or person to whom interest and dividends are to be sent.	Please forward, until further notice, all interest and dividends that may from time to time become due on any stock or shares now standing, or which may hereafter stand, in my (our) name(s) or in the name(s) of the survivor(s) of us in the company's books to: or, where payment is to be made to a bank, to such other branch of that bank as the bank may from time to time request. Your compliance with this request shall discharge the company's liability in respect of such interest or dividends.

1 .... 2 ....

[*signature(s) of shareholder(s)*]

3 ....

Date .... 4 ....

NOTES

(i) Executors or administrators must insert the name of the deceased holder.
(ii) This form must be signed by ALL the registered holders.
(iii) A body corporate should sign by means of authorised signatory(ies) whose capacity must be stated.
(iv) Directions to credit a particular account MUST be given to the bank direct and NOT INCLUDED in this form.
(v) WHERE INSTRUCTIONS ARE IN FAVOUR OF A BANK, THIS FORM SHOULD BE SENT DIRECT TO THE BANK BRANCH CONCERNED FOR COMPLETION OF THE SECTION BELOW.

BANK'S REFERENCE NUMBER AND DETAILS:	STAMP OF BANK BRANCH
(1) SORTING CODE NUMBER [| |] (2) NAME OF BANK .... TITLE OF BRANCH .... (3) ACCOUNT NUMBER (IF ANY) PLEASE QUOTE ALL DIGITS INCLUDING ZEROS [| | | | | | |]	

Precedent 8.11

Notice of Change of Branch or Account to which Dividends Mandated

MELMOTTE'S BANK PLC .... Branch

To the secretary or registrar 19

.... Ltd/plc

DIVIDENDS

Kindly note that dividends on stock or shares standing in the name(s) of our customer:
Name(s)

Present address:..
which were formerly sent to this branch should, in future, be addressed to our branch as shown below.

....
Manager

---

(1) If you use the Bulk Dividend Distribution Scheme to:

Code no

Melmotte's Bank PLC ....
(*Branch title as given in list of sorting code numbers*)

(2) If you post mandated dividends direct to branch banks to ....
.... [*full postal address of branch*]
* Will you please place our account number on tax dividend vouchers. It would be helpful if the account number could be shown after or below the name of the registered holder.

Confirmed by stamp of new branch, and authorised signature.

....
Manager

[*Branch stamp*]

(a) The transferring branch should complete the top half of this form and send it direct to the new branch – if appropriate with the dividend.
(b) The new branch should complete the rest of the form and return it.

EDITOR'S NOTE

* Delete if not applicable.

Precedent 8.12

Waiver of Dividend

To: The Directors,
Company Limited

I, [full names]. . . . .

of [address]. . . . .

HEREBY irrevocably waive my right to receive the under-mentioned dividend(s) on ordinary shares of £1 each in the capital of the company registered in my name.

Dividend(s) [eg 1st Interim in respect of the year ended 30 September 19].

Dated. . . . .

Signed . . . .

Precedent 8.13

Indemnity for Lost Dividend Warrant

INDEMNITY FOR LOST DIVIDEND WARRANT	(above this line for Registrar's use only)

To the directors of. . . . . Ltd/plc

The original dividend warrant(s) detailed below has/have been lost or destroyed.

I/We request you to issue a duplicate warrant(s) and in consideration of your doing so I/we undertake to indemnify you and the company against all claims and demands (and any expense thereof) which may be made against you or the company in consequence of your complying with this respect.

I/We undertake to deliver to the company for cancellation the said original warrant(s) should the same ever be recovered.

PARTICULARS OF DIVIDEND WARRANT(S)
LOST OR DESTROYED

Class of security	Div serial no	Warrant no (if known)	Date payable	Amount		In favour of
				£	p	

Dated . . . . 19. . . .

Signature:. . . . .

EDITOR'S NOTE

See Precedent 5C.13 for a bank endorsement of the shareholder's undertaking to indemnify the company, which may be appropriate to use in connection with this precedent also.

Precedent 8.14

Certificate for Tax Deducted for Loan Interest

(1) Notice of Interest and Tax Voucher

JS50

.... Limited

To

Address ....

....

....

....

Date .... 19 ....

Class and denomination of Security

[ ]

Period

[ ]

Rate of Tax applicable

Amount of Loan/Stock

Gross Interest

Income Tax

Net Amount [ ]

A cheque is enclosed for the net amount payable.

I certify that the income tax deducted from this interest will be accounted for to the proper officer for the receipt of taxes.

.... Secretary

IMPORTANT

This voucher should be kept. Stockholders claiming relief from tax may show it to the Inland Revenue who will accept it as evidence of payment of tax by deduction.

(2) Form R185

Certificate of deduction of income tax ***for payments under Deed of Covenant please use form R185(AP)***

Only use this form if income tax has been deducted from the payment

I certify that on paying to ______

of ______

the amount shown in column 3 below I deducted the income tax shown in column 4, and that this tax has been or will be paid by me either directly or by deduction from other income when received by me.

Nature of the payment eg bond, mortgage or loan interest, annuity, maintenance, rent, payments from a discretionary trust and single charitable donations by non-close companies 1	Profits or other source out of which paid 2	Gross payment 3	Income tax deducted by me 4	Net payment *see Note b.* 5	Period for which payment was due *see Note c.* From ______ to ______ 6
		£	£	£	Date on which payment due *see Note c.*

Enter here in CAPITAL letters please

- Payer's name and address *see Note a.*

  Postcode

- If you are employed, your employer's name and address **or** If a company or if you are in business the business address

  Postcode

- District and reference to which Tax Returns are made *if known*

day month year 7

Date payment actually made

day month year 8

Please do not write in the spaces below

District stamp

'Duty assessed' stamp

Signature ______ **Date** ______

The person deducting the tax and responsible for accounting for it to the Revenue should sign this form. They should say if they are deducting tax on behalf of their employer, for example as secretary or cashier.

Notes

a. Where the payment is made by a trustee give the full name of the trust together with the Tax District and reference.

b. In the case of a payment made by trustees of a discretionary trust in exercise of their discretion, enter in column 5 the actual amount paid, in column 4 the amount of tax treated as deducted at a rate equal to the basic rate and the additional rate for the year of payment, and in column 3 the corresponding gross amount ie the total of the amounts in columns 4 and 5.

c. Do not complete where payment is made upon the exercise of a trustee's discretion or as a single donation by a non-close company.

R185 ***The person receiving the payments should keep this form. It will be needed if a claim for repayment of income tax is made.***

5895/0877L Dd 8097836 400M 8/88 TP Gp607

Chapter 9

REGISTERED OFFICE

ns 287 CA 1989, s 136 Every company is required to have a registered office situated in that part of the United Kingdom in which it is registered.

If registered in England and Wales the registered office may be in either country unless its
s 21 memorandum states that the registered office must be in Wales.

Companies registered at the Scottish Registry must have a registered office in Scotland.

Initial Notification and Adoption of First Registered Office

s 10 ns 287(2) On formation, the proposed registered office will be notified to the Registrar of Companies on Form 10 with other particulars of the proposed company. The address of this first registered office will be adopted at the first Board meeting. (See Chapter 1, Precedent 1.1.)

Change of Registered Office

A change in the address of the registered office is effected by a resolution of the Board of directors.

See Precedent 9.1 (p 229) DIRECTORS' RESOLUTION TO CHANGE REGISTERED OFFICE

The change must be notified to the Registrar of Companies on Form G 287.

See Precedent 9.2 (p 229) FORM G 287 NOTICE OF CHANGE IN SITUATION OF REGISTERED OFFICE

It is extremely important that this notification takes place because:

ns 287(4) CA 1989, s 136
(1) the date on which the change takes place is that on which notification is registered by the Registrar of Companies;
(2) the address filed with the Registrar of Companies must correspond with that stated on the annual return;
(3) any writ or other notice delivered to the registered office is deemed to have been received by the company;
(4) the address filed is that to which official communications will be sent. Companies that are in active business have found themselves struck off the register because communications from the Registrar addressed to an outdated registered office have been returned marked 'unknown' (see Chapter 15).

SI 1991/1259 Notification of change of registered office will be accepted on the next annual return form if Form G 287 has not been completed at this time.

Display of Name and Address of Registered Office

The name of the company and address of the registered office must be shown on the company's letter headings and other documentation, as described in Chapter 3.

The name of the company must be displayed outside every office, or place at which it carries on business, including the registered office. Frequently, the display at the registered office will state not only the name, but the fact that this is the registered office address – although there is no statutory requirement to do so.

See Precedent 9.3 (p 230) DISPLAY OF NAME AT REGISTERED OFFICE

Most of the statutory registers must be kept at the registered office and made available for inspection (see Chapter 13).

Precedent 9.1

Directors' Resolution to Change Registered Office

That the situation of the registered office be changed to [*new address*].

Precedent 9.2

G

Notice of change in situation of registered office

287

Please do not write in this margin

Pursuant to section 287 of the Companies Act 1985
as substituted by section 136 of the Companies Act 1989

Please complete legibly, preferably in black type, or bold block lettering

To the Registrar of Companies
(Address overleaf)

Company number

Name of company

* insert full name of company

*

give notice of a change in the situation of the registered office of the company to:

Postcode

‡ Insert Director, Secretary, Administrator Administrative Receiver or Receiver (Scotland) as appropriate

Signed Designation‡ Date

Precedent 9.3

Display of Name at Registered Office

XYZ LTD Registered Office

The Registered Offices of XYZ Ltd ABC Ltd MPO Ltd

Normally on a plaque by the door of the office or on the wall of the reception area.

Alternatively, if there are a large number of companies registered at the address:

Registered Offices The companies whose registered office is at this address are recorded in a register which is available for inspection on request.

Chapter 10

DIRECTORS

10A Appointment and Cessation of Office

Introduction

This section assumes that the company is regulated by articles aligned to Table A of the Companies Act 1985. Many companies still operate under articles aligned to the 1948 Table A, or indeed Tables A to earlier Acts. In all such cases the articles must be carefully construed, particularly in relation to the 1929 and earlier Tables A and their interaction with current legislation.

Appointment

Directors may be appointed:

Table A, reg 79 (1) by co-option by the existing Board of directors. Under Table A directors so appointed are required to retire and seek re-election at the next annual general meeting;

(2) by the company in general meeting – by an ordinary resolution;

(3) by any special procedure provided in the articles, eg:
   (a) the articles of a subsidiary company may empower the parent company to appoint or remove a director by notice in writing sent to the registered office (see 10B below);
   (b) in companies used as the vehicle for a joint venture, each shareholder (or class of shareholder) may have power to appoint one or more directors.

A corporate body may be appointed a director and will act through its authorised representative(s). (As to form of appointment and notification of authorised representatives, see Precedent 10C.6D.) More usually, directors are individuals and there is no legal restriction on residence or nationality, although such may be imposed by a company's articles.

SI 1990/1707 Following the appointment of a director, Form 288 (see Precedent 10A.14) is filed with the Registrar of Companies within 14 days. The form must be signed by the new director confirming his acceptance of appointment. The company must also enter appropriate particulars in its own Register of Directors and, where appropriate, Register of Directors' Interests (see p 290). It will be noted that the date of birth of directors must now be entered on Form 288 and in the Register of Directors for *all* companies from 1 October 1990. Previously, this requirement was only relevant to public companies.

See Precedent 10A.1 (p 235) APPOINTMENT OF A DIRECTOR BY EXISTING DIRECTORS

See Precedent 10A.2 (p 235) APPOINTMENT BY COMPANY IN GENERAL MEETING: NOTICE

See Precedent 10A.3 (p 235) RESOLUTION OF GENERAL MEETING TO APPOINT A DIRECTOR

If several directors are being appointed, a separate resolution should be passed for each.

Often the articles of a subsidiary company give the parent company power to appoint or remove directors by notice in writing without recourse to other procedures (see Precedent 10B.1).

See Precedent 10A.4 (p 236) (1) APPOINTMENT UNDER TERMS OF ARTICLES
(2) DIRECTORS' MINUTES (SUBSIDIARY COMPANY)

See Precedent 10A.5 (p 237) REGISTER OF DIRECTORS

Before appointing an additional director it is important to check that such appointment does not result in exceeding the maximum number of directors for the company under the terms of the articles or any resolution pursuant thereto.

Table A, reg 64 — Table A provides for a minimum of two directors but no maximum, unless determined otherwise in general meeting. A private company may have just one director and articles may provide that a sole director may exercise all the powers of the Board. (See Jordans standard articles for a private company, at Appendix 2.)

See Precedent 10A.6 (p 238) RESOLUTION TO FIX NUMBER OF DIRECTORS

Other statutory and regulatory situations

In certain specialised circumstances, Governmental or regulatory authority consent may be required for appointment of directors to the Board of a company licensed to operate in sensitive circumstances (eg financial services).

An undischarged bankrupt, or a person disqualified under the Company Directors Disqualification Act 1986, may not be appointed. (See *Gore-Browne on Companies*, at § 25.7.)

Re-election of directors

Table A, reg 79 — As stated above, Table A provides that a director appointed by the Board must seek re-election at the next following annual general meeting. Such a re-election is additional and not taken into account in calculating which directors retire by rotation.

Table A, regs 73–80 — Table A also provides that one-third of the directors (or the nearest whole number below) shall retire at each annual general meeting. If two or more persons were originally appointed on the same day those to retire should be agreed between them or determined by lot.

Retiring directors are eligible for re-election.

Both above regulations may be excluded in the articles of a company. This is frequently done in smaller private companies and nearly always in joint venture companies which carry specific appointment powers in their articles. (See Appendix 2, Jordans standard articles for a private company.)

s 293 — In a public company a director attaining the age of 70 must likewise seek re-election on a special notice resolution (see Chapter 14). This does not apply to private companies.

See Precedent 10A.7 (p 238) WORDING FOR DIRECTORS' REPORT

See Precedent 10A.8 (p 238) RESOLUTION OF GENERAL MEETING FOR
RE-ELECTION OF A DIRECTOR

Retirement, resignation and vacation of office

s 288 In all circumstances in which a director resigns, or otherwise leaves the Board, appropriate entries must be made in the Register of Directors and a return made within 14 days to the Registrar of Companies on Form 288.

See Precedent 10A.9 (p 239) REGISTER OF DIRECTORS – DIRECTOR'S RESIGNATION ENTRY

In a company which has articles that provide for retirement by rotation a director may retire by not seeking re-election at the end of his term of office.

See Precedent 10A.10 (p 240) WORDING OF DIRECTORS' REPORT WHEN DIRECTOR DOES NOT SEEK RE-ELECTION

In other circumstances, a director may resign by notice in writing addressed to the chairman or secretary. Such letter must be precise as to the date of resignation, which cannot be retrospective. If there is any doubt the date of resignation will be taken as the date of the letter, unless delivery is postponed.

See Precedent 10A.11 (p 240) LETTER OF RESIGNATION

See Precedent 10A.12 (p 240) BOARD MINUTE RECORDING RESIGNATION

Table A, reg 81 There may be circumstances by which a director must vacate office under the terms of the articles.

See Precedent 10A.13 (p 240) BOARD MINUTE RECORDING VACATION OF OFFICE

Form 288 must be filed on the appointment of a director, or the cessation of such an appointment. If the particulars of a director, as originally filed, alter, notification should be given to the Registrar on Form 288. Alternatively, the annual return may be used once Form 363s (the final 'shuttle' version) is in use. The most usual alteration will be in other directorships held, ie additions or resignations.

See Precedent 10A.14 (p 241) FORM 288 CHANGE OF DIRECTOR OR SECRETARY OR CHANGE OF PARTICULARS

Dismissal

ss 303–304 The Act provides that a director can be removed during his term of office by an ordinary resolution at a general meeting of the company. Such a resolution must be proposed by a member (who, according to circumstances, may also be a director) under special notice (see Chapter 14A).

See Precedent 10A.15 (p 243) SPECIAL NOTICE OF RESOLUTION TO REMOVE A DIRECTOR

This notice should be given, forthwith, to the director whom the resolution proposes to remove, stating his rights of reply.

See Precedent 10A.16 (p 244) NOTICE OF RESOLUTION GIVEN BY COMPANY TO THE DIRECTOR

The time limit for receipt of any resultant representation must be such that the special notice time limit can be met for the sending of the notice of meeting to shareholders.

See Precedent 10A.17 (p 245) NOTICE OF MEETING TO REMOVE DIRECTOR

The full form of notice of meeting is included in this precedent so as to give the statutory references.

If the resolution is passed, appropriate entries will be made in the Register of Directors and Form 288 filed with the Registrar of Companies. (See Precedents 10A.10 and 10A.11 and adapt as appropriate.)

Generally

On the retirement or removal of directors, care should be taken to ensure that their signing powers on the company's bank account and elsewhere are cancelled.

Dismissal of a director may entitle the director to claim damages, if he is an employee, for breach of his service contract (if any), or he may be able to claim redundancy payment or compensation for unfair dismissal. If the director is also a shareholder, his dismissal may give grounds for presenting a winding-up petition, or a petition based on unfairly prejudicial conduct. See *Gore-Browne on Companies*, at § 32.5. If any of these, or similar, circumstances appear to apply, professional advice should be sought before acting to remove the director.

Compensation for loss of office

Sometimes circumstances arise in which compensation for loss of office is paid to a director who leaves. These notes deal only with Companies Act aspects of compensation payments. Employment law and taxation aspects must also be considered. Compensation for loss of office is a complicated matter and reference should be made to *Jordans Secretarial Administration*, at § 4.25.

Sch 5, para 29 If the compensation is for executive services and is a fair settlement of any claim the director may have under a service contract or contract of employment, then no Companies Act formalities are necessary save disclosure in the accounts.

ss 312, 314 If, however, the payment is excessive, or is on the occasion of an offer to purchase the share capital of the company, the payment must be approved by the shareholders before it is made.

See Precedent 10A.18 (p 246) BOARD RESOLUTION TO PAY COMPENSATION

s 312 Shareholders' approval for a compensation payment is given by ordinary resolution passed at a general meeting, but in order to meet the special requirements attached to compensation approval, notice of that resolution must be given to all shareholders, regardless of whether they are entitled to attend and vote at a general meeting.

If the resolution is in the context of a take-over bid, it is important to word it so that payment is conditional upon the bid being accepted by shareholders and, therefore, becoming unconditional.

See Precedent 10A.19 (p 246) SHAREHOLDERS' RESOLUTION TO APPROVE COMPENSATION PAYMENT

Precedent 10A.1

Appointment of a Director by Existing Directors

DIRECTORS' RESOLUTION

Resolved that [*name*] be and is hereby appointed a director of the company.

*With effect from [*date*].

EDITOR'S NOTE

* Add this clause if effective date is to be later than the date of the resolution, eg on appointment of a new executive joining the company at a future date or to fix appointment to a suitable date, ie commencement of a new accounting period.

Precedent 10A.2

Appointment by Company in General Meeting: Notice

NOTICE*

The business of the meeting will be to consider and if thought fit to appoint [*name*] a director of the company.

EDITOR'S NOTE

* See 14A (below) as to notice period and majorities required.

Precedent 10A.3

Resolution of General Meeting to Appoint a Director

PROPOSED AS AN ORDINARY RESOLUTION*

Resolved that [*name*] be and is hereby appointed a director of the company.

EDITOR'S NOTE

* Form 288 must be completed and filed with the Registrar of Companies. The company's Register of Directors and Register of Directors' Interests must be written up. Attention should be given to cheque signatures and, if appropriate, company stationery.

Precedent 10A.4

(1) Appointment under Terms of Articles

Pursuant to Article   in the articles of association of the company we hereby appoint [*name*] to be a director of the company.
*[In succession to [*name*] appointed by us under this article whose appointment we hereby terminate.]

(2) Directors' Minutes (Subsidiary Company)**

The secretary tabled a notice from the parent company pursuant to Article   appointing [*name*] a director of the company. The appointment was noted and the secretary asked to complete the necessary formalities.***

EDITOR'S NOTES

* Add as appropriate.
** This should be supported by a minute of the Board of the parent company.
*** Register of Directors, Form 288 and, perhaps, Register of Directors' Interests, will require amendment and filing, as appropriate. Attention may also need to be drawn to cheque signatures and stationery.

Precedent 10A.5
Register of Directors

Surname BLUE
(or Corporate Name)

Forename(s) PETER

Any former Forenames or Surnames

Nationality BRITISH Date of Birth 23/5/40

Residential Address THE HOLLIES
(or Registered or Principal Office)
25 RUFFORD ROAD

DILSBOROUGH

RUFFORDSHIRE RU3 9QE

Business Occupation CHARTERED ACCOUNTANT

Dates of:-

Appointment	20/9/1980	Resignation or Cessation	
Minute	37/80	Minute	
Filing Particulars	30/9/80	Filing Particulars	

Other Directorships	Date of Resignation
BLUE ASSOCIATES LTD	
RUFFORD INDUSTRIES PLC	

EDITOR'S NOTES

1. Other directorships do not include directorships in companies in the same groups or dormant or overseas companies.
overseas companies.
2. The date of resignation from another directorship must be recorded and the entry retained on the register for five years from that date (see CA 1985, s 289).

Precedent 10A.6

Resolution to Fix Number of Directors

ORDINARY RESOLUTION

(1) Notice

To fix the maximum number of directors at [six].

(2) Resolution

It is hereby resolved that (until otherwise decided by the company in general meeting) the maximum number of directors of the company shall be [six].

Precedent 10A.7

Wording for Directors' Report

DIRECTORS

[*Name*], appointed a director since the last annual general meeting, retired in accordance with the articles of association.

[*Name*] retires by rotation likewise.

Both being eligible, offer themselves for re-election.

EDITOR'S NOTE

The names only will be given in the notice of meeting.

Precedent 10A.8

Resolution of General Meeting for Re-election of a Director

Resolved that [*name*] be and is hereby reappointed a director of the company.

Precedent 10A.9
Register of Directors – Director's Resignation Entry

Surname GREEN
(or Corporate Name)

Forename(s) ERIC

Any former Forenames or Surnames

Nationality BRITISH Date of Birth 12/12/1937

Residential Address
(or Registered or Principal Office) GREEN LODGE

LONDON 4

Business Occupation COMPANY DIRECTOR

Dates of:-

Appointment	18/5/1959	Resignation or Cessation	1/12/86
Minute	18/5/1959	Minute	4/1/87
Filing Particulars	18/5/1959	Filing Particulars	11/12/86

Other Directorships	Date of Resignation
NONE	

Precedent 10A.10

Wording of Directors' Report when Director Does Not Seek Re-election

[*Name*] retires by rotation and does not seek re-election.

Precedent 10A.11

Letter of Resignation

I hereby resign as a director of [*name of company*] with effect from [*date*].

[I confirm that I have no claim whatsoever of any kind relating to my directorship or its termination.]*

EDITOR'S NOTE

* Add if appropriate.

Precedent 10A.12

Board Minute Recording Resignation

It is recorded that by letter dated [*date*], [*name*] resigned from the Board.

Precedent 10A.13

Board Minute Recording Vacation of Office

It was noted that [*name*] was declared bankrupt on [*date*] and thereby *(in accordance with reg 81 of Table A, which is included in the articles of association), vacated his position as a director of the company.

EDITOR'S NOTE

* Specify relevant regulation in Table A or special articles.

Precedent 10A.14

Printed and supplied by
Jordans
Jordan & Sons Limited
21 St. Thomas Street, Bristol BS1 6JS
Tel: 0272 230600 Telex 449119

288

Change of director or secretary or change of particulars

This form should be completed in black.

Company number CN 3 145 678

Company name

Appointment

(Turn over page for resignation and change of particulars).

	Day	Month	Year
Date of appointment DA	01	12	86

Appointment of director CD ✓

Appointment of secretary CS

Please mark the appropriate box. If appointment is as a director and secretary mark both boxes.

Name *Style/title MR

Forenames JACK

Surname JONES

*Honours etc

Previous forenames

Previous surname

Usual residential address AD 25 BLACK HILL

Post town DILSBOROUGH

County/region RUFFORDSHIRE

Postcode RU12 6JY Country

Date of birth† DO 02 02 56 Nationality† NA BRITISH

Business occupation† OC CHARTERED ACCOUNTANT

Other directorships† NONE

NOTES

Show the full forenames. **NOT INITIALS** If the director or secretary is a Corporation or Scottish firm, show the name on surname line and registered or principal office on the usual residential address line.

Give previous forenames or surname except:
- for a married woman the name before marriage need not be given.
- for names not used since the age of 18 or for at least 20 years.

A peer or individual known by a title may state the title instead of or in addition to the forenames and surname.

Other directorships.

Give the name of every company of which the person concerned is a director or has been a director at any time in the past 5 years. Exclude a company which either is, or at all times during the past 5 years when the person was a director, was
- dormant
- a parent company which wholly owned the company making the return
- a wholly owned subsidiary of the company making the return
- another wholly owned subsidiary of the same parent company.

I consent to act as director/secretary of the above named company

Consent signature Signed Jack Jones Date 1/12/86

*Voluntary details †Directors only

A serving director etc must also sign the form overleaf.

Resignation

(This includes any form of ceasing to hold office e.g. death or removal from office).

Date of resignation etc	DR 0 1 1 2 8 6	
Resignation etc, as director	XD ✓	*Please mark the appropriate box. If resignation etc is as a director and secretary mark both boxes.*
Resignation etc, as secretary	XS	
Forenames	ERIC	
Surname	GREEN	
Date of birth *(directors only)*	DO 1 2 1 2 3 7	
If cessation is other than resignation, please state reason *(eg death)*		

Change of particulars

Complete this section in all cases where particulars have changed and then the appropriate section below.

Date of change of particulars	DC	
Change of particulars, as director	ZD	*Please mark the appropriate box. If change of particulars is as a director and secretary mark both boxes.*
Change of particulars, as secretary	ZS	
Forenames *(name previously notified to Companies House)*		
Surname *(name previously notified to Companies House)*		
Date of birth *(directors only)*	DO	

Change of name *(enter new name)*	Forenames	NN
	Surname	
Change of usual residential address *(enter new address)*		AD
	Post town	
	County/region	
	Postcode	Country
Other change	*(please specify)*	

A serving director,secretary etc must sign the form below.

Signature

Signed ____________ Date ________

(by a serving director/secretary/administrator/ administrative receiver/receiver). *(Delete as appropriate)*

After signing please return the form to the Registrar of Companies at

Companies House, Crown Way, Cardiff CF4 3UZ
for companies registered in England and Wales

or **Companies House, 100-102 George Street, Edinburgh EH2 3DJ**
for companies registered in Scotland.

To whom should Companies House direct any enquiries about the information on this form?

Tel:

Precedent 10A.15

Special Notice of Resolution to Remove a Director

The Directors
Billbrook Enterprises Ltd

I hereby give special notice, pursuant to ss 379 and 303(2) of the Companies Act 1985, of my intention to propose the following resolution as an ordinary resolution at a general meeting of the company, to be held not earlier than 28 days from the date of this notice.

RESOLUTION

That Mr James Botsey be and is hereby removed from office as a director of the company.

Signed: A E Trefoil

Date: 10 December 1989

Precedent 10A.16

Notice of Resolution Given by Company to the Director

Billbrook Enterprises Ltd
[*address*]

11 December 1989
(Recorded delivery)

To James Botsey
[*address*]

Dear Sir

I hereby give notice that the enclosed special notice has been received, pursuant to s 303 of the Companies Act 1985, and that, accordingly, the following ordinary resolution will be proposed at an extraordinary general meeting of the company called for 10.30am on 30 January 19 at the registered office of this company (as above).

ORDINARY RESOLUTION

That Mr James Botsey be and is hereby removed from office as director of the company.

Pursuant to s 304 of the Companies Act 1985 you are entitled to be heard on the resolution at the aforesaid meeting and may request that representations in writing made by you (not exceeding a reasonable length) be sent to all members of the company to whom notices of the meeting are sent. If you wish representations to be so sent may I receive them not later than 5 January 1990.

Yours faithfully

G J Stickatit
Secretary

EDITOR'S NOTE

This letter should be sent immediately special notice is received and must be carefully dated. A copy of the special notice must be enclosed. The timing of the circulation of notice of meeting in relation to the receipt of special notice and the date of the meeting must be carefully checked. It is vital that procedures should be absolutely correct.

Precedent 10A.17

Notice of Meeting to Remove Director

BILLBROOK ENTERPRISES LTD

NOTICE IS HEREBY GIVEN that an extraordinary general meeting of the above-named company will be held at the registered office of the company on the 20 day of January 1990 at 10.30 am, for the purposes of considering, and if thought fit passing, the following resolution as an ordinary resolution, special notice having been given pursuant to ss 379 and 303(2) of the Companies Act 1985.

ORDINARY RESOLUTION

That Mr James Botsey be and is hereby removed from office as director of the company.

Dated this 29 day of December 1989.

By Order of the board.
G J Stickatit
Secretary

Registered Office:
The Mill
Billbrook
Ruffordshire

NOTE

A member entitled to attend and vote at the above-mentioned meeting is entitled to appoint a proxy, who need not be a member of the company, to attend and vote in his stead.

Precedent 10A.18

Board Resolution to Pay Compensation

(1) Without need of shareholders' approval.

£ be paid to [*name*] on his resignation from the Board and executive position with the company and in termination of his service contract dated in full and final settlement of any claims he may have against the company or otherwise.

(2) Subject to shareholders' approval.

It be recommended that an extraordinary general meeting of shareholders be called for [*date*] [*place*] [*time*] at which a resolution will be proposed that compensation of £ be paid to [*name*] on his resignation from the Board [if the offer of XYZ plc for the whole of the share capital of the company becomes unconditional].

EDITOR'S NOTE

[ ] Add if in context of an offer for share capital of the company.

Precedent 10A.19

Shareholders' Resolution to Approve Compensation Payment

That a payment of £ by the company to [*name*] in consideration for his retirement from office as a director of the company [on the occasion of the offer for the whole of the share capital of the company by XYZ plc and subject to that offer becoming unconditional be and is hereby approved*].

EDITOR'S NOTE

* Add this sentence if the payment is made in the context of an offer for the share capital of the company.

10B The Office of Director

Directors of subsidiary companies

Frequently, a holding company wishes to have control over the Board of its subsidiaries without recourse to the specific procedures of the Companies Acts which are designed for the circumstances of an independent company.

The following precedent articles are widely used for this purpose and are self-explanatory.

See Precedent 10B.1 (p 249) ARTICLE GIVING HOLDING COMPANY POWER TO APPOINT OR REMOVE DIRECTORS

These precedents are drafted to include within the articles a definition of 'holding' and 'subsidiary' company. In many circumstances, such definitions will be included in the interpretation regulation with which most articles commence. See Precedent 10A.4 for appointment of directors under terms of articles.

Alternate directors

Table A, regs 65–69

An alternate director is a person who is appointed by a director to attend and vote at any meeting of the directors or Board committee of which his appointor is a member and at which his appointor is not personally present. The position of an alternate director is covered in regs 65–69 of Table A. (See also article 9 of Jordans standard articles of association in Appendix 2.) Frequently, another director is appointed to be an alternate director for a colleague.

Table A, reg 65

Articles usually provide that a person appointed as alternate, if not himself a director, must be approved by resolution of the directors.

See Precedent 10B.2 (p 250) NOTICE OF APPOINTMENT OF ALTERNATE DIRECTOR

See Precedent 10B.3 (p 250) BOARD MINUTE AS TO ALTERNATE APPOINTMENT

The appointment of an alternate is revoked by notice by the appointor to the company.

See Precedent 10B.4 (p 251) NOTICE OF REVOCATION OF APPOINTMENT OF ALTERNATE DIRECTOR

The appointor should likewise inform the alternate.

The revocation and date thereof should be reported at the next meeting of the directors and minuted (see Precedent 10B.4).

Table A, reg 68 s 288

An alternate director is deemed for all purposes to be a director of the company and thus Form 288 should be filed covering appointment or revocation unless the alternate is already a director of the company. Likewise, entries should be made in the Register of Directors but endorsed 'alternate director'.

See Precedent 10B.5 (p 252) FORM 288 CHANGE OF DIRECTOR OR SECRETARY OR CHANGE OF PARTICULARS (AMENDED FOR AN ALTERNATE DIRECTOR)

Managing directors

Table A, reg 72

The Board may appoint one or more of their number to the office of managing director or to any other executive office under the company and may remunerate him or grant him a service contract.

The appointment terminates if he ceases to be a director.

Table A, reg 84

Such a director is not subject to retirement by rotation under Table A articles.

See Precedent 10B.6 (p 253) MINUTE OF DIRECTORS APPOINTING A MANAGING DIRECTOR

See Precedent 10B.7 (p 254) SPECIMEN SERVICE AGREEMENT FOR A MANAGING DIRECTOR

A director's service contract of more than five years fixed term is required to be approved in general meeting. See *Jordans Secretarial Administration*, at § 4.6.

Associate directors

It is sometimes convenient to create a class of 'associate' or 'management' directors who are in fact senior managers, but able to represent themselves to customers and others as a director. This is a recognised formula for creating a limited category which does not carry the rights and responsibilities of a director under the Companies Acts.

See Appendix 2, additional optional Article IV, for specimen article creating a class of associate directors.

It will be seen that associate directors are created and hold office at the will of the Board and their function is to advise the Board as it may request. They have no personal right to attend Board meetings and no vote if they are invited to attend.

Since associate directors appointed in accordance with this draft article are not directors of the company under the Companies Acts, there is no requirement to maintain entries in the Register of Directors or file Form 288 in respect of them.

Precedent 10B.1

Article Giving Holding Company Power to Appoint or Remove Directors

(a) Notwithstanding any other provisions of these articles, for so long as the company is a subsidiary company, its holding company may appoint any person to be a director or remove any director from office howsoever appointed.

(b) For so long as the company is a subsidiary company, no transfer of a share shall be registered without the prior consent of the company's holding company.

(c) The first sentence of reg 24 in Table A shall not apply to the company.

(d) Every consent or any appointment or removal of a director under the powers conferred upon a holding company by these articles shall be made by instrument in writing and signed by a director or the secretary of such holding company and such instrument shall only take effect on the service thereof at the registered office of the company. Every such instrument shall be annexed to the directors' minute book as soon as practicable after such service.

(e) No person dealing with the company shall be concerned to see or enquire as to whether the powers of the directors have been in any way restricted hereunder or as to whether any requisite consent of a holding company has been obtained and shall not be affected or in any way prejudiced by any such restriction or lack of consent unless such person had at the time expressed notice that any act or transaction effected by or with the authority of the directors was in excess of their powers.

(f) If the company has more than one holding company then for the purpose of these articles references to its holding company shall be read and construed as references to its immediate holding company and the definitions of subsidiary company and holding company in the Companies Act shall apply.

Precedent 10B.2

Notice of Appointment of Alternate Director*

The Directors [*date*]
.... Limited

I hereby give notice that I have appointed [*name*] of [*address*] (**who is also a director of this company) to be my alternate as a director (†and request that this appointment receive your approval which could you please confirm to me).

Signed: ....
Director

EDITOR'S NOTE

*See Table A, reg 65.
**Delete if not so.
†This wording should be added if the articles of association provide that the appointment requires the approval of the Board.

Precedent 10B.3

Board Minute as to Alternate Appointment

A notice in writing was tabled by [*name*] by which he appointed [*name*] his alternate as a director of the company pursuant to Article   of the articles of association.

(It was resolved that the appointment of [*name*] as alternate director for [*name*] be and is hereby approved.)

EDITOR'S NOTE

This resolution must be checked against the articles of association (see Table A, reg 65, which provides that an appointment requires approval of the Board if the alternate is not already a director).

Precedent 10B.4

Notice of Revocation of Appointment of Alternate Director

To the Directors: Ltd [*date*]

I hereby give notice that I revoke the appointment of [*name*] as my alternate as a director of the company with effect from this date.

Precedent 10B.5

288

Change of director or secretary or change of particulars

This form should be completed in black.

Company number CN

Company name BUSH HOTEL (DILSBOROUGH) LTD

Appointment

(Turn over page for resignation and change of particulars).

Date of appointment DA (Day Month Year) 3 0 1 1 9 0

Appointment of alternate director CD

Appointment of secretary CS

Please mark the appropriate box.
If appointment is as a director and secretary mark both boxes.

NOTES

Show the full forenames. **NOT INITIALS**
If the director or secretary is a Corporation or Scottish firm, show the name on surname line and registered or principal office on the usual residential address line.

Give previous forenames or surname except:
- for a married woman the name before marriage need not be given.
- for names not used since the age of 18 or for at least 20 years.

A peer or individual known by a title may state the title instead of or in addition to the forenames and surname.

Name *Style/title MRS

Forenames JANE

Surname SMITH

*Honours etc

Previous forenames

Previous surname

Usual residential address AD BUSH HOTEL

Post town DILSBOROUGH

County/region RUFFORDSHIRE

Postcode

Country

Date of birth† DO 2 0 0 6 5 6 Nationality† NA BRITISH

Business occupation† OC CHEF

Other directorships†

Other directorships.

Give the name of every company of which the person concerned is a director or has been a director at any time in the past 5 years. Exclude a company which either is, or at all times during the past 5 years when the person was a director, was
- dormant
- a parent company which wholly owned the company making the return
- a wholly owned subsidiary of the company making the return
- another wholly owned subsidiary of the same parent company.

I consent to act as director/secretary of the above named company

Consent signature Signed J Smith Date 30/11/91

*Voluntary details †Directors only

Precedent 10B.6

Minute of Directors Appointing a Managing Director

There was produced the draft of a [service agreement] [letter of appointment]* between the company and [*name*] whereby the company appoints [*name*] a managing director from 19 , upon the terms and conditions set out in the [agreement] [letter]*.

Resolved (appointee not voting):

That the said [agreement] [letter]* be approved and that the chairman be and is hereby authorised to sign it on behalf of the company.

EDITOR'S NOTE

*Adapt as necessary.

Precedent 10B.7

Specimen Service Agreement for a Managing Director

AN AGREEMENT made the day of 19 BETWEEN Ltd whose registered office is situate at (hereinafter called 'the company') of the one part and of (hereinafter called 'the director') of the other part.

WHEREBY IT IS AGREED as follows.

1. The company shall employ the director and the director shall serve the company as managing director of the company for the term commencing on 19 and ending on 19 and continuing thereafter unless or until terminated by not less than 12 months' notice in writing by either party to the other given to expire at 19 or at the end of any subsequent calendar month.
2. During the continuance of this Agreement the director shall perform all such duties and exercise all such powers in relation to the business and affairs of the company and such other companies as may from time to time be subsidiary companies of the company (hereinafter together called 'the subsidiary companies') as may from time to time be reasonably assigned to him by the Board of directors of the company (hereinafter called 'the Board'). In carrying out his duties the director shall comply with all such lawful and reasonable instructions as may from time to time be given to him by the Board and he shall give the Board all such explanations, information and assistance as they may reasonably require.
3. During the continuance of this Agreement:
   (1) the director shall well and faithfully serve the company to the best of his ability and shall use his best endeavours to promote the interests of the company and the subsidiary companies;
   (2) the director shall not engage in any activities which detract from the proper performance of his duties hereunder or (without the written consent of the Board first being obtained) either solely or jointly with or as manager or agent for any other person, firm or company directly or indirectly carry on or be engaged in or (save as a holder of shares or securities issued by a public company and listed on the Stock Exchange) be concerned in any other business, trade or calling whatsoever.
4. As remuneration for his services hereunder the director shall be entitled to a salary at the rate of £ pounds per annum or at such other rate as may from time to time be agreed. Such salary which will be payable monthly in arrear shall be deemed to accrue from day to day and shall be inclusive of all director's fees.
5. The company shall pay all reasonable travelling, entertainment and other expenses properly incurred by the director in the performance of his duties hereunder.

6. The company shall during the term of this Agreement provide the director with a suitable motor car for use in the performance of his duties hereunder and shall pay motor tax, insurance premiums and the running expenses of such motor car including petrol, lubrication, maintenance and repairs. The director shall also be permitted to use the said motor car for his own private purposes including use on holidays at his own expense in relation to petrol and lubrication.
7. In addition to the usual bank and public holidays the director shall be entitled to weeks holiday in each year.
8. If the director shall during the continuance of this Agreement make or become possessed of any invention, discovery or process (or any improvement of any kind) relating to or which could be applied to the business of any of the company and the subsidiary companies, then any such invention, discovery, process or improvement shall become the property of the company and the director shall at the request and expense of the company do all acts and things necessary for obtaining a patent or patents for the same if patentable or otherwise making the same available to the company.
9. If the director shall be guilty of any serious misconduct or any serious breach or non-observance of any of the provisions of this Agreement or shall neglect or fail or refuse to carry out the duties assigned to him hereunder the company shall be entitled summarily to terminate his employment hereunder without notice and without payment in lieu of notice.
10. (a) In case the director shall at any time be prevented by illness or accident or other disability from properly performing his duties hereunder (and shall if required furnish the Board with evidence satisfactory to them of such incapacity) for a longer period than 13 consecutive weeks then in such case the company shall be entitled forthwith by giving written notice to the director to discontinue for the period the disability exists any further payment of salary, but so that, notwithstanding the discontinuance of the payment of such salary, the employment of the director hereunder shall continue for the purposes of any term of any insurance policy taken out to provide the benefits referred to under subclause (b) of this clause.

    (b) The company shall without cost to the director use its best endeavours to procure that the group permanent health insurance Policy No effected by the company with the Insurance Company PLC and dated 19 shall remain in full force and effect or that another or other policy providing benefits not less favourable than the benefits provided under such policy be effected and maintained and that in the event of the director's salary being discontinued pursuant to subclause (a) of this clause the director shall thereafter with immediate effect be paid sums equivalent to and for the duration of the benefits payable under such policy.

    (c) Notwithstanding any other provision of this Agreement if the director shall have been disabled from performing his duties hereunder (and whether or not the director's salary shall have been discontinued in accordance with subclause (a) of this clause) for a longer period than 12 consecutive months then the company shall be entitled forthwith by giving written notice to the director to procure the appointment of another person or persons to the office described under clause 1 hereof in place of and to the exclusion of the director. No such appointment shall be deemed to be a breach of this Agreement or to be grounds for any claim for unfair dismissal pursuant to the Employment Protection (Consolidation) Act 1978 or any regulations made thereunder or statutory modification or re-enactment thereof.

11. The director shall be a member of the company's Pension and Assurance Scheme.
12. The director shall not during his employment hereunder or after the determination hereof (however caused) except in the proper course of his duties hereunder use or divulge to any person whomsoever and shall use his best endeavours to prevent the publication or disclosure of any trade secret or any confidential information concerning the products or businesses or finances or customers or trade connection of the company or any of the subsidiary companies or any such company's dealings, transactions or affairs.
13. The director shall not either on his own account or for any other person, firm or company solicit, interfere with or endeavour to entice away from the company or any of the subsidiary companies:
    (1) during the continuance of his employment hereunder any person, firm or company who at any time during such period is or has been customer of or in the habit of dealing with such company;
    (2) for a period of two years after the termination of his employment hereunder howsoever occasioned any person, firm or company who at the date of such termination were customers of or in the habit of dealing with any such company.
14. For the purposes of s 1 of the Employment Protection (Consolidation) Act 1978 it is hereby agreed and declared that the terms and conditions of the director's employment include the provision that the hours of work shall be such hours as may be requisite for the proper discharge of his duties hereunder and subject thereto shall be at the director's discretion.
15. Any notice to be given under the terms of this Agreement shall be in writing and may either be given personally or sent by post addressed in the case of notice to the company to its registered office and in the case of notice to the director to his last known place of abode and any notice given by post shall be deemed to have been served on the expiration of 48 hours after the same was posted.

AS WITNESS this agreement has been signed by or on behalf of the parties hereto the day and year first before written.

SIGNED by
for and on behalf of Limited
in the presence of

....
....
....

SIGNED by the said [*the director*]
in the presence of

....

....

....

EDITOR'S NOTE

Clause 6 provides for full benefits from use of a company car. Clauses 10 and 11 cover insurance and pension schemes of types frequently found. These clauses must be adjusted to the specific situation. Benefits in kind (including a company car) are assessed to tax on the director and must be returned to the Inland Revenue on Form P.II.D.

10C Meetings of the Directors

Table A, reg 70 The management of the company and the exercise of all the powers of the company are vested in its Board of directors.

Matters of policy and importance which transcend any reasonable definition of personal executive responsibility must be decided by the Board at a meeting or at a duly constituted committee of the Board acting within the terms of its authority. The proceedings of directors are covered by regs 88–98 of Table A.

A meeting of the directors will be called by the secretary at the request of any director, but usually on the instructions of the chairman. It is usual to give formal written notice, but valid meetings can be arranged informally, by telephone for instance, so long as all directors agree. The period of notice to be given of a meeting is not laid down by the Companies Acts, but it must be reasonable and in accordance with the company's practice. Under Table A regulations it is not necessary to give notice to a director who is absent from the UK – a provision which is not appropriate to many companies. (Table A, reg 88)

The notice of meeting will normally have an agenda attached and be accompanied by reports, accounts and other documents which are to be discussed at the meeting.

See Precedent 10C.1 (p 260) NOTICE OF BOARD MEETING AND AGENDA

Alternatively, a resolution in writing signed by all directors entitled to receive notice of a meeting or a committee of the directors is as valid as if it had been passed at a meeting. It may consist of several documents in like form, each signed by one or more directors. (Table A, reg 93)

See Precedent 10C.2 (p 260) WRITTEN RESOLUTION IN LIEU OF A MEETING OF DIRECTORS

After the document(s) have been signed by all directors the secretary will date it and place it in the directors' minute book. The ability to use several documents in like form avoids delays in circulating a single document by post amongst the directors and subject to appropriate verifications, fax and other methods of instant communication, can be used to accelerate the process.

A director has a statutory duty to disclose any interests he may have in matters discussed at Board meetings (see Chapter 10D 'Conflicts of Interest').

Committees of the directors

Table A, reg 72 Frequently, the directors will appoint committees from amongst themselves, either with continuing responsibility for a specific activity or to handle a special situation. Such committee will be either general (eg 'any two members of the Board') or specific as to membership (eg 'Mr A and Mrs B'). A committee may comprise only one person. It is of course necessary to define with exactitude the authority of any committee and its powers to act, without reference back to the full Board.

See Precedent 10C.3 (p 261) MINUTES TO APPOINT A COMMITTEE OF THE DIRECTORS

Circumstances may also arise where it is desirable to authorise persons specifically to sign documents on behalf of the company and where the other party is desirous of confirmation that the signatories are properly authorised to do so by the company.

See Precedent 10C.4 (p 261) MINUTE APPOINTING AUTHORISED SIGNATORIES

ns 233 CA 1989, s 7 There are circumstances when individual members of the Board are required to sign documents to confirm that they have been positively approved by the directors, eg signatories to the annual accounts (see Chapter 7).

Minutes of meetings of the directors

s 382 Table A, reg 100 The directors are required to keep minutes of their meetings and committee meetings and this is the responsibility of the secretary. The style of the minutes will vary with the minute taker, but emphasis should be on recording decisions, not general discussion. The form of the minutes will tend to follow a set pattern, recording first the date and place of meeting and who was present and then following through the various agenda items discussed.

See Precedent 10C.5 (p 262) STANDARD FORM OF MINUTES OF A DIRECTORS' MEETING

Within this format, minutes will be written to cover the specific business of the meeting and the following precedents set out suitable minutes for circumstances that frequently occur.

See Precedent 10C.6 (p 263) STANDARD MINUTES COVERING SPECIFIC CIRCUMSTANCES

Other minutes will be found in the sections of the text dealing with their subject matter.

Sometimes circumstances arise in which there may be a lack of clarity as to whether the appointment or reappointment of directors has been strictly in accordance with the provisions of the Companies Act and the articles of association. The following precedent can then prove useful. The resolution should be proposed in general meeting of the company as an ordinary resolution of which due notice needs to be given. It is only suitable for the smaller company with a close-knit shareholder list.

See Precedent 10C.7 (p 266) RESOLUTION VALIDATING ACTS OF DIRECTORS

See Precedent 14A.17 (p 312) for form of special resolution by shareholders giving directions to the directors, pursuant to reg 70 of Table A.

Precedent 10C.1

Notice of Board Meeting and Agenda

Notice is hereby given that a meeting of the directors of the company will be held at [*address*] at [*time*] [*date*] at which your attendance is requested.

[*date*]

Secretary

AGENDA

1. Apologies for absence.
2. Minutes of meeting held on [*date*].
3. Matters arising therefrom.
4. Management accounts for the three months ended 30 June 19 .
5. Divisional reports.
6. Audit review.
7. Employment policy.
8. Share transfers.
9. Other business.

Precedent 10C.2

Written Resolution in Lieu of a Meeting of Directors

Pursuant to the articles of association of the company the undersigned, being all the directors of the company, hereby resolve:

....
....
....

Signed: Dated:

Precedent 10C.3

Minutes to Appoint a Committee of the Directors

(1) Any two directors be and are hereby appointed a committee of the Board with power to act in respect of .

(2) [*Name*] and [*name*] are hereby appointed a committee of the Board to review the salaries and terms of employment of the senior staff of the company [and make recommendations to the Board in this respect] with full power to give effect to their decision in this respect.

Precedent 10C.4

Minute Appointing Authorised Signatories

[*Name*] and [*name*] are hereby authorised [to execute] [to seal] the proposed contract between the company and Ltd.

Precedent 10C.5

Standard Form of Minutes of a Directors' Meeting

XYZ LTD

Minutes of a meeting of the directors held on [*date*] at [*address*]

PRESENT

A	(*Chairman*)
B	
C	
D	
F	(*Secretary*)
[*in attendance*]	
G	(*Auditors' item*)

*20. Apologies for absence

E

21. The minutes of the meeting held on [*date*] were confirmed and signed by the chairman.

22. Arising from these minutes it was reported:

[*details of report.*]

23. Management accounts and current trading accounts for the three months ended were reviewed and reports were made by the divisional directors in respect of their respective responsibilities.

Audit review

24. Mr G, representing the company's auditors, introduced his firm's detailed comments arising from their recent audit and answered questions thereon.

Employment policy

25. The secretary outlined the proposed alterations to the company's standard contracts of employment to take account of current legislation and pension scheme amendments.

Share transfers

26. The share transfers listed on the schedule appended were tabled and it was resolved that they be approved (if duly stamped) for registration [it being confirmed that they all fall within categories unrestricted in the articles].

EDITOR'S NOTE

*It is usual to number minutes consecutively. Often a calendar year basis is used, prefixing year minute with that year, eg 91/20.

Precedent 10C.6

Standard Minutes Covering Specific Circumstances

[*On certain occasions the Board will be asked by an outside party doing business with the company to pass a resolution in a specific standard form setting out the arrangement between them. In such circumstances it is usual to minute a summary and attach the formal resolution as an appendix.*]

A. Opening a bank account/amending bank mandate

It was resolved to open an account with   Bank plc on the terms of the minutes hereto appended and initialled by the chairman for purposes of identification.

It was resolved to amend the mandate [signatories] on the company's accounts with   Bank plc in accordance with the minutes hereto appended and initialled by the chairman for purposes of identification.

B. Specimen formal minutes to open bank account

These minutes will be supplied by the bank in stated form and a certified copy will be required to be attached to it.

[The following example is illustrative and is included by courtesy of the National Westminster Bank Plc.]

National Westminster Bank Plc

NWB1010 (*Revised February 1982*) Company Mandate

Instructions for completion

1 At a meeting of the Board of Directors, Resolutions in the form set out in the attached document should be passed by the Board, entered in the Minute Book of the Company and signed by the Chairman. The attached document should then be compared with the Minute Book, certified a true copy by the Chairman and Secretary, detached from these instructions and forwarded to the Bank.

2 At the same time the Company should forward to the Bank:

(a) An up-to-date copy of the Company's Memorandum and Articles of Association;
(b) The Company's Certificate of Incorporation.

3 The persons authorised to sign on behalf of the Company should preferably be referred to in the Resolution as 'any one Director **for the time being**', or (as the case may be) as 'any two Directors **for the time being**'; or in the case of the Secretary as 'the Secretary **for the time being**'. That is, Directors or the Secretary should not be named personally in the Resolutions.

4 If the Company does not wish to give instructions to the Bank, in regard to any of the Special Transactions referred to in the Schedule, it or they should be deleted.

NWB1010 (*Revised February 1982*) **Company Mandate**

Name of Company ______________________________

Registered Office ______________________________

Address for Statements ______________________________

____

At a meeting of the Directors of the above Company held on the ____________

day of ______________ 19 ___

it was resolved:

1 That **National Westminster Bank Plc** (the Bank) as bankers to the Company be and are hereby authorised to honour all cheques or other orders for payment drawn on behalf of the Company including bills and promissory notes accepted or made on behalf of the Company and payable at the Bank notwithstanding that any such payment may cause any account or accounts of the Company to be overdrawn or increase any existing overdraft provided such documents are signed by*

2 That as regards the special transactions referred to in the Schedule to these Resolutions the Bank be and are hereby authorised to accept on behalf of the Company only the signatures of the respective officials therein mentioned.

3 That the Company give the Bank a list of the names of the Directors, Secretary and other officers of the Company and advise the Bank in writing of any changes that may take place and the Bank shall be entitled to act upon the information so given.†

4 That these Resolutions be communicated to the Bank and shall constitute the Company's Mandate to the Bank to remain in force until revoked by notice in writing to the Bank signed by the Chairman or any Director or the Secretary acting or purporting to act on behalf of the Company and for this purpose any instruction varying or purporting to vary the Mandate contained in these Resolutions shall be deemed a revocation.

*Complete by description of the authorised official(s) eg 'any two Directors for the time being.'

†Any change of signatory should be notified on form NWB1012, Change of Signatures, which may be obtained from your branch.

- -

C. Approving a contract

Resolved that the terms of the proposed contract between this company and   Ltd for the purchase of the business trading as   be all hereby approved and [*name*] and [*name*] [*any two directors*] be authorised to approve such detailed alterations to the draft documentation as they may think fit and sign the contract on behalf of the company.

D. Appointment of authorised representatives to act for the company when the company is a corporate director

The company being a director of   Limited, it was resolved that [*name*] be and is hereby appointed its authorised representative to act on its behalf in all matters in relation to such directorship subject to any instructions that this board may give him.

To the secretary of the company

Dear Sir

This is to confirm that by resolution of the directors of this company on [*date*] [*name*] was appointed authorised representative to act on behalf of this company in any matters pertaining to its position as a director of your company.

Yours faithfully

Director

Precedent 10C.7

Resolution Validating Acts of Directors

That all appointments and reappointments of directors of the company made and all acts of the directors done prior to the date of this resolution be and are hereby confirmed and ratified, notwithstanding any defects in any such appointments or reappointments that might otherwise cause their validity to be in doubt.

EDITOR'S NOTE

This resolution should be proposed at a general meeting of the company as an ordinary resolution.

10D Conflicts of Interest and Related Matters

Directors' general duties

Directors owe fiduciary duties and duties of care and skill. The directors' position of control over the company's assets makes them subject to legal requirements rather like those of trustees, the most important of which is that they should always act in what they honestly believe to be the best interests of the company. This is an overriding duty and failure to observe it can result in the directors incurring serious personal liabilities. This will be particularly important in any circumstance where the directors, collectively or individually, stand to gain personally from a proposed course of action, or are connected with someone who may do so. In some such circumstances there are specific statutory rules or provisions under the company's memorandum and articles which must be observed. Quite apart from these, it is important that any potential conflict of interest should be made known to the Board, that any profit made by individual directors should be authorised by specific provisions of the articles or approved by the members, and that these facts should be clearly recorded in the minutes of the appropriate meetings. Legal advice should be sought if there is ever any doubt about such matters.

Apart from their fiduciary duties, directors are required to exercise reasonable care and skill in the conduct of the company's business.

Statutory requirements

s 317 A director who is in any way, directly or indirectly, interested in a transaction with the
Table A, reg 85 company, must disclose the nature and extent of that interest to the Board. Because of the
general fiduciary duty the disclosure should be made at the earliest opportunity, but under
s 317(2) the Act disclosure should take place no later than the first Board meeting at which the
s 317(4) matter is discussed, or the first Board meeting after the director acquired the interest.
Disclosure to a committee of the directors will not usually suffice. The Act specifically provides that the notice is not effective unless it is given at a Board meeting, or the director takes reasonable steps to secure that it is brought up and read at the next meeting.

See Precedent 10D.1 (p 271) DECLARATION OF INTEREST BY A DIRECTOR PURSUANT TO SECTION 317 AND TABLE A, REG 85

The disclosure should be minuted as part of the record of the proceedings of the meeting. The fact that the disclosure was made could prove to be important if the transaction, or the directors' interest in it, should subsequently be challenged, so the secretary should ensure that the disclosure is made and minuted, even if it appears that all the directors in fact know the circumstances. A director must not enter into a transaction with the company until any disclosure of interest has been made and minuted.

See Precedent 10D.2 (p 271) MINUTE OF DIRECTORS RECORDING DECLARATION OF SPECIFIC INTEREST

A director may make a general disclosure, eg that he has an interest in another company
s 317(3) or firm, or is connected with a certain person, and should be regarded as being interested
in all future transactions with that company or person.

See Precedent 10D.3 (p 272) NOTICE OF GENERAL DISCLOSURE UNDER SECTION 317(3)

See Precedent 10D.4 (p 272) MINUTE OF NOTICE OF GENERAL DISCLOSURE

Substantial property transactions

The above requirement to disclose an interest applies to all transactions in which a s 320 director has a personal interest. Where the company wishes to dispose of, or acquire, a non-cash asset (the value of which must be more than £100,000 or 10 per cent of the company's asset value, subject in the latter case to a minimum of £2,000) then the arrangement must first be approved by the members, if a director, or any person connected with a director, is a party to the acquisition or disposal. The amount of a company's asset value is the value of its net assets as determined by reference to its last annual accounts or its called-up share capital if no such accounts have been prepared.

s 346 The definition in the Act of 'connected persons' for these purposes is lengthy and complex and should be consulted specifically in case of doubt, but the main circumstances where a person is regarded as connected are:

(1) spouse, child or step child;
(2) family trustees;
(3) partner of a director or other connected person;
(4) (director's) associated company.

An associated company for these purposes is one in which the director (either alone or with other connected persons) is interested in one-fifth or more of its equity share capital or of the votes in general meeting.

Where a director of the company's holding company (or a 'connected person' of such a director) is the other party to the acquisition or disposal, the transaction must be s 736 approved by the members of the holding company. If the company making the acquisition or disposal is a wholly owned subsidiary there is no need for the transaction to be approved by the members of the subsidiary company as well. If it is not a wholly owned subsidiary, then approval must be given by the members of both the subsidiary and the holding company.

The approval may be given by an ordinary resolution of the general meeting or by written resolution.

See Precedent 10D.5 (p 272) ORDINARY RESOLUTION TO APPROVE A PROPERTY TRANSACTION IN WHICH A DIRECTOR HAS AN INTEREST

s 322 Failure to comply with these provisions can make the transaction voidable at the instance of the company and may impose personal liability on the director interested in the acquisition or disposal to account for any profit made on the transaction, and can render that director and any director who authorised the transaction liable to indemnify the company for any loss or damage it has suffered on the deal.

It should be noted that transactions not falling within the scope of these provisions may require approval by the members for other reasons, eg under the general fiduciary duties owed by directors at common law where the director has a conflict of interest or stands to make personal profit on the transaction.

Provisions in the company's articles

The requirements of the Companies Act given above are mandatory and cannot be excluded by the company's articles. Subject to these, an individual company may have provisions in its articles of association which impose additional requirements. Very many companies adopt Table A articles, either wholly or in part, and so the following provisions of Table A will be applicable to many companies. It should be noted, however, that it is commonplace for companies adopting Table A generally to exclude or modify the provisions on directors' interests, and so the articles of the individual company should be consulted to ascertain the provisions applicable.

Table A, reg 94 — Regulation 94 of Table A requires that a director shall not vote at a meeting of directors or committee of directors on any resolution concerning a matter in which he has, directly or indirectly, an interest or duty which is material and which conflicts or may conflict with the interests of the company.

Table A, reg 95 — By reg 95, a director shall not be counted in the quorum present at a meeting in relation to a resolution on which he is not entitled to vote.

For these purposes a director is treated as having the same interest as that of any person connected with him. 'Connected person' has the same meaning as in the Act (see above).

Certain situations are excluded from the restrictions on voting and counting in the quorum, for which reference should be made to reg 94.

If these provisions apply, the minutes of the meeting should record the fact that the director abstained from voting on the matter and that a quorum was still present despite the disqualification of the interested director from it.

See Precedent 10D.6 (p 273) MINUTE THAT AN INTERESTED DIRECTOR DID NOT VOTE OR COUNT IN THE QUORUM ON A PARTICULAR TRANSACTION

If so many directors are interested in a transaction that a quorum cannot be obtained the Board will be unable to proceed on the transaction and the matter should be referred to a general meeting, where the restrictions do not apply, or the company may pass an ordinary resolution under reg 96 to relax these provisions. This may be a useful provision in a tightly held company with a small Board, or to enable a particular class of transactions to be free of the restrictions, while retaining the restrictions in respect of other matters.

Table A, reg 96

See Precedent 10D.7 (p 273) ORDINARY RESOLUTION TO ENABLE INTERESTED DIRECTOR TO VOTE ON CONTRACTS

Loans to directors

s 330 — There are strict prohibitions in the Act on loans and related dealings between the company and its directors or those of its holding company, which may give rise to civil or criminal penalties.

s 334, CA 1989, s 138 — There are complex exceptions, including an overall exemption where the aggregate indebtedness of a director does not exceed £5,000. (See generally, *Jordans Secretarial Administration*, at § 4.24.) Any such transaction must be within the exceptions and carefully minuted.

See Precedent 10D.8 (p 274) MINUTE APPROVING LOAN TO A DIRECTOR

Sometimes directors have a current account with the company and sometimes such an account may be overdrawn. It is important that any such accounts be minuted.

See Precedent 10D.9 (p 274) MINUTE APPROVING DIRECTOR'S CURRENT ACCOUNT

Sometimes it may be appropriate to capitalise a director's current or loan account which the company is unable to repay and which has become part of its working capital. Care, however, must be taken that any pre-emptive articles are duly varied before such transaction takes place.

See Precedent 10D.10 (p 274) RESOLUTION TO CAPITALISE DIRECTOR'S LOAN ACCOUNT

Register of Directors' Interests

Every company is required to maintain a register of the interests of its directors in shares and debentures of the company or of other companies in the same group (except wholly owned subsidiaries). The definition of 'interest' is widely drawn and reference should be
s 324 made to *Jordans Secretarial Administration*, at §4.28 for an analysis thereof.

A director is required to notify the company in writing within five days of acquiring or disposing of any interest (as defined in the Act) he has in the company's shares or debentures or any interest he has when appointed to the Board.

When the company receives such information it must, within three days, enter it on the Register of Directors' Interests. This is a statutory register and must be available for inspection.

It is convenient to use a standard layout for the provision of information by the directors and to give them a suitable form for this purpose.

See Precedent 10D.11 (p 275) FORM J324/328 NOTIFICATION BY A DIRECTOR OF HIS INTERESTS IN SHARES OR DEBENTURES OR ANY CHANGE THEREIN

A separate register page will be kept for each director even if it remains blank, thus making a positive statement that no interest has been notified.

See Precedent 10D.12 (p 277) REGISTER OF DIRECTORS' INTERESTS

Precedent 10D.1

Declaration of Interest by a Director Pursuant to Section 317 and Table A, Reg 85

To the Directors

I give notice that I am interested in the contract that the company proposes to consider entering into with   Ltd [as I am a director and controlling shareholder of   Ltd].

Date ....   Signature ....

Precedent 10D.2

Minute of Directors Recording Declaration of Specific Interest

At the commencement of the meeting [*name*] tabled notice that as a director and controlling shareholder in   Ltd he was interested in the proposed contract between that company and the company.

EDITOR'S NOTE

CA 1985, Sch 6, para 9 CA 1989, s 6, Sch 4

Payment for a director's services made to a third party must be disclosed in the accounts.

Precedent 10D.3

Notice of General Disclosure under Section 317(3)

To the Directors

Pursuant to s 317(3) of the Companies Act 1985, I give notice that I am to be regarded as interested in any contract which may from this date be made with any of the undermentioned companies and firms.

Name of company or firm	Nature of interest
	[Director] [Partner] [Controlling shareholder]

Precedent 10D.4

Minute of Notice of General Disclosure

There was placed before the meeting and duly noted a statement dated [*date*] by [*name*] pursuant to s 317(3) of the Companies Act 1985 declaring interests of his which might conflict with those of the company, a copy of which is appended to this minute.

Precedent 10D.5

Ordinary Resolution to Approve a Property Transaction in which a Director has an Interest

That the purchase by the company of the freehold premises known as from the trustees of the will of in which proposed purchases [*name*], a director of the company, has an interest as a beneficiary under the said will, be approved.

Precedent 10D.6

Minute that an Interested Director did not Vote or Count in the Quorum on a Particular Transaction

(At the relevant agenda item)

(1) [*Name*] left the meeting while this matter, in which he had declared an interest, was discussed and resolved upon. The remaining directors constituted sufficient quorum under the articles of association.

[*or*]

(2) [*Name*], who had declared an interest in this matter, abstained from voting on the resolution. The remaining directors constituted sufficient quorum under the articles of association.

Precedent 10D.7

Ordinary Resolution to Enable Interested Director to Vote on Contracts

RESOLVED that pursuant to reg 96 of Table A (which is incorporated in the articles of association of the company) [*name*], who is a director of this company, may vote on contracts between this company and Ltd, notwithstanding that he has declared his interest as a director of Ltd.

Precedent 10D.8

Minute Approving Loan to a Director

That the sum of £5,000 be loaned by the company to [*name*] no other loans to him being outstanding and the transaction falling within s 334 of the Companies Act 1985, as amended by s 138 of the Companies Act 1989.

Precedent 10D.9

Minute Approving Director's Current Account

That a current account with the company be opened for [*name*] and that the account may from time to time be overdrawn to the maximum sum of [£5,000] provided that at any such time the total indebtedness of [*name*] to the company shall not exceed [£5,000].

Precedent 10D.10

Resolution to Capitalise Director's Loan Account

That the amount of £ being the [*whole*] [*part*] of the company's indebtedness to [*name*] a director of the company, shall with his consent and in accordance with the application lodged with the company be applied to paying up in full ordinary shares in the capital of the company which shall be allotted to him on [*date*] [at a price of per share] ranking pari passu with the existing ordinary shares in the capital of the company and interest on the aforesaid loan shall be paid up to the date of allotment stated above.

Precedent 10D.11
Notification by Director of his Interests in Shares or Debentures, or any Change Therein (Pursuant to s 324 (1) and (2), and s 328 of the Act)

J324/328

To ______________________________ Limited

Date of appointment or event	Name of company (1)	Description of interest (2)	Name of registered holder	Nature of event	Price or consideration	Additional statements (3)
24/7/90	XYZ Ltd	Beneficial owners	James Bond	Purchase of 50	£50	
				ordinary shares		
24/7/90	XYZ Ltd	Shares beneficially	Jane Bond	Purchase of 50	£50	
		owned by wife		ordinary shares		

Dated ______________ *Signed* ______________ *Name of Director* James Bond

(1) *Insert name of company whose shares or debentures are involved.*
(2) *Insert number or amount, and class, of shares or debentures involved.*
(3) *Section 325 (5) of the Act provides that the nature and extent of a director's interest must be recorded in the register if he so requires. This and other additional information should be written in this column.*

NOTES

These notes are offered as a guide to those completing this form but are not intended as an authoritative interpretation of the relevant provisions of the Act.

Directors and company secretaries are referred to the Companies Act 1985, ss 324 to 328. Companies with a Stock Exchange listing are also referred to ss 329 and 732 in respect of duty to notify the Stock Exchange.

1. Every person, who, or whose spouse or child under 18 years old (not being a director), has an interest in shares or debentures in a company or its associated companies and who becomes a director must give written notice to the company of the subsistence of that interest within five 'working' days (ie excluding Saturdays, Sundays and Bank Holidays).
   A director must notify the company in writing, within five 'working' days, of the occurrence of certain events affecting his interest in its shares or those of its associated companies, or the interest of his spouse or child under 18 years old (not being a director).
   These events include:—
   (a) events in consequence of which such an interest arises or ceases;
   (b) entering into a contract to sell any such shares or debentures;
   (c) assignment of any right to subscribe for shares or debentures of the company;
   (d) the grant of a right to subscribe for shares or debentures of an associated company, the exercise or the assignment of such right.

3. See Sch 13, Part III for circumstances in which a notification obligation is not discharged. In particular notification requires:—
   (i) where a contract to purchase or sell shares or debentures, or the assignment of a right to subscribe is notified the consideration must be stated, or if no consideration, that fact;
   (ii) Where the grant of a right to subscribe for shares or debentures in an associated company is notified, there must be stated (a) the date of grant (b) when it is exercisable (c) the consideration for the grant and (d) the subscription price. Where the exercise of such a right is notified the number of shares or debentures and the name(s) in which they are registered must be given.

4. An associated company to which these notes refer is defined as the subsidiary or holding company, or another subsidiary of the holding company of the company to which notice is to be given, but notice need not be given in respect of holdings in wholly owned subsidiaries.

5. The relevant interests of a director and his spouse or children are defined in Sch 13, Pt I. They include interests which subsist through the medium of certain kinds of trust or through another company controlled by the director. They also include contracts to purchase or call for delivery of an interest, and to exercise voting rights (otherwise than as a mere proxy), and joint interests.

6. A 'director' is defined as including a person in accordance with whose instructions the Board is accustomed to act.

7. 'Child' (under 18 years old) includes step-child and adopted child.

8 In general, the period of five 'working' days for fulfilment of an obligation to notify commences with the time the existence of an interest or the occurrence of an event comes to the knowledge of the director. See Sch 13, Part II for definition of periods, within which obligations imposed by s 324 must be fulfilled.

Precedent 10D.12
Register of Directors' Interests

Name & Address of Person interested	Classes of Share Capital of Debenture
JAMES BOND	(a) ORDINARY SHARES
	(b)

Entry		Date of			No of Shares involved				
No	Date	Event	Notification	Nature of Event	Acquisitions	Disposals	No of Shares in which interested after event	Price or consideration	Remarks
1	25/7/90	24/7/90	25/7/90	PURCHASE OF SHARES BY DIRECTOR	50		50	£50	
2	25/7/90	24/7/90	25/7/90	PURCHASE OF SHARES BY SPOUSE	50		50	£50	

Chapter 11

THE SECRETARY

Introduction

s 283 The Companies Act 1985 requires every company to have a secretary. Table A provides
Table A, reg 99 that the secretary be appointed by the directors for such term, at such remuneration and upon such conditions as they think fit and a secretary so appointed may be removed by them.

s 288 The company must keep at its registered office a register of its secretaries.

See Precedent 11.1 (p 279) REGISTER OF SECRETARIES

The secretary may be an individual, a company or a partnership; in this latter case unless it is a Scottish partnership, which is a corporate entity, the individual members of the partnership will be appointed to act jointly.

The secretary can be a director of the company, but if the company has only one director he cannot also be secretary.

s 286 There is no requirement in the Companies Acts in respect of the qualifications of the secretary of a private company. There are specific rules for public companies.

The appointment of the secretary on incorporation of a company is dealt with in Chapter 1.

See Precedent 11.2 (p 279) DIRECTORS' MINUTE APPOINTING SECRETARY

A change of secretary must be notified to the Registrar of Companies on Form 288 within 14 days.

See Precedent 11.3 (p 280) FORM 288 CHANGE OF DIRECTOR OR SECRETARY OR CHANGE OF PARTICULARS

Note, when completing the details on Form 288 it is not necessary to list the professional qualification or directorships held by the secretary, nor is it necessary to state the nationality of the secretary on which there is no restriction. The appointee must signify acceptance by signing the form.

See Precedent 11.4 (p 282) DIRECTORS' MINUTE REMOVING SECRETARY

The manner in which the secretary will sign documents is set out in Precedent 11.5.

See Precedent 11.5 (p 282) SIGNATURE OF DOCUMENTS

Precedent 11.1

Register of Secretaries

Surname (or Corporate Name): STICKATIT

Forename(s): GEORGE JOHN

Any former Forenames or Surnames: NONE

Residential Address (or Registered or Principal Office): 13 BULLOCK HILL DRIVE

DILSBOROUGH

RUFFORDSHIRE

RU15 8SE

DATES OF:—

Appointment	1 APRIL 1990	Resignation or Cessation	
Minute	1 APRIL 1990	Minute	
Filing Particulars	3 APRIL 1990	Filing Particulars	

Precedent 11.2

Directors' Minute Appointing Secretary

Mr G J Stickatit is hereby appointed secretary of the company [in place of Mr T Snape who has resigned].

EDITOR'S NOTE

It is not usual to include in such minute remuneration or other conditions of appointment, nor is it usual to appoint a secretary for a fixed term.

Precedent 11.3

Printed and supplied by
Jordans
Jordan & Sons Limited
21 St. Thomas Street, Bristol BS1 6JS
Tel: 0272 230600 Telex 449119

288

Change of director or secretary or change of particulars.

This form should be completed in black.

Company number	CN 3 257 934
Company name	BILLBROOK ENTERPRISES LTD

Appointment

(Turn over page for resignation and change of particulars).

Date of appointment	DA Day 01 Month 04 Year 90
Appointment of director	CD
Appointment of secretary	CS ✓

Please mark the appropriate box. If appointment is as a director and secretary mark both boxes.

Name *Style/title	MR
Forenames	GEORGE JOHN
Surname	STICKATIT
*Honours etc	NONE
Previous forenames	NONE
Previous surname	NONE
Usual residential address	AD 13 BULLOCK HILL LANE
Post town	DILSBOROUGH
County/region	RUFFORDSHIRE
Postcode	RU15 8SE Country
Date of birth†	DO Nationality† NA
Business occupation†	OC
Other directorships†	

NOTES

Show the full forenames. **NOT INITIALS** If the director or secretary is a Corporation or Scottish firm, show the name on surname line and registered or principal office on the usual residential address line.

Give previous forenames or surname except:
- for a married woman the name before marriage need not be given.
- for names not used since the age of 18 or for at least 20 years.

A peer or individual known by a title may state the title instead of or in addition to the forenames and surname.

Other directorships.

Give the name of every company of which the person concerned is a director or has been a director at any time in the past 5 years. Exclude a company which either is, or at all times during the past 5 years when the person was a director, was
- dormant
- a parent company which wholly owned the company making the return
- a wholly owned subsidiary of the company making the return
- another wholly owned subsidiary of the same parent company.

I consent to act as ~~director~~/secretary of the above named company

Consent signature Signed G. J. Stickatit Date 3 APRIL 1990

*Voluntary details †Directors only

A serving director etc must also sign the form overleaf.

Resignation

(This includes any form of ceasing to hold office e.g. death or removal from office).

Date of resignation etc	DR 01 04 90
Resignation etc, as director	XD
Resignation etc, as secretary	XS ✓
Forenames	THOMAS
Surname	SNAPE
Date of birth *(directors only)*	DO
If cessation is other than resignation, please state reason *(eg death)*	

Please mark the appropriate box. If resignation etc is as a director and secretary mark both boxes.

Change of particulars

Complete this section in all cases where particulars have changed and then the appropriate section below.

Date of change of particulars	DC
Change of particulars, as director	ZD
Change of particulars, as secretary	ZS
Forenames *(name previously notified to Companies House)*	
Surname *(name previously notified to Companies House)*	
Date of birth *(directors only)*	DO

Please mark the appropriate box. If change of particulars is as a director and secretary mark both boxes.

Change of name *(enter new name)* Forenames	NN
Surname	
Change of usual residential address *(enter new address)*	AD
Post town	
County/region	
Postcode	Country
Other change *(please specify)*	

A serving director,secretary etc must sign the form below.

Signature

Signed J. F. Runciman Date 3 APRIL 1990

(by a serving director/~~secretary/administrator/ administrative receiver/receiver~~). *(Delete as appropriate)*

After signing please return the form to the Registrar of Companies at

Companies House, Crown Way, Cardiff CF4 3UZ
for companies registered in England and Wales

or **Companies House, 100-102 George Street, Edinburgh EH2 3DJ**
for companies registered in Scotland.

To whom should Companies House direct any enquiries about the information on this form?

JORDAN & SONS LIMITED
21 ST THOMAS STREET
BRISTOL Tel: 0272 230600

Precedent 11.4

Directors' Minute Removing Secretary

Mr T Snape shall cease to be secretary of the company as from this date [and Mr G J Stickatit be and is hereby appointed secretary in his place].

Precedent 11.5

Signature of Documents

[*Documents such as notices to shareholders are to be signed by the secretary as follows:*]

By order of the Board

G J Stickatit

Secretary

[*If the secretary is a company the form is usually as follows:*]

G J Stickatit

For Gazebee Ltd
Secretary

[*If the secretary is a partnership it will sign in its partnership name.*]

[*On other documents or cheques the secretary will sign in a representative capacity as follows:*]

For Billbrook Enterprises Ltd
G J Stickatit
Secretary

Chapter 12

EXECUTION OF DOCUMENTS AND THE COMPANY SEAL

Introduction

A company no longer requires a common seal. When executing documents the company has the choice of whether to use its seal or not. Provided that the document is executed in accordance with the Companies Act 1989, s 130, the effect will be the same. Section 130 (inserting new s 36A in the 1985 Act) sets out the procedure for executing documents without a seal. Section 36A(4) states:

> 'A document signed by a director and the secretary or by two directors of a company and expressed (in whatever form of words) to be executed by the company has the same effect as if executed under the common seal of the company.'

This chapter deals with:
(1) the company seal;
(2) execution of documents without using a seal;
(3) procedures common to both methods of executing documents and deeds; and
(4) dispensation with the seal.

(1) The Company Seal

The seal must carry the exact registered name of the company. Sometimes a logo or other appropriate symbol is incorporated in the design. The seal must be adopted as the common seal of the company by a Board resolution.

See Precedent 12.1 (p 285) RESOLUTION OF COMPANY TO ADOPT A SEAL

Any change in the design of the seal or change in the name of the company leading to a new seal will require a similar resolution.

Use of the seal is attested in accordance with the provisions of the articles.

Table A, reg 101, provides that attestation be by any two directors or one director and the secretary or otherwise as the directors may determine.

See Precedent 12.2 (p 285) STANDARD FORM OF ATTESTATION OF A SEALING

(2) Execution of Documents Without Using Seal

ns 36 CA 1989, s 130

As stated above, documents expressed to be executed by the company and signed by a director and the secretary or any two directors have the same effect as if executed under seal.

If the document makes clear on its face that it is intended by those making it to be a deed, it shall be regarded as such.

See Precedent 12.3 (p 285) EXECUTION OF A DOCUMENT WITHOUT USING A SEAL AND AS A DEED

A document executed in this manner as a deed is treated as delivered (ie effective) upon being executed, but this assumption can be rebutted if it can be shown that such was not the intention. All documents under seal are regarded as delivered by the action of sealing unless stated to be *in escrow* (ie conditional) until a stated date or event.

(3) Procedures Common to Both Methods of Executing Documents or Deeds

The authorisation of the execution or sealing of a document will be by resolution of the Board.

In a small company the resolution will be specific and this is also usually the case with larger companies on important transactions. In other cases, the directors of a larger company will appoint a committee to seal or execute documents in the normal course of business and record such acts in a register which will be inspected at each Board meeting.

See Precedent 12.4 (p 286) BOARD MINUTE AUTHORISING SEALING/EXECUTION OF A DOCUMENT

See Precedent 12.5 (p 286) BOARD MINUTE APPOINTING COMMITTEE TO SEAL/EXECUTE DOCUMENTS

See Precedent 12.6 (p 287) REGISTER OF SEALINGS/EXECUTIONS

See Precedent 12.7 (p 288) MINUTE OF BOARD FOLLOWING INSPECTION OF REGISTER

(4) Dispensation with the Seal

A company in existence prior to July 1990 (the commencement date of CA 1989, s 130) will, by the requirements of the Companies Act and its own articles, have a common seal. It will probably retain that seal, and, if appropriate, execute documents under the alternative provisions of s 130.

There is no statutory requirement for a company incorporated after July 1990 to have a seal.

In both cases it will be necessary to disapply the relevant provisions of Table A if the company wishes to dispense entirely with the use of a seal.

Table A, reg 6, requires share certificates to be sealed and reflects CA 1985, s 186 (which has not been specifically amended by CA 1989) which states that share certificates under the common seal of the company are prima facie evidence of title. Provisions of CA 1989, s 130, seem to make clear that the use of a seal for this one purpose is not intended.

Table A, reg 101, covers the use of the company seal.

See Precedent 12.8 (p 288) DISAPPLICATION OF TABLE A, REGS 6 AND 101 RELATING TO USE OF COMPANY SEAL

See Precedent 12.9 (p 288) EXAMPLE OF A COMPANY SEAL

The seal must contain the exact name of the company as registered. If wished, a logo or other design may be added.

Precedent 12.1

Resolution of Company to Adopt a Seal

Resolved that the seal of which there is an impression below is hereby adopted as the common seal of the company to the exclusion of any other seal.

Precedent 12.2

Standard Form of Attestation of a Sealing

The seal of Ltd
was affixed hereto in the
presence of:

.... Director(s)
.... Secretary

Precedent 12.3

Execution of a Document Without Using a Seal and as a Deed

Executed by the company [as a deed]
on [*date*].

for XYZ Ltd

.... Director
.... Secretary

Precedent 12.4

Board Minute Authorising Sealing/Execution of a Document

. . . . and it was resolved that [the seal be impressed thereon] [this document be executed by the company]*.

EDITOR'S NOTE

*Delete as appropriate.

Precedent 12.5

Board Minute Appointing Committee to Seal/Execute Documents

Resolved that any two directors be and are hereby constituted a committee of the Board to approve the sealing or the execution of documents by the company arising in the normal course of business and entered in the register of such documents.

Precedent 12.6
Register of Sealings/Executions

Consecutive No	Date of Sealing Document	Date of Authority	Description of Documents Sealed or Executed	Persons attesting
1	21/3/91	20/3/91	CONVEYANCE OF FREEHOLD	AB/CD
			25 THE PLAIN	
			LIPTOWN	

Precedent 12.7

Minute of Board Following Inspection of Register

The Register of Sealings/Documents sealed or executed by the company was tabled and entry nos   to   were noted.

Precedent 12.8

Disapplication of Table A, Regs 6 and 101 Relating to Use of Company Seal

*[That the articles of association be amended by the addition of the following article numbered   .]

Regulation 101 in Table A shall not apply to the company. Regulation 6 in Table A (share certificates) shall be read and construed as if the words 'shall be sealed with the seal and' were deleted from the second sentence.

EDITOR'S NOTE

*For companies in existence at the commencement date of the Companies Act 1989, s 130, which have need to change their articles. Companies incorporated after that date should incorporate the specimen clause in their articles.

Precedent 12.9

Example of a Company Seal

Chapter 13

STATUTORY AND OTHER REGISTERS

Introduction

The Companies Acts require companies to maintain and make available to the public registers known as 'Statutory Registers'. These are:

(1) Register of Members;
(2) Register of Directors and Secretaries (often kept as separate Registers);
(3) Register of Directors' Interests; and
(4) Register of Charges.

(A company may also keep other Registers (including a Register of Debenture Holders) and these are covered below. A public company may also have to keep a Register of Substantial Interests, but this is outside the scope of this book.)

(1) Register of Members

Every company must keep a Register of its members showing their names and addresses
and the date of becoming and of ceasing to be a member. If the company has a share
capital the Register of Members must also contain a statement of the shares held by
s 352 each member, showing the share numbers (if any), classes of shares and amounts paid on
them. If the company has bearer shares the fact of the issue of a warrant must appear on
the Register, with details of the number and class of shares it covers, but with no
s 353 personal details of the holder. If the company has more than 50 members the Register
must have an index or be in the form of an index.

The Register of Members is prima facie evidence of the matters directed or authorised by
s 361 the Act to be inserted in it. As it is a public record of who owns the shares and the extent
to which they are paid up, entries on the Register, or deletions or alterations, may be
s 359 made only in accordance with proper procedures (eg on an allotment or transfer or
redemption of shares, or when payment is made for the issue of shares). It should be
noted that any other entry (eg because an error has been discovered) should be made only
with the consent of the court granted on an application for rectification of the Register.

Although comments relevant to the administration of the Register (eg 'subscriber's share')
may be made in the Register against individual entries, generally only the statutory
s 360 information should be shown and, in particular, no notice of any trust or beneficial
interest should appear. Acceptance of a simple designation reference is not regarded as
notice of a trust.

For further details of the Register of Members and entries on allotment and transfer of shares, see Chapter 5.

(2) Register of Directors and Secretaries

Every company must keep a Register of Directors and Register of Secretaries.

The Register of Directors must show for each director:

(a) full name;
(b) any former name (other than where a woman has changed her name on marriage);
(c) usual residential address;
(d) nationality;
(e) occupation;
(f) other directorships;
(g) date of birth which now extends to all companies, not only those subject to s 293 (age limit).

s 289 Only directorships in other companies incorporated in Great Britain need be recorded, including any directorships held within the previous five years. Dormant companies, or those wholly owned within the same group, need not be listed.

SI 1990/1706 If the director is a corporation, only its corporate name and registered or principal office need be shown.

s 290 See Chapter 10 for precedents.

The Register of Secretaries shows less information than that for directors, ie:

(a) name;
(b) former name;
(c) usual residential address.

If the secretary is a corporation or Scottish firm, its corporate or firm name and the address of its registered or principal office should be shown. Where all the partners of a firm are joint secretaries, the name and principal office of the firm may be stated instead of the particulars listed above.

See Chapter 11 for precedents.

(3) Register of Directors' Interests

s 352 This is a Register of directors' interests in the company's own shares or debentures, or those of its subsidiary or holding companies, as disclosed by each director under s 324, and should not be confused with the requirement to disclose interests in other companies where there may be a conflict of interest for directors.

See Chapter 10 for further details and precedents.

(4) Register of Charges

ns 411 CA 1989, s 101 Every company must keep a Register of all charges affecting the company's property, showing for each charge a short description of the property charged, the amount charged and (unless to bearer) the name of the chargee.

The company is also bound to keep a copy of every instrument creating or evidencing a charge affecting its property.

See Chapter 8 for details and precedents.

Inspection of Registers

The intention is that the Statutory Registers should be available as a source of essential information to any member of the public who cares to inspect them. While much of the information they contain is also available by undertaking a search at Companies House, some of the information, notably the details of current shareholders and of directors' interests is available only from these Registers.

ss 353, 356 The Registers are kept at the company's registered office except that the Register of Members may be kept at some other office (either of the company or some other person or company if they have undertaken the task of making up the Register) provided this is within the same country as the registered office and a notice is filed with the Registrar of Companies stating where the Register is kept.

See Precedent 13.1 (p 292) FORM G 353 NOTICE OF PLACE WHERE REGISTER OF MEMBERS IS KEPT OR OF ANY CHANGE IN THAT PLACE

If the Register is kept in non-legible form (eg on a computer) Form G 353a should be lodged. The equivalent forms for the Register of Debenture Holders are Forms G 190 and G 190a.

Sch 13 The Register of Directors' Interests should be kept with the Register of Members. If this is somewhere other than the company's registered office the address should be notified to the Registrar of Companies on Form G 325.

The Register of Directors and Secretaries and the Register of Charges (and copies of charges) must be kept at the registered office.

The Registers must be open to inspection by members and non-members during business hours, on which the company in general meeting may impose reasonable restrictions
s 356 provided that the Registers are available for no less than two hours each (working) day. Members may inspect without charge. Non-members may be required to pay a prescribed fee. Any person may require a copy of entries on the Register, which the company must supply within 10 days, and for which a prescribed fee may be levied.

Other Registers

Although not required by the Companies Acts, it is usual for companies to keep the following additional Registers:

(1) Register of Applications and Allotments (see Chapter 5);
(2) Register of Transfers (see Chapter 5);
(3) Register of Sealings (see Chapter 12).

s 190 If the company has issued debentures it must keep a Register of Debenture Holders, in which case rules equivalent to those applicable to the Register of Members apply.

Precedent 13.1

Notice of place where register of members is kept or of any change in that place

Note: This notice is not required where the register is and has, since 1 July 1948, always been kept at the Registered Office

353

Please do not write in this margin

Pursuant to section 353 of the Companies Act 1985

Please complete legibly, preferably in black type, or bold block lettering

To the Registrar of Companies

For official use

Company number

Name of company

* insert full name of company

*

gives notice that the register of members is [now] kept at:

Postcode

‡ Insert Director, Secretary, Administrator, Administrative Receiver or Receiver (Scotland) as appropriate

Signed Designation‡ Date

Chapter 14

COMPANY MEETINGS

14A General Meetings and Class Meetings

General meetings are meetings of the members of the company as listed in the Register of Members, although in any particular company there may, under the terms of the articles of association, be classes of members who are not entitled to attend general meetings or vote.

There are two types of general meetings: annual general meetings and extraordinary general meetings. There may also be class meetings confined to a particular class of members.

Annual general meeting

Subject to the provisions of the elective regime (if adopted by the company) every company is required to hold an annual general meeting (AGM). The first AGM must be
s 366 held within 18 months after the date of incorporation. Subsequent AGMs must be held in each calendar year (ie in 1991, in 1992, etc) and must be held not more than 15 months after the last AGM.

Notice

The Board of directors will decide the date of the AGM and resolve to call it.

See Precedent 14A.1 (p 299) BOARD RESOLUTION CONVENING AGM

If the Board fails to call an AGM and the statutory time limit of 15 months between meetings expires, the members can convene an AGM.

Notice must then be given to those members entitled to attend and to the auditors.

See Precedent 14A.2 (p 299) MEMBERS' NOTICE CONVENING AGM

See Precedent 14A.3 (p 300) NOTICE OF AGM

The notice must specify the date, time and place of the meeting, the agenda, the fact that it is the AGM and that proxies may be appointed (except in the case of a company limited by guarantee where there is no statutory right to appoint proxies – but the articles may permit them).

s 369 The period of notice for an AGM is 21 clear days, but shorter notice will be valid if it is so agreed by all the members entitled to attend and vote at the meeting. The notice period
Table A, regs 111–115 must not include the date of service and the date of the meeting. If notice is sent by post, 48 hours must be allowed for posting. (The earlier version of Table A, which many companies still have, specifies 24 hours.) Notices must be in writing and either posted or given to the member personally. If shares are held in joint names, only the first named holder need be sent notice. A member whose registered address is outside the UK need not

Table A, reg 112 be sent notice unless a UK address for the purpose has been supplied. Notice should also be given to all directors and the auditors.

s 240 Documents such as the annual report and accounts are usually circulated with the notice of the AGM for consideration. Such documents may carry specific notice periods which must be observed and if a waiver of notice is given for the AGM then additional waivers of these separate notice requirements must be included.

Resolutions removing directors or auditors require special notice (see Chapters 10A and
s 379 7B respectively, and Precedents 14A.13 and 14A.14 below) and notice to the persons concerned which cannot be curtailed by a waiver of notice by shareholders.

See Precedent 14A.4 (p 301) CONSENT TO SHORT NOTICE FOR AGM

The business usually conducted at an AGM is that shown in the agenda in Precedent 14A.2. Additional business may be conducted provided this is included in the agenda. If
s 378 any special resolution is to be passed the agenda must state that it is to be proposed as a special resolution and the exact wording of the resolution must be given. Copies of all
s 380 special resolutions and some other resolutions must be sent to the Registrar of Companies.

s 382 Table A, reg 100 Minutes of the meeting must be taken. If purported to be signed by the chairman of the meeting, or of the next meeting, they are evidence of the proceedings and, until the contrary is proved, the meeting is deemed duly convened and held and all proceedings duly conducted.

See Precedent 14A.5 (p 302) SPECIMEN MINUTES OF AGM

Extraordinary general meeting

Any general meeting other than an annual general meeting is an extraordinary general
Table A, reg 37 meeting (EGM). The directors may call an EGM whenever they think fit, subject to giving proper notice.

See Precedent 14A.6 (p 304) RESOLUTION OF BOARD TO CONVENE AN EGM

s 368 Members holding one-tenth of the voting shares or one-tenth of the voting rights at general meetings may requisition the calling of an EGM. The requisition must be deposited at the company's registered office. It may consist of several documents in like form.

See Precedent 14A.7 (p 304) MEMBERS' REQUISITION FOR EGM

On receipt of such a requisition the directors must proceed to call the EGM within 21 days, ie within that period they must send out notices of the meeting. The directors determine the period of notice to be given (subject to the statutory minimum periods) but
s 368(8) will be deemed not to have duly convened the meeting if it is held more than 28 days after the date of the notice convening the meeting. If the directors do not call the EGM the requisitionists (or one-half of them) may themselves call the meeting to be held within three months, and reclaim their reasonable expenses from the company. The company may deduct this cost from the directors' remuneration.

s 369 The period of notice required for an EGM depends on the business to be conducted. If any special resolutions or resolution appointing a director is to be passed, 21 days'

Table A, reg 115 notice must be given. If not, then only 14 days' notice is required, which period must not include the day of service or the date of the meeting. If notice is sent by post, 48 hours must be allowed for posting (earlier versions of Table A which many companies still have, specify 24 hours). Notices must be in writing and either posted or given to the member personally. If shares are held in joint names, only the first named need be sent notice. A Table A, reg 112 member whose registered address is outside the UK need not be sent notice unless a UK address for the purpose has been supplied. Notice should also be given to all directors and the auditors.

See Precedent 14A.8 (p 305) FORM OF NOTICE TO PROPOSE SPECIAL OR EXTRAORDINARY RESOLUTION

s 369 The meeting can be held on short notice if this is agreed by a majority in number of the members who hold 95 per cent of the voting shares. This may be reduced to a majority who hold not less than 90 per cent by means of an elective resolution (see Chapter 14C and Precedent 14C.9).

See Precedent 14A.9 (p 306) NOTICE OF AGREEMENT BY MEMBERS TO SHORT NOTICE FOR GENERAL MEETINGS

Minutes of all general meetings must be kept (see note above on minutes of AGM).

See Precedent 14A.10 (p 306) MINUTES OF EGM

Resolutions removing directors and auditors (or not re-appointing auditors) may require special notice (see p 294).

Copies of all special resolutions and some other resolutions must be sent to the Registrar of Companies.

Proxies

s 372 Every member of a company limited by shares who is entitled to attend and vote at general meetings may appoint a proxy. The proxy need not be a member of the company. The notice of any general meeting must state the members' rights to appoint proxies (see Precedents 14A.3 and 14A.8). In a private company (although not a plc) the proxy may speak at the meeting (subject to the chairman's general power to control the conduct of the meeting). A proxy may vote only on a poll although he has the same right as the member appointing him to demand a poll.

Table A, reg 62 s 372(5) Proxies must be appointed in writing and this must be delivered to the registered office of the company 48 hours before the start of the meeting. The company cannot specify a longer period than this. The instrument appointing the proxy may confer either a general power (to vote as the proxy thinks fit) or a special power (instructing the proxy how to vote).

Table A, regs 60, 61 Forms of proxy are prescribed in Table A and will apply to companies which use Table A based articles and do not exclude these clauses.

See Precedent 14A.11 (p 307) FORM OF PROXY (GENERAL POWER)

See Precedent 14A.12 (p 308) FORM OF PROXY (SPECIAL OR GENERAL POWER)

Corporate representatives

s 375 Where the shareholder is a company, it may send a representative to the general meeting. Such a representative is not a proxy. The representative must be authorised to act by the Board of directors of the company appointing him.

See Precedent 14A.13 (p 309) NOTICE OF APPOINTMENT OF CORPORATE REPRESENTATIVE

Types of resolutions passed at meetings of a company

Ordinary resolution

An ordinary resolution requires 14 days' clear notice to those entitled to attend and vote and is passed by a simple majority of those voting in person and by proxy or of shares voted on a poll.

Special resolution

s 378 A special resolution requires 21 days' clear notice to those entitled to attend and vote and is passed by a majority of not less than 75 per cent of those voting in person and by proxy or of shares voted on a poll.

Extraordinary resolution

An extraordinary resolution requires 14 days' clear notice and a majority of not less than 75 per cent.

All of the above periods of notice are subject to the ability of all, or a specified majority, of members to agree to short notice (see above, Precedents 14A.4 and 14A.9). The procedure and circumstance of use are dealt with in Precedent 14C below.

Elective resolution

CA 1989 ss 115–116 An elective resolution requires 21 days' clear notice and a vote of 100 per cent of the members.

Special notice resolutions

s 379 Certain ordinary resolutions require the special notice procedure to be followed before they may be properly passed. The procedure and circumstance of use are dealt with below.

Form of notice of resolution

s 378 For a resolution to be validly passed the notice of meeting must in all cases other than an ordinary resolution specify the intention to pass the resolution as 'special', 'extraordinary' or 'elective', as the case may be.

Special notice

s 379 The special notice procedure must be observed before an ordinary resolution can be passed in the following circumstances.

s 303 (1) To remove a director before his period of office expires or to appoint someone else in his place at a meeting at which he is removed.

s 293(5) (2) To appoint or approve appointment of a director who is or will be over the age limit (70). This applies to public companies and their subsidiaries only.

ns 391A CA 1989, s 122 (3) To remove an auditor before his term of office expires, to appoint an auditor other than the retiring one, to fill a casual vacancy in the office of auditors or re-appoint an auditor appointed by the directors to fill a casual vacancy.

The procedure is covered in detail in *Jordans Secretarial Administration*, at § 5.9.4, but basically it is as follows.

(1) Notice must be given by a member to the company to propose this resolution not less than 28 days before the meeting at which it is to be proposed.

See Precedent 14A.14 (p 309) SPECIAL NOTICE TO PROPOSE RESOLUTION

(2) The company must give notice of the resolution to members at the same time as it gives notice of the meeting. Twenty-one days' notice of meeting must be given if a special notice resolution is to be proposed. The resolution must be set out in full in the notice of meeting.

See Precedent 14A.15 (p 310) NOTICE OF EGM TO PASS ORDINARY, EXTRAORDINARY OR SPECIAL RESOLUTION UNDER SPECIAL NOTICE

(3) If the special notice resolution proposes to remove a director or auditor or appoint an auditor other than the retiring auditor, a copy of the special notice must be sent to the directors or auditors who have the right to make written representations to the company and request their circulation to the members. If the company fails to circulate the representations it can be made to read them out at the meeting before the resolution is put.

See Precedent 14A.16 (p 311) NOTICE TO DIRECTOR/AUDITOR OF SPECIAL NOTICE RESOLUTION

Directions to the Board by shareholders

Table A, reg 70 Table A provides that shareholders may by special resolution give directions to the directors on how the business of the company be managed and its powers exercised. Such directions should be given sparingly and it would be inappropriate for shareholders to attempt to use this power to interfere with the day-to-day management. However, the following precedent gives an example of its use.

See Precedent 14A.17 (p 312) SPECIAL RESOLUTION GIVING DIRECTIONS TO DIRECTORS

Class meetings

If the company has different classes of members it may sometimes be necessary to hold separate class meetings.

s 125 The commonest circumstance where this occurs is if there is to be a variation of the rights of a particular class of shares (see p 20).

s 125(6) The regulations for the calling and conduct of EGMs apply to class meetings.

If a resolution requires both class consent and consent in a general meeting of the company, the class meeting should be held first or alternatively the resolution passed in general meeting made conditional on approval at a subsequent class meeting.

See Precedent 14A.18 (p 312) (1) NOTICE OF CLASS MEETING
(p 313) (2) SPECIMEN CLASS RESOLUTION
(3) PROVISO IF COMPANY RESOLUTION ALSO REQUIRED

Precedent 14A.1

Board Resolution Convening AGM

Resolved that the annual general meeting of the company be held at [*place*] on [*date*] at [*time*] and that the secretary be instructed to attend to all necessary arrangements in this respect.

Precedent 14A.2

Members' Notice Convening AGM

We   and   , being members of the aforesaid company do hereby convene the (10th) annual general meeting of the company which will be held at [*place*] on [*date*] at [*time*]. We so convene this meeting because the directors have failed to do so.

The business of the meeting will be:

[*agenda.*]

EDITOR'S NOTE

This notice will be served by the members on the secretary at the registered office. The secretary will then send out a notice of meeting in the usual form but signed:

'At the requisition of   , members of the company.

. . . .
Secretary'

Precedent 14A.3

Notice of AGM

Limited

NOTICE IS HEREBY GIVEN that the annual general meeting of the company will be held at [*place*] on [*date*] at [*time*] for the following purposes.

1. To receive the report of the directors and the audited accounts for the year ended 19 (and to declare a dividend).
2. To elect the directors in place of those retiring (see the directors' report).
3. To re-elect the auditors and authorise the directors to fix their remuneration.
4. To transact any other ordinary business of the company.

By order of the Board

....

Secretary

[*registered office address*]

Dated 19

A member entitled to attend and vote at the above-mentioned meeting is entitled to appoint a proxy, who need not be a member of the company, to attend and vote in his stead.

NOTE – Copies of service contracts of the directors with the company and any subsidiaries not expiring or determinable without payment of compensation within one year will be available for inspection at the registered office during normal business hours, from the date of this notice until the conclusion of the meeting.

EDITOR'S NOTE

For forms of proxy see Precedents 14A.11 and 14A.12.

Precedent 14A.4

Consent to Short Notice for AGM

To the Directors of   Limited

We, the undersigned, being all the members entitled to attend and vote at general meetings of the above-named company, do hereby signify our consent to the annual general meeting of the company being held on [*date*] notwithstanding that the meeting is called by shorter notice than that specified in s 369 of the Companies Act 1985 (*and do hereby agree that copies of the documents required to be sent in accordance with s 238(1) of the Companies Act 1985 shall be deemed to have been duly sent notwithstanding that they are sent less than 21 days before the date of the said meeting).

Dated   19

EDITOR'S NOTE

*Delete if inapplicable.

Precedent 14A.5

Specimen Minutes of AGM

Minutes of the [10th] AGM held at [*place*] on 19 .

PRESENT: .... (Chairman)

(and the Directors who signed the attendance sheet attached to these minutes).

IN ATTENDANCE:

.... (Secretary
.... (Auditors)
(and ....
..................)

1. The secretary read the notice of meeting.
2. [*Name*] on behalf of the auditors, read the report of the auditors.
3. The chairman proposed:

   'That the report of the directors and the audited accounts for the year 19 now submitted to this meeting, be and are hereby received; and

   *That the final dividend of p per share recommended therein be and is hereby declared payable on 19 to holders of ordinary shares registered at the close of business on 19 '.

   [*Name*] seconded the resolution, which was put to the meeting and declared carried.

4. The chairman proposed:

   'That ....
   the director(s) retiring by rotation be and is (are) hereby re-elected (a) director(s) of the company'.

   [*Name*] seconded the resolution, which was put to the meeting and declared carried.

5. The chairman proposed:

   'That the appointment(s) of [*names*] to the Board on 19 be confirmed'.

   [*Name*] seconded the resolution, which was put to the meeting and declared carried.

6. The chairman proposed:

   'That Messrs be re-appointed as auditors of the company, to hold office until the conclusion of the next general meeting at which accounts are laid and the directors be authorised to fix their remuneration'.

[*Name*] seconded the resolution which was put to the meeting and declared carried.

7. There being no further business the meeting was closed.

....
Chairman

EDITOR'S NOTES

Under Table A any director appointed by the directors since the previous AGM retires at the AGM, but may stand for re-election.

Precedent 14A.6

Resolution of Board to Convene an EGM

THAT an extraordinary general meeting of the company be convened at which the following shall be proposed:

[*proposed resolution*]

[and that the members be requested to agree to the meeting being held on short notice*].
The secretary was instructed to give the notice of the meeting to the members of the company entitled thereto and to the company's auditors and to the directors.

EDITOR'S NOTE

*Delete if inapplicable.

Precedent 14A.7

Members' Requisition For EGM

[*Date*]

To Limited and its Directors

We, the undersigned, being shareholders who, at the date of deposit of this requisition at the registered office of the company, hold not less than one-tenth of the paid up capital of the company hereby, pursuant to s 368 of the Companies Act 1985, requisition an extraordinary general meeting of the company to consider and if thought fit to pass the resolutions set out below as special resolutions.

The resolutions to be proposed are as follows.

*1. [That the articles of association of the company be amended by the deletion of subclause (c) of Article 7 from the said articles.]
2. That the company meet the costs of convening and holding this meeting and circulating the statement of the requisitionists with respect to the resolutions to be proposed.

Should Resolution No 2 not be passed, we undertake to meet the costs of the company in giving effect to this requisition.

Yours faithfully

.....

.....

[*Signatures*]

EDITOR'S NOTE

*Words in brackets used as an example.

Precedent 14A.8

Form of Notice to Propose Special or Extraordinary Resolution

Notice is hereby given that an extraordinary general meeting of the company will be held at [*place*] on [*date*] at [*time*] when the following resolution will be proposed as an (*extraordinary) (*special) resolution:

[*resolution.*]

By order of the Board

.....

Secretary

[*registered office address*]

[*date of notice*]

A member entitled to attend and vote at the above-mentioned meeting is entitled to appoint a proxy, who need not be a member of the company, to attend and vote in his stead.

EDITOR'S NOTES

*Delete as appropriate.

For forms of proxies, see Precedents 14A.11 and 14A.12.

Precedent 14A.9

Notice of Agreement by Members to Short Notice for General Meetings

To the Directors of Limited

We, the undersigned, being all the members entitled to attend and vote at general meetings of the above named company, do hereby signify our consent to the [*annual/extraordinary*] general meeting of the company being held on [*date*], notwithstanding that the meeting is called by shorter notice than that specified in section 369 of the Companies Act 1985.

Dated 19 .

Precedent 14A.10

Minutes of EGM

.... Limited

MINUTES of an extraordinary general meeting of the members of the above-named company, duly convened and held at on the day of 19 .

The following resolution was duly proposed and passed as an ORDINARY RESOLUTION:

That [*name*] be appointed auditor in place of the retiring auditor, [*name*] to act as such until the conclusion of the next general meeting of the company at which the requirements of s 238(1) of the Companies Act 1985 should be complied with and that the directors of the company be authorised to fix their remunerations.*

EDITOR'S NOTE

*Example resolution.

Precedent 14A.11

Form of Proxy
(GENERAL POWER)

pursuant to section 372 of the Companies Act 1985
and Table A, reg 60

J 372

. . . . Limited.

I . . . .

of . . . .

in the County of . . . . being a Member of

. . . . LIMITED,

hereby appoint . . . .

of . . . .

or failing him . . . .

of . . . .

as my Proxy, to vote for me on my behalf at the* . . . .

GENERAL MEETING of the Company to be held on the . . . .

day of . . . . 19 . . . . , and at any adjournment thereof.

Signed on [*date*].

. . . . *Signature of Member*

EDITOR'S NOTE

*Annual or extraordinary, as the case may be.

Precedent 14A.12

Form of Proxy

(SPECIAL OR GENERAL POWER)

pursuant to section 372(a) of the Companies Act 1985
and Table A, reg 61

J 372a

. . . . Limited.

I . . . .

of . . . .

in the County of . . . . being a Member of

. . . . LIMITED,

hereby appoint . . . .

of . . . .

or failing him . . . .

of . . . .

as my Proxy, to vote for me on my behalf at the* . . . .

GENERAL MEETING of the Company to be held on the . . . .

day of . . . . 19 . . . . , and at any adjournment thereof.

This form is to be used in respect of the resolutions mentioned below as follows:

Resolution No 1 †for †against
Resolution No 2 †for †against

[*dated*]

. . . . *Signature of Member*

N.B. – This form must be deposited at the Registered Office of the Company at ....

.... not less than [forty eight] .... hours before the time for holding the meeting.

* "Annual" or "Extraordinary" as the case may be. † Strike out whichever is not desired.

Unless otherwise instructed, the proxy will vote as he thinks fit.

Precedent 14A.13

Notice of Appointment of Corporate Representative

We, XYZ Limited being a member of the above named company, hereby appoint [*name*] to act as our representative for the purpose of s 375 of the Companies Act 1985 at [any general meeting of the company until further notice]* [the (annual) extraordinary general meeting of the company to be held on [*date*] and at any adjournment thereof]*.

[*date*]

Signed .... [*authorised signatory*]
For XYZ Ltd

EDITOR'S NOTE

*Delete as applicable for permanent appointment or appointment for a specific meeting.

Precedent 14A.14

Special Notice to Propose Resolution

The Directors

Limited

I hereby give special notice, pursuant to ss 379 and 388 of the Companies Act 1985, of my intention to propose the following resolution as an ordinary resolution at an extraordinary general meeting of the company:

[*resolution.*]

[*Date*]

EDITOR'S NOTE

The following words should be included against the resolution in the notice of meeting:

'Special Notice has been received of the intention to propose this resolution'.

Precedent 14A.15

Notice of Extraordinary General Meeting to Pass Ordinary, Extraordinary or Special Resolution under Special Notice

NOTICE IS HEREBY GIVEN that an EXTRAORDINARY GENERAL MEETING of the Company will be held at [*place*] on [*date*] at [*time*] at which meeting special notice has been given for the following resolution to be proposed as an [ordinary/extraordinary/special]* resolution.

A member entitled to attend and vote at the above-mentioned meeting is entitled to appoint a proxy who need not be a member of the company, to vote in his stead.

By Order of the Board

Secretary

[*registered office address*]
[*date of notice*]

EDITOR'S NOTE

* Delete as appropriate.

Precedent 14A.16

Notice to Director/Auditor of Special Notice Resolution

Dear Sir

I hereby give notice that the company has received special notice (a copy of which is enclosed) that the following ordinary resolution will be proposed at an extraordinary general meeting of the company called for [*date*] at [*time*] at [*address*].

[To appoint auditors, special notice having been given, pursuant to ss 379 and 388 of the Companies Act, of the intention to propose the following resolution as an ordinary resolution:

'That [*name*] be appointed auditor in place of the retiring auditor, [*name*], to act as such until the conclusion of the next general meeting of the company at which the requirements of s 241(1) of the Companies Act 1985 should be complied with and that the directors of the company be authorised to fix their remunerations.']

[[*Name*], be and is hereby removed from office as a director of the company.]

Pursuant to s 388(3) of the Companies Act 1985, you are entitled to be heard on the resolution at the aforesaid meeting and may request that representations in writing made by you (not exceeding a reasonable length) be sent to all members of the company to whom notice of the meeting is sent. If you wish representations to be made, I should be obliged to receive them no later than [*date*].

Yours faithfully

....
Secretary

EDITOR'S NOTE

*Adjust according to circumstances.

For a precedent giving notice to a director whose removal is proposed, see Precedent 10A.16.

Precedent 14A.17

Special Resolution Giving Directions to Directors

Pursuant to regulation 70 of the 1985 Table A (which is incorporated in the articles of association of the company) it is hereby resolved that a direction be given to the directors of the company to institute a profit-sharing scheme for the benefit of all categories of the company's employees.

Precedent 14A.18

(1) Notice of Class Meeting

Notice is hereby given that a separate general meeting of the holders of the five per cent preference shares of £1 each in the capital of the company will be held at [*place*] on [*date*] at 12.15 pm or as soon thereafter as the (*annual general meeting) (*extraordinary general meeting) of the company called for 12 noon on the same day and at the same place shall have been concluded or adjourned. At this meeting the following resolution will be proposed as a/n (*special/extraordinary) resolution.

[*resolution.*]

By order of the Board

....
Secretary
[*registered office address*]

[*date*]

Every holder of five per cent preference shares is entitled to attend and vote at this class meeting or to appoint a proxy to attend and vote in his stead. A proxy need not be a member of the company.

EDITOR'S NOTE

*Alter as appropriate.

(2) Specimen Class Resolution*

EXTRAORDINARY RESOLUTION

That this separate general meeting of the holders of all the [five per cent preference shares] in the capital of the company sanctions on behalf of the aforesaid class of shareholders every variation and abrogation of the special rights attached to such shares in the capital of the company which may result from the passing of the special resolution to adopt new articles of association proposed at the extraordinary general meeting of the company convened for [*date*] notice of which accompanied notice of this separate general meeting and any subsequent purchase redemption and/or conciliation of shares in the capital of the company or issue of redeemable shares pursuant to such articles of association.

(3) Proviso if Company Resolution Also Required**

PROVIDED THAT this resolution (save for this proviso) shall be passed as an (extraordinary) resolution at the separate class meeting of the holders of the five per cent preference shares in the capital of the company called for the same day and at the same place or at any adjournment thereof.

EDITOR'S NOTE

*This specimen class resolution is illustrative of that suitable to update articles from those based on 1948 Table A to those based on 1985 Table A.
**The resolution at the class meeting will not include this proviso which assumes that the meeting of the company is held before the class meeting (see Precedent 14A.18(1)).

14B Written Resolutions in Place of a Meeting

Introduction

Written resolutions instead of a meeting of the company may be organised under:

CA 1989, s 113 (a) the provisions of s 113 of the Companies Act 1989, whereby, if the necessary procedures are completed a private company may, by a written resolution, do anything that may be done by a resolution passed at a general or class meeting; or

Table A, reg 53 (b) the articles of association of the company (see Table A, reg 53).

The written resolution provisions of s 113 do not prevent a company using, as an alternative, appropriate procedures under Table A. However, s 113 procedures are wider in scope and expressly cover any sort of resolution, including elective resolutions. The section also covers situations where the Companies Act itself would have prevented the use of a written resolution.

Sch 15A Written resolutions may not be used to remove a director or auditor before expiration of term of office, when they have a right to make representations to a general meeting of the company.

Written resolutions under s 113 of the Companies Act 1989

The procedure under s 113 (which inserts ss 381A–381C, 382A and Sch 15A into the Companies Act 1985) requires that:

s 381A (1) the written resolution is signed by or on behalf of all members who, at the date of the resolution, would be entitled to attend and vote at a meeting of the company necessary to pass such a resolution;

s 381B (2) notice of the resolution be given to the auditors and if in their opinion it concerns them as auditors and should be considered in general meeting, they must reply to such effect within seven days.

See Precedent 14B.1 (p 317) BOARD MINUTE TO PROPOSE WRITTEN RESOLUTION

See Precedent 14B.2 (p 318) FORM OF WRITTEN RESOLUTION

Signatures of members may be on separate documents, provided that each sets out in full the terms of the resolution.

See Precedent 14B.3 (p 319) LETTER SENDING WRITTEN RESOLUTION TO MEMBERS

Sch 15A Where information has to be given with the notice of meeting, or documents made available for inspection if a meeting is to be held, it will suffice, under the s 113 procedure, if such information is supplied to the members at or before the time when the resolution is circulated for signature.

When the 1985 Act provides that a resolution is ineffective because it was only passed as a result of votes cast by an interested party, the consent of the member(s) concerned is not needed for a unanimous resolution. (See, eg Sch 15A, para 5(2), in relation to an off-market purchase by a company of its own shares.)

The seven-day-period within which the auditors must respond is regarded as commencing on the day on which the auditors receive the notice and terminating on the day on which counter-notice is received by the company. If the auditors do not respond within seven days they are regarded as having no objection to the resolution being passed as a written resolution.

Until the auditors have replied, or the seven days elapsed, a written resolution under these procedures cannot take effect. In some circumstances it could be essential to involve the auditors at an earlier stage so as to avoid delays in their consideration of the resolution or indeed to give prior consent.

See Precedent 14B.4 (p 320) (1) LETTER SENDING STATUTORY WRITTEN RESOLUTION TO AUDITORS

(p 321) (2) RESPONSE BY AUDITORS TO STATUTORY WRITTEN RESOLUTION

A copy of the written resolution required to be sent to the auditors may be transmitted by fax which will save time and fix a firm date of receipt for the purpose of the subsequent procedural time scale.

Once agreed in the above manner, a written resolution is as effective as if it had been passed at an appropriate meeting, although no meeting has been held. No previous notice of the resolution need be given.

Written resolutions under Table A

The written resolution procedure under Table A, or similar article, will rarely provide for notice to and consent from the auditors and may be simpler to use, but its extent depends on the manner in which the relevant clause is drafted.

It cannot replace such circumstances referred to in the introduction above where the Companies Acts require a meeting. Unless it is clear that the powers under Table A are adequate the statutory written resolution procedure should be used. It should be noted that the statutory procedures are only available to private companies. There is no such restriction to procedures under Table A which, if practical, may be used by a public limited company.

Precedents 14B.1, 14B.2 and 14B.3 will be used with the necessary substitution of references to the articles and Table A, instead of the Companies Act, and an addendum to the written resolution, which makes it clear that Table A, as opposed to statutory procedures, is being used. See addendum to Precedent 14B.2 for use in such circumstances.

Minuting and dating of written resolutions

s 381A A written resolution is effective when all the members have signed and any statutory formalities with the auditors are completed.

s 382A An appropriate memorandum should be entered in the minute book recording the completion of the procedures and if this resolution is passed under the statutory provisions a memorandum should be entered detailing the dealings with the auditors.

See Precedent 14B.5 (p 322) RECORD OF MEMBERS' STATUTORY WRITTEN RESOLUTION FOR MINUTE BOOK

The copies of the resolution signed by the individual members must be carefully preserved and, unless there are too many, are best placed in the minute book.

If the resolution would, if passed at a meeting, require to be notified to the Registrar of Companies, a copy of the written resolution will also require filing within 15 days of the effective date of the resolution.

Written resolutions instead of a class meeting

Written resolutions under s 113 of the Companies Act 1989 may be used instead of a meeting of a class of members.

s 125 In the case of a variation of class rights, the Act specifically provides for consent to be given by the appropriate majority in writing or at a class meeting.

Precedent 14B.1

Board Minute to Propose Written Resolution

Resolved that [the written resolution procedures pursuant to s 381A of the Companies Act 1985]* be used to pass (if members think fit) the resolution set out below which is proposed as a [an] [†] resolution and the secretary is instructed to give effect to the statutory procedures including notice to the auditors.

EDITOR'S NOTES

*The following minute may be adopted for a written resolution passed under the provisions of Table A in the following manner, instead of the words in brackets.

['the written resolution procedures pursuant to regulation 53 of Table A to the Companies Act 1985 which is embodied in the articles of association of the company'].

†Special, extraordinary or ordinary or, in the case of the 1989 Act procedures, an elective resolution.

Precedent 14B.2

Form of Written Resolution

Company No

THE COMPANIES ACTS 1985 TO 1989

PRIVATE COMPANY LIMITED BY SHARES

WRITTEN RESOLUTION(S) OF LIMITED

Dated this day of 19 .

We, the undersigned, being all the members* of the company who, at the date of this resolution would be entitled to attend and vote at general meetings of the company, HEREBY PASS the following resolutions as a [an] [†] resolution(s)** and agree that the said resolution(s) shall, for all purposes be as valid and effective as if the same had been passed by us all at a general meeting of the company duly convened and held.

EDITOR'S NOTES

*If a class resolution is sent, detail here, eg 'of the class of seven per cent cumulative preference shares in the capital of the'.

**If the resolution is passed under the provisions of Table A, as opposed to the statutory procedures under s 113 of the Companies Act 1989, the following first paragraph should be added to the written resolution.

> 'We confirm that this written resolution is passed in accordance with regulation 53 of Table A to the Companies Act 1985, which is embodied in the articles of association of the company'.

†Special, extraordinary, ordinary or, in the case of the 1989 Act procedures, an elective resolution.

Precedent 14B.3

Letter Sending Written Resolution to Members

Dear Shareholder,

Enclosed with this letter is a form of written resolution which if you and all other shareholders approve, and signify such approval by signing and returning the document to the secretary of the company in the attached envelope, will, subject to agreement of the auditors, be passed without the necessity of holding a meeting of the company for the purpose.

The reasons for the proposed resolution are:

[*here detail the exact reasons.*]

*[Enclosed are the following documents which, if a meeting were held, would be available for prior inspection. (*Here list documents*).]

*[Set out below are details of the matters which, if a meeting were held, would be required to be disclosed at the meeting. (*Here describe such matters*).]

In order that matters may be completed expeditiously it is hoped shareholders will return the documents duly signed or otherwise communicate with the secretary not later than [*date*].

Yours sincerely
[Chairman]

EDITOR'S NOTE

*Include as appropriate.

Precedent 14B.4

(1) Letter Sending Statutory Written Resolution to Auditors

To: The Auditors

RECORDED DELIVERY

Dear Sirs,

Proposed Written Resolution(s)

We enclose a copy of a written resolution of the above company, proposed to be agreed to pursuant to s 381A of the Companies Act 1985, without holding a general meeting of the company.

If you consider that the proposed resolution concerns you as auditors you may, within seven days from the day upon which you receive the copy of the resolution, give notice to the company at its registered office stating your opinion that the resolution should be considered by the company in general meeting.

Unless you give notice within the seven-day-period specified stating your opinion as aforesaid we are entitled, upon expiry of the seven-day-period referred to above, to proceed to pass the resolution as a written resolution in any event.

Alternatively, you may notify the company that in your opinion the resolution:

(a) does not concern you as auditors; or
(b) does so concern you, but need not be considered by the company in general meeting.

In order that the resolution may be dealt with as quickly as possible we would be grateful for your prompt reply addressed to the company at [*address*]. Specimen alternative responses are enclosed for your guidance.

If you have any queries, please contact us.

Yours faithfully,

for Limited

Secretary

(2) Response by Auditors to Statutory Written Resolution

To: The company [*address to which notice is to be given*].

Dear Sirs,

Proposed Written Resolutions

We acknowledge receipt of your letter of [*date*] and the enclosed copy of [a] written resolution(s) of the above company proposed to be agreed and sent to us pursuant to s 381B of the Companies Act 1985.

[The resolution(s) [does] [do] not concern us as auditors.]*

OR

[The resolution(s) concern(s) us as auditors but need not be considered by the company in general meeting.]*

OR

[The resolution(s) concern(s) us as auditors and we are of the opinion that the resolution(s) should be considered by the company in general meeting.]*

Yours faithfully,

Auditors

EDITOR'S NOTE

*Delete if inapplicable.

Precedent 14B.5

Record of Members' Statutory Written Resolution for Minute Book

RECORD OF (A) WRITTEN RESOLUTION(S) OF LIMITED

The resolution(s) set out on the attached copy document was (were) passed as (a) Written Resolution(s) pursuant to s 381A of the Companies Act 1985. The date of the resolution(s) being the date of the last signature, was the day of 19 .

A copy of the proposed resolution(s) having been delivered to the auditors of the company on the day of 19 , the resolutions became effective on the day of 19 , pursuant to s 381B of the Companies Act 1985, when [the Company received notice from its auditors that the resolution(s) did not concern them as auditors]* [the company received notice from its auditors that the resolution(s) did concern them as auditors but need not be considered by the company in general meeting]* [a period of seven days from the day on which the auditors received a copy of the proposed resolution(s) expired without any notice being given to the company by its auditor, pursuant to s 381B(2) of the Companies Act 1985]*.

Names of Signatories ....
....
....
....

Signed: .... (Director) (Secretary)
Date: ....

EDITOR'S NOTE

* [ ] Select and delete as appropriate.

14C Elective Resolutions

s 116 The Companies Act 1989 enacts an elective resolution procedure by which a private company may disapply certain Companies Acts requirements. The 1989 Act covers five specific requirements and gives the Secretary of State power to extend elective resolutions
s 117 to cover other areas of internal administration and procedure.

The requirements covered by the Act are dealt with below.

An elective resolution is a specific type of resolution similar to a special or extraordinary resolution and likewise only effective if the necessary procedures and majorities are met.

Passing an elective resolution

s 116 The procedure is similar to a special resolution except that *all* members entitled to attend and vote at meetings of the company must agree to the passing of the resolution either in person or by proxy. Notice of 21 days in writing must be given for the meeting at which an elective resolution is to be passed – the notice must set out the resolution and state it is to be proposed as an elective resolution. Waiver of notice and holding a meeting on less than 21 days' notice is not permitted. The 1989 Act procedures for written resolutions may, however, be used to pass an elective resolution.

The commencement date for these provisions of the Companies Act 1989 was 1 April 1990 and no amendments to the articles of association of a company are necessary to authorise the passing of elective resolutions.

Elective resolutions continue in force until revoked by an ordinary resolution (see Precedent 14C.10) or the company ceases to be a private company, but there are certain circumstances in which they can be overruled (see below).

See Precedent 14C.1 (p 326) DIRECTORS' MINUTES TO PROPOSE ELECTIVE RESOLUTION

See Precedent 14C.2 (p 326) NOTICE OF MEETING FOR ELECTIVE RESOLUTION

After an elective resolution is passed a copy must be filed with the Registrar of Companies within 15 days.

See Precedent 14C.3 (p 327) FORM OF ELECTIVE RESOLUTION FOR FILING WITH THE REGISTRAR OF COMPANIES

The following precedents cover the five circumstances for the use of elective resolutions provided in the Companies Act 1989. A separate resolution must be passed for each circumstance. It is not possible to pass one omnibus elective resolution covering all five circumstances.

See Precedent 14C.4 (p 327) ELECTION TO DISPENSE WITH AGM

This election has effect in the year in which it is made and subsequent years but does not affect any liability already incurred by reason of default in holding an annual general meeting (AGM).

Table A, regs 73–80 If the articles provide for retirement and rotation of directors at the AGM, the relevant provisions must be disapplied by a special resolution altering the articles before the elective resolution is passed. This resolution should not be passed unless the laying of accounts at an AGM is dispensed with by a second elective resolution.

See Precedent 14C.5 (p 328) ELECTION TO DISPENSE WITH LAYING OF ACCOUNTS AND REPORTS BEFORE GENERAL MEETING

This election has effect in relation to the accounts and reports in respect of the financial year in which it is passed and subsequent financial years, but not in respect of any previous financial year, even if accounts for that year have not been completed.

In certain circumstances, a member or the auditors can enforce the requirements disapplied by an elective resolution as to the AGM and laying of accounts in spite of such a resolution being in force.

s 386 *See* Precedent 14C.6 (p 328) ELECTION TO DISPENSE WITH ANNUAL APPOINTMENT OF AUDITORS

s 80 *See* Precedent 14C.7 (p 329) ELECTION AS TO DURATION OF DIRECTORS' AUTHORITY TO ALLOT SHARES

The letter accompanying the notice of meeting or written resolution to pass this elective resolution should explain that the references to the Companies Act in the elective resolution allow the allotment of shares by the directors without reference to shareholders for a period in excess of five years. Such an elective resolution must be followed by an ordinary resolution granting the directors the requisite authority. The fixed period or indefinite period will be set out in the ordinary resolution.

See Precedent 14C.8 (p 329) ORDINARY RESOLUTION AS TO ALLOTMENT OF SHARES

ss 369(4), 378(3) *See* Precedent 14C.9 (p 330) ELECTION TO REDUCE MAJORITY REQUIRED TO SANCTION SHORT NOTICE OF MEETING

The election enables the majority to be reduced from 95 per cent to not less than 90 per cent.

An elective resolution may be revoked at any time by an ordinary resolution.

See Precedent 14C.10 (p 330) ORDINARY RESOLUTION REVOKING ELECTIVE RESOLUTION

A copy of an ordinary resolution revoking an elective resolution must be filed within 15 days with the Registrar of Companies. A separate ordinary resolution must be passed for each elective resolution revoked.

Circumstances in which an elective resolution can be overruled while in force

(a) Holding an annual general meeting

ns 366A CA 1989, s 115 In any year when an elective resolution is in force to dispense with the holding of an annual general meeting, any member may give notice to the company not later than three months before the end of the year to require the company to hold a meeting in that year.

See Precedent 14C.11 (p 331) NOTICE TO COMPANY TO REQUIRE THAT AGM BE HELD WHILE ELECTIVE RESOLUTION IS IN FORCE

(b) Laying accounts and reports before a general meeting

If an elective resolution has been passed to dispense with the need to lay accounts and reports before a general meeting, the accounts must instead be sent to the members at least 28 days before the end of the period within which they should have been laid.

ns 253 CA 1989, s 16

Any member or auditor of the company may, within 28 days after the day on which the account and reports of the company are actually sent out to members, require that a general meeting be held for the purpose of laying the accounts and reports before the company.

The accounts must be accompanied by a notice informing each member of his right to require the laying of the reports and accounts before a general meeting.

See Precedent 14C.12 (p 331) NOTICE TO MEMBERS INFORMING THEM OF RIGHTS IN RELATION TO REPORTS AND ACCOUNTS

See Precedent 14C.13 (p 332) NOTICE TO REQUIRE LAYING OF ACCOUNTS AND REPORTS AT A GENERAL MEETING WHILE ELECTIVE RESOLUTION IS IN FORCE

Precedent 14C.1

Directors' Minutes to Propose Elective Resolution

That an [extraordinary] general meeting of the company be called for [*date*] at which will be proposed an elective resolution pursuant to s 379A of the Companies Act 1985 to

[*here set out which of the statutory circumstances the resolution is to cover. If more than one circumstance is to be covered each must be the subject of a separate resolution.*]

EDITOR'S NOTES

Adjust to circumstances. The resolution may be proposed as a separate agenda item at an AGM. The form of notice in the agenda will be as follows.

> To consider, and if thought fit, to pass, the following resolution(s) which will be proposed as [an] elective resolution(s):
>
> [1]
> [2] } [*here set out full text of resolution.*]
> [3]

Precedent 14C.2

Notice of Meeting for Elective Resolution

LIMITED

NOTICE IS HEREBY GIVEN that an extraordinary general meeting of the above-named company will be held at on the day of 19 , at am/pm for the purposes of considering, and if thought fit, passing the following resolution(s) which [is] [are] proposed as [an] ELECTIVE RESOLUTION(S):

[*here set out resolution.*]

Dated this day of 19 .

By Order of the Board

Registered Office: Secretary

A member entitled to attend and vote at the above-mentioned meeting is entitled to appoint a proxy, who need not be a member of the company, to attend and vote in his stead.

Precedent 14C.3

Form of Elective Resolution for Filing with the Registrar of Companies

Company No

THE COMPANIES ACTS 1985 TO 1989

COMPANY LIMITED BY SHARES

ELECTIVE RESOLUTION(S) OF LIMITED

At an extraordinary general meeting of the members of the above-named company, duly convened and held at on [*date*] the following elective resolution(s) [was] [were] passed by agreement, in person or by proxy, of all the members entitled to attend and vote at the meeting:

ELECTIVE RESOLUTION(S).

....
[Director] [Secretary] [Chairman]

Precedent 14C.4

Election to Dispense with AGM

ELECTIVE RESOLUTION

'That pursuant to s 366A of the Companies Act 1985, the company hereby elects to dispense with the holding of annual general meetings in 19 and subsequent years (until this election is revoked).'

EDITOR'S NOTE

This election has effect in the year in which it is made and subsequent years, but does not affect any liability already incurred by reason of default in holding an AGM.

Precedent 14C.5

Election to Dispense with Laying of Accounts and Reports Before General Meeting

ELECTIVE RESOLUTION

'That pursuant to s 252 of the Companies Act 1985, the company hereby elects to dispense with the laying of accounts and reports before the company in general meeting.'

EDITOR'S NOTE

This election has effect in relation to the accounts and reports in respect of the financial year in which it is passed, and subsequent financial years, but *not* previous financial years.

Precedent 14C.6

Election to Dispense with Annual Appointment of Auditors

ELECTIVE RESOLUTION

'That pursuant to s 386 of the Companies Act 1985 the company hereby elects to dispense with the obligation to appoint auditors annually.'

Precedent 14C.7

Election as to Duration of Directors' Authority to Allot Shares

ELECTIVE RESOLUTION

That [the company elects that] the provisions of s 80A of the Companies Act 1985 apply instead of the provisions of ss 80(4) and 80(5) in relation to [the giving] [the renewal] after the said election of authority to allot shares.

Precedent 14C.8

Ordinary Resolution as to Allotment of Shares

ORDINARY RESOLUTION*

That the directors be and they are hereby generally and unconditionally authorised, pursuant to s 80 of the Companies Act 1985, to exercise any power of the company to allot and grant rights to subscribe for or to convert securities into shares of the company up to a maximum nominal amount equal to the nominal amount of the authorised but unissued share capital at the date of the passing of this resolution. [Provided that the authority hereby given shall expire [ ] year(s) after the passing of this resolution unless previously renewed or varied save that the directors may, notwithstanding such expiry, allot any shares or grant any such rights under this authority in pursuance of an offer or agreement so to do made by the company before the expiry of this authority.] *Or*
[The authority hereby given shall be for an indefinite period.]**

EDITOR'S NOTE

*The ordinary resolution is given here so as to provide complete documentation. The elective resolution should be passed first and followed by the ordinary resolution.

The circular accompanying notice of meeting to propose this resolution should explain that the references to the Act allow the allotment of shares without reference to shareholders for a period greater than five years.

**The authority may be for any fixed period or for an indefinite period, but must state which applies.

Precedent 14C.9

Election to Reduce Majority Required to Sanction Short Notice of Meeting

ELECTIVE RESOLUTION

That pursuant to ss 369(4) and 378(3) of the Companies Act 1985 the company hereby elects that the said provisions shall have effect in relation to the company as if for the references to 95 per cent therein there were substituted references to [ ] per cent, being a percentage not less than 90 per cent.

Precedent 14C.10

Ordinary Resolution Revoking Elective Resolution

That pursuant to s 379A of the Companies Act 1985 the company hereby revokes the elective resolution of the company made on [*date*] whereby the company [dispensed with the laying of accounts and reports before the company in general meeting] [dispensed with the holding of annual general meetings] [dispensed with the annual appointment of auditors] [elected that the provisions of s 80A of the Companies Act 1985 should apply in relation to the [giving] [renewal] of an authority to allot shares] [elected to reduce the majority required to sanction short notice of general meetings].

Precedent 14C.11

Notice to Company to Require that AGM be Held while Elective Resolution is in Force

To The Directors
[at Registered Office
of Company]

Recorded Delivery

I/We holder(s) of [ordinary] shares in the capital of the company hereby give notice pursuant to s 366A(3) of the Companies Act 1985 that I/we require an annual general meeting of the company to be held for this year ending [*date*]* notwithstanding that an elective resolution to dispense with the annual general meeting is in force.

dated** ....

**Not less than three months before the date * above.

Precedent 14C.12

Notice to Members Informing Them of Rights in Relation to Reports and Accounts

TO ALL SHAREHOLDERS

A copy of the audited accounts and report of the directors for the year ended 19 is enclosed.

An elective resolution is in force which dispenses with the need for the accounts and reports to be laid before the company in general meeting unless any member requires a general meeting to be held for this purpose.

Any shareholder requiring such a meeting must give notice in writing thereof to the secretary of the company to reach him at this registered office within 28 days of the date of this letter.

Chairman

EDITOR'S NOTE

1. This circular must accompany the report and accounts and be dated with the day of dispatch.
2. The circular should be addressed from the registered office and state that it is such.
3. A similar letter, suitably adjusted, should be sent to the auditors.

Precedent 14C.13

Notice to Require Laying of Accounts and Reports at a General Meeting while Elective Resolution is in Force

To The Directors
[at Registered Office
of Company]

Recorded Delivery

I/We [holder(s) of   [ordinary] shares in the capital of the company] [auditors of the company] hereby give notice pursuant to s 253(2) of the Companies Act 1985 that I/we require a general meeting of the company be called at which the accounts and reports for the accounting reference period ended [*date*] be laid, notwithstanding that an elective resolution to dispense with the laying of accounts and reports is in force.

Chapter 15

WINDING UP AND STRIKING OFF

15A Members' Voluntary Winding Up

Introduction

The winding up or striking off of a company is a highly technical process and no steps to progress it should be taken by a Board of directors unless professional advice has been obtained first. Substantial liabilities may attach to directors who contravene this complicated and detailed legislation.

This process of members' voluntary winding up may be used only if the company is solvent. To ensure that this is so the first stage of such a winding up is for the directors to make a statutory declaration at a meeting of all the directors, or a majority of them, that they have made a full enquiry into the company's affairs and they are of the opinion that the company will be able to pay all its debts in full, with interest at the official rate, within 12 months of the commencement of the winding up (or such shorter period as they specify). The statutory declaration (including the statement of assets and liabilities which forms part of it) must be sent to the Registrar of Companies.

IA 1986, s 89 The directors must be sure of the solvency of the company before making the declaration of solvency. Making such a declaration without reasonable grounds is an offence which may be punished by a fine or imprisonment. If the company does not in fact pay all its debts within the 12 months (or specified shorter period) there is a presumption that the declaration was made without reasonable grounds, although this may be rebutted by showing that the declaration was reasonable on the facts available to the directors at the time.

The statutory declaration will usually be made at the Board meeting at which the directors resolve to call an extraordinary general meeting so that the members can pass a special resolution to wind up the company.

See Precedent 15A.1 (p 335) MINUTES OF BOARD MEETING

See Precedent 15A.2 (p 336) DIRECTORS' DECLARATION OF SOLVENCY

IA 1986, s 84 Within five weeks after the date of the declaration of solvency the members must pass a special resolution to wind up the company. As with any other special resolution, the full period of notice for the meeting is 21 days, but it may be held on short notice if so agreed by the requisite majority.

The written resolution procedure under the Companies Act 1989 may be adopted (see Chapter 14B). The winding up is deemed to commence at the date of the special resolution.

IA 1986, s 109; IA 1986, Pt XIII In addition to resolving to wind up the company the members will usually appoint a liquidator who must be an authorised insolvency practitioner, and must give the chairman of the meeting a written statement to that effect. If no liquidator has agreed to act by the date of the meeting the appointment could be made at a later meeting.

See Precedent 15A.3 (p 339) NOTICE TO MEMBERS OF MEETING TO PASS SPECIAL RESOLUTION TO WIND UP COMPANY VOLUNTARILY

Within 15 days after the date of the meeting a copy of the special resolution accompanied by the declaration of solvency must be delivered to the Registrar of Companies and advertised in the *London Gazette* within 14 days.

See Precedent 15A.4 (p 340) COPY OF SPECIAL RESOLUTION FOR REGISTRAR OF COMPANIES AND FOR ADVERTISEMENT FOR *LONDON GAZETTE*

The chairman of the meeting must provide the liquidator with a written certificate of his appointment.

See Precedent 15A.5 (p 341) CERTIFICATE OF APPOINTMENT OF LIQUIDATOR BY MEETING

The liquidator must, within 14 days of his appointment, send notice of it to the Registrar of Companies and advertise it in the *London Gazette.*

See Precedent 15A.6 (p 342) FORM G 600 NOTICE OF APPOINTMENT OF LIQUIDATOR – VOLUNTARY WINDING UP (MEMBERS OR CREDITORS)

See Precedent 15A.7 (p 343) FORM 600A NOTICE OF APPOINTMENT OF LIQUIDATOR [MEMBERS'] [CREDITORS']† VOLUNTARY WINDING UP

Once appointed, the liquidator will wind up the company. This will involve the collection and realisation of all its assets and applying the proceeds in satisfaction of his own costs and remuneration, the payment of creditors in full and the payment of any balance to the shareholders in accordance with the rights attached to their shares. The formalities and processes will be handled by the liquidator and precedents are not included here.

When the company's affairs are fully wound up the liquidator must prepare a final account showing how the liquidation has been conducted and the company's property disposed of. The liquidators must call a final meeting of the company for the purpose of laying before it the account and giving an explanation of it.

Within one month after the meeting the liquidator must lodge a copy of his account with the Registrar of Companies with a return stating the date when the meeting was held. The company will be struck off the register three months later.

If at any time the liquidator forms the opinion that the company will not be able to pay all its debts within 12 months (or the shorter time specified in the declaration of solvency) he must notify all the creditors and call a meeting of these. The winding up will then continue as a creditors' voluntary winding up.

At the termination of the liquidation the shareholders should pass a resolution determining the disposal of the books and records of the company.

See Precedent 15A.8 (p 343) EXTRAORDINARY RESOLUTION FOR DISPOSAL OF BOOKS AND PAPERS AFTER LIQUIDATION

Precedent 15A.1

Minutes of Board Meeting

Minutes of a meeting of the directors of   Ltd held at [*address*] on [*date*].

PRESENT:

It was resolved:

1. That the company be put into voluntary liquidation.
2. Having made full enquiry into the company's affairs and on the basis of the statement of assets and liabilities circulated at the meeting, that the directors can make a statutory declaration pursuant to s 89(3) of the Insolvency Act 1986.
3. That an extraordinary general meeting be convened for the purpose of considering, and if agreed, passing, a special resolution that the company be put into members' voluntary winding up and that [*name*], an insolvency practitioner, be appointed as liquidator of the company.

....
(Chairman)

Precedent 15A.2

Directors' Declaration of Solvency

Form 4.70

Section 89(3)

The Insolvency Act 1986

Members' Voluntary Winding Up
Declaration of Solvency Embodying
a Statement of Assets and Liabilities

S.89(3)

Pursuant to section 89(3) of the Insolvency Act 1986

To the Registrar of Companies

For official use

Company Number

Name of company

(a) Insert full name of company

(a)

Limited

(b) Insert full name(s) and address(es)

I/We (b)

attach a declaration of solvency embodying a statement of assets and liabilities

Signed

Date

Presenter's name, address and reference (if any)

For Official Use	
Liquidation Section	Post Room

Form 4.70 contd.

Section 89(3)

The Insolvency Act 1986

Members' Voluntary Winding Up Declaration of Solvency Embodying a Statement of Assets and Liabilities

Company number ______________________

Name of company ______________________

Limited

____

Presented by ______________________

Declaration of Solvency

(a) Insert names and addresses

We (a) ______________________

____

(b) Delete as applicable
(c) Insert name of company
(d) Insert a period of months not exceeding 12

being (b) [all the] [the majority of the] directors of (c) ________ do solemnly and sincerely declare that we have made a full inquiry into the affairs of this company, and that, having done so, we have formed the opinion that this company will be able to pay its debts in full together with interest at the official rate within a period of (d) ________ months, from the commencement of the winding up.

(e) Insert date

We append a statement of the company's assets and liabilities as at (e) ________, being the latest practicable date before the making of this declaration.

We make this solemn declaration, conscientiously believing it to be true, and by virtue of the provisions of the Statutory Declarations Act 1835.

Declared at ______________________

this ______ day of ____________ 19__

Before me,

Solicitor or Commissioner of Oaths

4.70 contd.

Statement as at ____________________ showing assets at estimated realisable values and liabilities expected to rank

Assets and liabilities			Estimated to realise or to rank for payment to nearest £
Assets:			£
Balance at Bank			
Cash in Hand			
Marketable Securities			
Bills Receivable			
Trade Debtors			
Loans and Advances			
Unpaid Calls			
Stock in Trade			
Work in Progress			
Freehold Property			
Leasehold Property			
Plant and Machinery			
Furniture, Fittings, Utensils etc			
Patents, Trade Marks etc			
Investments other than Marketable Securities			
Other Property, viz			
Estimated Realisable Value of Assets £			
Liabilities			£
Secured on specific assets, viz			
Secured by a Floating Charge(s)			
Estimated Cost of Liquidation and other expenses including interest accruing until payment of debts in full			
Unsecured creditors (amounts estimated to rank for payment)	£	£	
Trade accounts			
Bills payable			
Accrued expenses			
Other liabilities			
Contingent liabilities			
Estimated Surplus after paying Debts in full £			

Remarks:

Precedent 15A.3

Notice to members of meeting to pass special resolution to wind up company voluntarily

J71

Company Number

name of company

....

.... Limited

NOTICE IS HEREBY GIVEN that an Extraordinary General Meeting of the above-named

Company will be held at ....

.... [*place*]

on .... [*date*]

at .... [*time*] for the purpose of considering and, if thought fit, passing the

following Resolution as a SPECIAL RESOLUTION:—

"That the Company be wound up voluntarily, and that ....

.... [and](1) ....

of ....

....

be and he is/they are(2) hereby appointed Liquidator(s)(1) for the purpose of such winding-up."

A Member entitled to attend and vote at the above-mentioned Meeting is entitled to appoint a proxy, who need not be a Member of the Company, to attend and vote instead of him.

Dated .... 19 ....

By order of the Board

.... Secretary

NOTES:
(1) Delete if it does not apply.
(2) Delete that which does not apply.

Precedent 15A.4

[COPY]

special resolution

pursuant to sections 378(2) of the Companies Act 1985 and 84(1)(b) of the Insolvency Act 1986

J84a

name of company

Company Number

....

.... Limited

Passed .... 19 ....

At an Extraordinary General Meeting of the members of the above-named Company duly convened and held at ....

....

on .... 19 ...., the following SPECIAL RESOLUTION was duly passed:–

"That the Company be wound up voluntarily, and that

....

[and] (1) ....

of ....

....

be and he is/they are (2) hereby appointed Liquidator(s) (1) for the purposes of such winding-up".

Signature (3) ....

Description ....

NOTES:
(1) Delete if it does not apply.
(2) Delete that which does not apply.
(3) This form should be signed by the Chairman of the meeting at which the Resolution was passed, or by a Director or the Secretary of the Company.

This copy resolution must be filed with the Registrar of Companies within 15 days after it was passed. It must also be published in the *London Gazette* within 14 days.

Presented by ....

....

....

Presenter's Reference ....

EDITOR'S NOTE

The *London Gazette* copy should be authenticated by the company's solicitor or other professional advisor and name of the signatory at (3) typed in capitals.

Precedent 15A.5

Rule 4.100, 4.101-CVL, 4.139

Certificate of Appointment of Liquidator by Meeting

* Insert the name of the company

IN THE MATTER OF*

and

IN THE MATTER OF THE INSOLVENCY ACT 1986

(a) Delete depending upon whether meeting of creditors, contributories, or company

(b) Insert date

(c) State full name and address of liquidator

This is to certify that at a meeting (a) [of the creditors] [of the contributories] of the above-named company held on (b)

(c)

having provided a written statement that he is qualified to act as an insolvency practitioner in relation to the above-named company under the provisions of the Insolvency Act 1986 and that he consents so to act, was appointed liquidator of the company.

Date ____________________

Signed ____________________
Chairman

Name in BLOCK LETTERS ____________________

____

Precedent 15A.6

Notice of appointment of liquidator Voluntary winding up (Members or Creditors)

Pursuant to section 109 of the Insolvency Act 1986

Please do not write in this margin

To the Registrar of Companies

For official use	Company number

Please complete legibly, preferably in black type, or bold block lettering

Name of company

*

* insert full name of company

Nature of Business

I/We give notice that I/we have been appointed liquidator(s) of the above company

on ____________________ 19 __________.

The appointment was by [the company][the creditors]†

Type of liquidation [Members] [Creditors] †

† delete as appropriate

Name of Liquidator	
Office holder number	
Address	
Signature	Date

Name of Liquidator	
Office holder number	
Address	
Signature	Date

Presentor's name address and reference (if any):

Time Critical Reference

For official Use

General Section	Post room

Precedent 15A.7

Notice of appointment of liquidator [Members'][Creditors']† voluntary winding up

† delete as appropriate

Pursuant to section 109 of the Insolvency Act 1986

For insertion in the [London][Edinburgh]† Gazette

Company Number
Name of company
Previous name(s) of company (if any)
Nature of business
Type of liquidation [Members] [Creditors] †
Address of registered office

Liquidator(s) name(s) and address(es)	
Office holder number(s)	
Date of appointment	
By whom appointed	
Signature(s)	Date
(Liquidator(s))	
Attested by	
Description	

Precedent 15A.8

Extraordinary Resolution for Disposal of Books and Papers after Liquidation

That all books, accounts, papers and documents of the company, and of the liquidator, be retained by the liquidator for a period of years* from the dissolution of the company, after which they shall be destroyed.

EDITOR'S NOTE

* Complete as appropriate. Six years is the normal practice.

15B Striking a Company Off the Register

s 652 The Companies Act provides that the Registrar of Companies may strike a company off the register if he has cause to believe that it is not carrying on business now in operation.

A company that is struck off the register is automatically dissolved, but the liability of every director, managing officer or member continues and may be enforced.

IA 1986, s 388 Some thousands of companies are struck off each year. Many because the Registrar of Companies can get no reply to repeated official requests for compliance filings, others because it is a convenient and cheap procedure for terminating a dormant or disused company if its affairs are so simple that the use of a liquidator (who must be an authorised insolvency practitioner) is unnecessary, and it has no outstanding liabilities actual or contingent.

Any assets belonging to a company at the date it is struck off or later accruing to it are
s 653 forfeit to the Crown *in bona vacantia*. An application to the court by a company struck off, for its restoration to the register, may be made by members or creditors within 20 years of the date the advertisement of striking off appears in the *London Gazette*.

The procedure to attain an intentional striking off is as follows.

1. Ensure the company is not now carrying on business or in operation.
2. Ensure all creditors have been paid and that tax affairs are up-to-date and that there are no known contingent liabilities.
3. Strip company as far as possible of all assets (on which professional advice must be taken).
4. After consultation with shareholders, hold Board meeting to decide to apply to the Registrar of Companies for the company to be struck off.

See Precedent 15B.1 (p 345) BOARD MINUTES

5. Apply to the Registrar of Companies for company to be struck off.

See Precedent 15B.2 (p 345) LETTER OF REQUEST TO REGISTRAR OF COMPANIES

6. The Registrar will reply making the statutory enquiries of the company, to which a director must respond.

See Precedent 15B.3 (p 346) REGISTRAR'S FORMAL INQUIRY LETTER

7. After checking with the Inland Revenue that there is no outstanding taxation position the Registrar will proceed with striking off the company and advertising it in the *London Gazette*.
8. If no objections received by the Registrar the company is dissolved after three months.

It must be realised that once the Registrar has commenced the striking off procedure it is unlikely that it will be reversed at the request of the company if there is a change of mind.

Precedent 15B.1

Board Minutes

Discussions with the shareholders were reported and it was their unanimous view that the company should apply to be struck off the Register of Companies and dissolved as it was not carrying on business or otherwise in operation.

The directors agreed that such was an appropriate course and resolved that the necessary steps be taken for this purpose.

Precedent 15B.2

Letter of Request to Registrar of Companies

The Registrar of Companies (Default Section)
Companies House
Crown Way
Cardiff
CF4 3UZ

[*date*]

Dear Sir,

Re   Limited – Company No:

The directors and shareholders of the above-named company wish the company to be dissolved. Please would you therefore send a DISS 1 form to the directors for signature.

Yours faithfully

Precedent 15B.3

Registrar's Formal Inquiry Letter

COMPANIES HOUSE

Please address any reply to
quoting reference DISS 1/[*company no*]

[*date*]

Companies House
Crown Way
CARDIFF CF4 3UZ

Telephone:

Telex:
Fax:

Dear Sirs

Re Limited

Thank you for your letter of [*date*]

Before the Registrar can take action under section 652 of the Companies Act 1985, he must write formally to inquire whether or not the company is carrying on business or in operation. Please accept this letter as such formal inquiry.

Would you please complete and return the attached slip, which must be signed by a director of the company.

Yours faithfully

To: Companies House
PO Box No 310
Cardiff
CF4 3UZ

Your ref DISS 1/

[*date*]

Dear Sir

.... Limited

I, being a director of the above named company, confirm that it is not in business or operation and request that it be struck off the register.

Yours faithfully

Director

15C Restoration to the Register

s 653 The Companies Acts provide a procedure for the restoration to the register if a company is struck off as described above. Such procedure involves an application to the court and is outside the scope of this book (see *Jordans Secretarial Administration*, at § 7.40 for an outline).

s 651 There are also procedures for the restoration of a company which has been dissolved on liquidation, for which see *Gore-Browne on Companies*, at § 34.27.

Appendix 1

Companies Act 1985 – Tables A to F

These tables set out the form of memorandum and articles of association for companies formed under Companies Act 1985. The articles apply to every company unless special articles have been adopted to replace or amend them.

These tables are prescribed by the Companies (Tables A to F) Regulations 1985 (SI 1985 No 805) amended by the Companies (Tables A to F) (Amendment) Regulations 1985 (SI 1985 No 1052) and came into effect on 1 August 1985. No amendments to these Tables are contained in the Companies Act 1989 and associated legislation though the Act affects certain of their provisions. See Appendix 2 for Jordans Standard Form of Memorandum and Articles of Association which contains special articles enabling advantage to be taken of the 1989 Act. Section 128 of the Companies Act 1989 provides for a Table G (partnership company) but no such table has yet been prescribed.

Table A
Regulations for Management of a Company Limited by Shares

Interpretation

1. In these regulations –

'the Act' means the Companies Act 1985 including any statutory modification or re-enactment thereof for the time being in force.

'the articles' means the articles of the company.

'clear days' in relation to the period of a notice means that period excluding the day when the notice is given or deemed to be given and the day for which it is given or on which it is to take effect.

'executed' includes any mode of execution.

'office' means the registered office of the company.

'the holder' in relation to shares means the member whose name is entered in the register of members as the holder of the shares.

'the seal' means the common seal of the company.

'secretary' means the secretary of the company or any other person appointed to perform the duties of the secretary of the company, including a joint, assistant or deputy secretary.

'the United Kingdom' means Great Britain and Northern Ireland.

Unless the context otherwise requires, words or expressions contained in these regulations bear the same meaning as in the Act but excluding any statutory modification thereof not in force when these regulations become binding on the company.

Share capital

2. Subject to the provisions of the Act and without prejudice to any rights attached to any existing shares, any share may be issued with such rights or restrictions as the company may by ordinary resolution determine.

3. Subject to the provisions of the Act, shares may be issued which are to be redeemed or are to be liable to be redeemed at the option of the company or the holder on such terms and in such manner as may be provided by the articles.

4. The company may exercise the powers of paying commissions conferred by the Act. Subject to the provisions of the Act, any such commission may be satisfied by the payment of cash or by the allotment of fully or partly paid shares or partly in one way and partly in the other.

5. Except as required by law, no person shall be recognised by the company as holding any share upon any trust and (except as otherwise provided by the articles or by law) the company shall not be bound by or recognise any interest in any share except an absolute right to the entirety thereof in the holder.

Share certificates

6. Every member, upon becoming the holder of any shares, shall be entitled without payment to one certificate for all the shares of each class held by him (and, upon transferring a part of his holding of shares of any class, to a certificate for the balance of such holding) or several certificates each for one or more of his shares upon payment for every certificate after the first of such reasonable sum as the directors may determine. Every certificate shall be sealed with the seal and shall specify the number, class and distinguishing numbers (if any) of the shares to which it relates and the amount or respective amounts paid up thereon. The company shall not be bound to issue more than one certificate for shares held jointly by several persons and delivery of a certificate to one joint holder shall be a sufficient delivery to all of them.

7. If a share certificate is defaced, worn-out, lost or destroyed, it may be renewed on such terms (if any) as to evidence and indemnity and payment of the expenses reasonably incurred by the company in investigating evidence as the directors may determine but otherwise free of charge, and (in the case of defacement or wearing-out) on delivery up of the old certificate.

Lien

8. The company shall have a first and paramount lien on every share (not being a fully paid share) for all moneys (whether presently payable or not) payable at a fixed time or called in respect of that share. The directors may at any time declare any share to be wholly or in part exempt from the provisions of this regulation. The company's lien on a share shall extend to any amount payable in respect of it.

9. The company may sell in such manner as the directors determine any shares on which the company has a lien if a sum in respect of which the lien exists is presently payable and is not paid within fourteen clear days after notice has been given to the holder of the share or to the person entitled to it in consequence of the death or bankruptcy of the

holder, demanding payment and stating that if the notice is not complied with the shares may be sold.

10. To give effect to a sale the directors may authorise some person to execute an instrument of transfer of the shares sold to, or in accordance with the directions of, the purchaser. The title of the transferee to the shares shall not be affected by any irregularity in or invalidity of the proceedings in reference to the sale.

11. The net proceeds of the sale, after payment of the costs, shall be applied in payment of so much of the sum for which the lien exists as is presently payable, and any residue shall (upon surrender to the company for cancellation of the certificate for the shares sold and subject to a like lien for any moneys not presently payable as existed upon the shares before the sale) be paid to the person entitled to the shares at the date of the sale.

Calls on shares and forfeiture

12. Subject to the terms of allotment, the directors may make calls upon the members in respect of any moneys unpaid on their shares (whether in respect of nominal value or premium) and each member shall (subject to receiving at least fourteen clear days' notice specifying when and where payment is to be made) pay to thc company as required by the notice the amount called on his shares. A call may be required to be paid by instalments. A call may, before receipt by the company of any sum due thereunder, be revoked in whole or part and payment of a call may be postponed in whole or part. A person upon whom a call is made shall remain liable for calls made upon him notwithstanding the subsequent transfer of the shares in respect whereof the call was made.

13. A call shall be deemed to have been made at the time when the resolution of the directors authorising the call was passed.

14. The joint holders of a share shall be jointly and severally liable to pay all calls in respect thereof.

15. If a call remains unpaid after it has become due and payable the person from whom it is due and payable shall pay interest in the amount unpaid from the day it became due and payable until it is paid at the rate fixed by the terms of allotment of the share or in the notice of the call or, if no rate is fixed, at the appropriate rate (as defined by the Act) but the directors may waive payment of the interest wholly or in part.

16. An amount payable in respect of a share on allotment or at any fixed date, whether in respect of nominal value or premium or as an instalment of a call, shall be deemed to be a call and if it is not paid the provisions of the articles shall apply as if that amount had become due and payable by virtue of a call.

17. Subject to the terms of allotment, the directors may make arrangements on the issue of shares for a difference between the holders in the amounts and times of payment of calls on their shares.

18. If a call remains unpaid after it has become due and payable the directors may give to the person from whom it is due not less than fourteen clear days' notice requiring payment of the amount unpaid together with any interest which may have accrued. The notice shall name the place where payment is to be made and shall state that if the notice is not complied with the shares in respect of which the call was made will be liable to be forfeited.

19. If the notice is not complied with any share in respect of which it was given may, before the payment required by the notice has been made, be forfeited by a resolution of the directors and the forfeiture shall include all dividends or other moneys payable in respect of the forfeited shares and not paid before the forfeiture.

20. Subject to the provisions of the Act, a forfeited share may be sold, re-allotted or otherwise disposed of on such terms and in such manner as the directors determine either to the person who was before the forfeiture the holder or to any other person and at any time before sale, re-allotment or other disposition, the forfeiture may be cancelled on such terms as the directors think fit. Where for the purposes of its disposal a forfeited share is to be transferred to any person the directors may authorise some person to execute an instrument of transfer of the share to that person.

21. A person any of whose shares have been forfeited shall cease to be a member in respect of them and shall surrender to the company for cancellation the certificate for the shares forfeited but shall remain liable to the company for all moneys which at the date of forfeiture were presently payable by him to the company in respect of those shares with interest at the rate at which interest was payable on those moneys before the forfeiture or, if no interest was so payable, at the appropriate rate (as defined in the Act) from the date of forfeiture until payment but the directors may waive payment wholly or in part or enforce payment without any allowance for the value of the shares at the time of forfeiture or for any consideration received on their disposal.

22. A statutory declaration by a director or the secretary that a share has been forfeited on a specified date shall be conclusive evidence of the facts stated in it as against all persons claiming to be entitled to the share and the declaration shall (subject to the execution of an instrument of transfer if necessary) constitute a good title to the share and the person to whom the share is disposed of shall not be bound to see to the application of the consideration, if any, nor shall his title to the share be affected by any irregularity in or invalidity of the proceedings in reference to the forfeiture or disposal of the share.

Transfer of shares

23. The instrument of transfer of a share may be in any usual form or in any other form which the directors may approve and shall be executed by or on behalf of the transferor and, unless the share is fully paid, by or on behalf of the transferee.

24. The directors may refuse to register the transfer of a share which is not fully paid to a person of whom they do not approve and they may refuse to register the transfer of a share on which the company has a lien. They may also refuse to register a transfer unless –

(a) it is lodged at the office or at such other place as the directors may appoint and is accompanied by the certificate for the shares to which it relates and such other evidence as the directors may reasonably require to show the right of the transferor to make the transfer;
(b) it is in respect of only one class of shares; and
(c) it is in favour of not more than four transferees.

25. If the directors refuse to register a transfer of a share, they shall within two months after the date on which the transfer was lodged with the company send to the transferee notice of the refusal.

26. The registration of transfers of shares or of transfers of any class of shares may be suspended at such times and for such periods (not exceeding 30 days in any year) as the directors may determine.

27. No fee shall be charged for the registration of any instrument of transfer or other document relating to or affecting the title to any share.

28. The company shall be entitled to retain any instrument of transfer which is registered, but any instrument of transfer which the directors refuse to register shall be returned to the person lodging it when notice of the refusal is given.

Transmission of shares

29. If a member dies the survivor or survivors where he was a joint holder, and his personal representatives where he was a sole holder or the only survivor of joint holders, shall be the only persons recognised by the company as having any title to his interest; but nothing herein contained shall release the estate of a deceased member from any liability in respect of any share which had been jointly held by him.

30. A person becoming entitled to a share in consequence of the death or bankruptcy of a member may, upon such evidence being produced as the directors may properly require, elect either to become the holder of the share or to have some person nominated by him registered as the transferee. If he elects to become the holder he shall give notice to the company to that effect. If he elects to have another person registered he shall execute an instrument of transfer of the share to that person. All the articles relating to the transfer of shares shall apply to the notice or instrument of transfer as if it were an instrument of transfer executed by the member and the death or bankruptcy of the member had not occurred.

31. A person becoming entitled to a share in consequence of the death or bankruptcy of a member shall have the rights to which he would be entitled if he were the holder of the share, except that he shall not, before being registered as the holder of the share, be entitled in respect of it to attend or vote at any meeting of the company or at any separate meeting of the holders of any class of shares in the company.

Alteration of share capital

32. The company may by ordinary resolution —

(a) increase its share capital by new shares of such amount as the resolution prescribes;
(b) consolidate and divide all or any of its share capital into shares of larger amount than its existing shares;
(c) subject to the provisions of the Act, sub-divide its shares, or any of them, into shares of smaller amount and the resolution may determine that, as between the shares resulting from the sub-division, any of them may have any preference or advantage as compared with the others; and
(d) cancel shares which, at the date of the passing of the resolution, have not been taken or agreed to be taken by any person and diminish the amount of its share capital by the amount of the shares so cancelled.

33. Whenever as a result of a consolidation of shares any members would become

entitled to fractions of a share, the directors may, on behalf of those members, sell the shares representing the fractions for the best price reasonably obtainable to any person (including, subject to the provisions of the Act, the company) and distribute the net proceeds of sale in due proportion among those members, and the directors may authorise some person to execute an instrument of transfer of the shares to, or in accordance with the directions of, the purchaser. The transferee shall not be bound to see to the application of the purchase money nor shall his title to the shares be affected by any irregularity in or invalidity of the proceedings in reference to the sale.

34. Subject to the provisions of the Act, the company may by special resolution reduce its share capital, any capital redemption reserve and any share premium account in any way.

Purchase of own shares

35. Subject to the provisions of the Act, the company may purchase its own shares (including any redeemable shares) and, if it is a private company, make a payment in respect of the redemption or purchase of its own shares otherwise than out of distributable profits of the company or the proceeds of a fresh issue of shares.

General meetings

36. All general meetings other than annual general meetings shall be called extraordinary general meetings.

37. The directors may call general meetings and, on the requisition of members pursuant to the provisions of the Act, shall forthwith proceed to convene an extraordinary general meeting for a date not later than eight weeks after receipt of the requisition. If there are not within the United Kingdom sufficient directors to call a general meeting, any director or any member of the company may call a general meeting.

Notice of general meetings

38. An annual general meeting and an extraordinary general meeting called for the passing of a special resolution or a resolution appointing a person as a director shall be called by at least twenty-one clear days' notice. All other extraordinary general meetings shall be called by at least fourteen clear days' notice but a general meeting may be called by shorter notice if it is so agreed –

(a) in the case of an annual general meeting, by all the members entitled to attend and vote thereat; and
(b) in the case of any other meeting by a majority in number of the members having a right to attend and vote being a majority together holding not less than ninety-five per cent. in nominal value of the shares giving that right.

The notice shall specify the time and place of the meeting and the general nature of the business to be transacted and, in the case of an annual general meeting, shall specify the meeting as such.

Subject to the provisions of the articles and to any restrictions imposed on any shares, the notice shall be given to all the members, to all persons entitled to a share in consequence of the death or bankruptcy of a member and to the directors and auditors.

39. The accidental omission to give notice of a meeting to, or the non-receipt of notice of a meeting by, any person entitled to receive notice shall not invalidate the proceedings at that meeting.

Proceedings at general meetings

40. No business shall be transacted at any meeting unless a quorum is present. Two persons entitled to vote upon the business to be transacted, each being a member or a proxy for a member or a duly authorised representative of a corporation, shall be a quorum.

41. If such a quorum is not present within half an hour from the time appointed for the meeting, or if during a meeting such a quorum ceases to be present, the meeting shall stand adjourned to the same day in the next week at the same time and place or to such time and place as the directors may determine.

42. The chairman, if any, of the board of directors or in his absence some other director nominated by the directors shall preside as chairman of the meeting, but if neither the chairman nor such other director (if any) be present within fifteen minutes after the time appointed for holding the meeting and willing to act, the directors present shall elect one of their number to be chairman and, if there is only one director present and willing to act, he shall be chairman.

43. If no director is willing to act as chairman, or if no director is present within fifteen minutes after the time appointed for holding the meeting, the members present and entitled to vote shall choose one of their number to be chairman.

44. A director shall, notwithstanding that he is not a member, be entitled to attend and speak at any general meeting and at any separate meeting of the holders of any class of shares in the company.

45. The chairman may, with the consent of a meeting at which a quorum is present (and shall if so directed by the meeting), adjourn the meeting from time to time and from place to place, but no business shall be transacted at an adjourned meeting other than business which might properly have been transacted at the meeting had the adjournment not taken place. When a meeting is adjourned for fourteen days or more, at least seven clear days' notice shall be given specifying the time and place of the adjourned meeting and the general nature of the business to be transacted. Otherwise it shall not be necessary to give any such notice.

46. A resolution put to the vote of a meeting shall be decided on a show of hands unless before, or on the declaration of the result of, the show of hands a poll is duly demanded. Subject to the provisions of the Act, a poll may be demanded –

- (a) by the chairman; or
- (b) by at least two members having the right to vote at the meeting; or;
- (c) by a member or members representing not less than one-tenth of the total voting rights of all the members having the right to vote at the meeting; or
- (d) by a member or members holding shares conferring a right to vote at the meeting being shares on which an aggregate sum has been paid up equal to not less than one-tenth of the total sum paid up on all the shares conferring that right;

and a demand by a person as proxy for a member shall be the same as a demand by the member.

47. Unless a poll is duly demanded a declaration by the chairman that a resolution has been carried or carried unanimously, or by a particular majority, or lost, or not carried by a particular majority and an entry to that effect in the minutes of the meeting shall be conclusive evidence of the fact without proof of the number or proportion of the votes recorded in favour of or against the resolution.

48. The demand for a poll may, before the poll is taken, be withdrawn but only with the consent of the chairman and a demand so withdrawn shall not be taken to have invalidated the result of a show of hands declared before the demand was made.

49. A poll shall be taken as the chairman directs and he may appoint scrutineers (who need not be members) and fix a time and place for declaring the result of the poll. The result of the poll shall be deemed to be the resolution of the meeting at which the poll was demanded.

50. In the case of an equality of votes, whether on a show of hands or on a poll, the chairman shall be entitled to a casting vote in addition to any other vote he may have.

51. A poll demanded on the election of a chairman or on a question of adjournment shall be taken forthwith. A poll demanded on any other question shall be taken either forthwith or at such time and place as the chairman directs not being more than thirty days after the poll is demanded. The demand for a poll shall not prevent the continuance of a meeting for the transaction of any business other than the question on which the poll was demanded. If a poll is demanded before the declaration of the result of a show of hands and the demand is duly withdrawn, the meeting shall continue as if the demand had not been made.

52. No notice need be given of a poll not taken forthwith if the time and place at which it is to be taken are announced at the meeting at which it is demanded. In any other case at least seven clear days' notice shall be given specifying the time and place at which the poll is to be taken.

53. A resolution in writing executed by or on behalf of each member who would have been entitled to vote upon it if it had been proposed at a general meeting at which he was present shall be as effectual as if it had been passed at a general meeting duly convened and held and may consist of several instruments in the like form each executed by or on behalf of one or more members.

Votes of members

54. Subject to any rights or restrictions attached to any shares, on a show of hands every member who (being an individual) is present in person or (being a corporation) is present by a duly authorised representative, not being himself a member entitled to vote, shall have one vote and on a poll every member shall have one vote for every share of which he is the holder.

55. In the case of joint holders the vote of the senior who tenders a vote, whether in person or by proxy, shall be accepted to the exclusion of the votes of the other joint holders; and seniority shall be determined by the order in which the names of the holders stand in the register of members.

56. A member in respect of whom an order has been made by any court having jurisdiction (whether in the United Kingdom or elsewhere) in matters concerning mental

disorder may vote, whether on a show of hands or on a poll, by his receiver, curator bonis or other person authorised in that behalf appointed by that court, and any such receiver, curator bonis or other person may, on a poll, vote by proxy. Evidence to the satisfaction of the directors of the authority of the person claiming to exercise the right to vote shall be deposited at the office, or at such other place as is specified in accordance with the articles for the deposit of instruments of proxy, not less than 48 hours before the time appointed for holding the meeting or adjourned meeting at which the right to vote is to be exercised and in default the right to vote shall not be exercisable.

57. No member shall vote at any general meeting or at any separate meeting of the holders of any class of shares in the company, either in person or by proxy, in respect of any share held by him unless all moneys presently payable by him in respect of that share have been paid.

58. No objection shall be raised to the qualification of any voter except at the meeting or adjourned meeting at which the vote objected to is tendered, and every vote not disallowed at the meeting shall be valid. Any objection made in due time shall be referred to the chairman whose decision shall be final and conclusive.

59. On a poll votes may be given either personally or by proxy. A member may appoint more than one proxy to attend on the same occasion.

60. An instrument appointing a proxy shall be in writing, executed by or on behalf of the appointor and shall be in the following form (or in a form as near thereto as circumstances allow or in any other form which is usual or which the directors may approve) –

'   PLC/Limited
I/We,   , of   , being a member/members of the above-named company, hereby appoint   of   , or failing him,   of   , as my/our proxy to vote in my/our name[s] and on my/our behalf at the annual/extraordinary general meeting of the company to be held on   19   , and at any adjournment thereof.
Signed on   19   .'

61. Where it is desired to afford members an opportunity of instructing the proxy how he shall act the instrument appointing a proxy shall be in the following form (or in a form as near thereto as circumstances allow or in any other form which is usual or which the directors may approve) –

'   PLC/Limited
I/We,   , of   , being a member/members of the above-named company, hereby appoint   of   , or failing him,   of   , as my/our proxy to vote in my/our name[s] and on my/our behalf at the annual/extraordinary general meeting of the company to be held on   19   , and at any adjournment thereof.

This form is to be used in respect of the resolutions mentioned below as follows:
Resolution No. 1 *for *against.
Resolution No. 2 *for *against.
* Strike out whichever is not desired.
Unless otherwise instructed, the proxy may vote as he thinks fit or abstain from voting.
Signed this   day of   19   .'

62. The instrument appointing a proxy and any authority under which it is executed or a

copy of such authority certified notarially or in some other way approved by the directors may –

(a) be deposited at the office or at such other place within the United Kingdom as is specified in the notice convening the meeting or in any instrument of proxy sent out by the company in relation to the meeting not less than 48 hours before the time for holding the meeting or adjourned meeting at which the person named in the instrument proposes to vote; or
(b) in the case of a poll taken more than 48 hours after it is demanded, be deposited as aforesaid after the poll has been demanded and not less than 24 hours before the time appointed for the taking of the poll; or
(c) where the poll is not taken forthwith but is taken not more than 48 hours after it was demanded, be delivered at the meeting at which the poll was demanded to the chairman or to the secretary or to any director;

and an instrument of proxy which is not deposited or delivered in a manner so permitted shall be invalid.

63. A vote given or poll demanded by proxy or by the duly authorised representative of a corporation shall be valid notwithstanding the previous determination of the authority of the person voting or demanding a poll unless notice of the determination was received by the company at the office or at such other place at which the instrument of proxy was duly deposited before the commencement of the meeting or adjourned meeting at which the vote is given or the poll demanded or (in the case of a poll taken otherwise than on the same day as the meeting or adjourned meeting) the time appointed for taking the poll.

Number of directors

64. Unless otherwise determined by ordinary resolution, the number of directors (other than alternate directors) shall not be subject to any maximum but shall be not less than two.

Alternate directors

65. Any director (other than an alternate director) may appoint any other director, or any other person approved by resolution of the directors and willing to act, to be an alternate director and may remove from office an alternate director so appointed by him.

66. An alternate director shall be entitled to receive notice of all meetings of directors and of all meetings of committees of directors of which his appointor is a member, to attend and vote at any such meeting at which the director appointing him is not personally present, and generally to perform all the functions of his appointor as a director in his absence but shall not be entitled to receive any remuneration from the company for his services as an alternate director. But it shall not be necessary to give notice of such a meeting to an alternate director who is absent from the United Kingdom.

67. An alternate director shall cease to be an alternate director if his appointor ceases to be a director; but, if a director retires by rotation or otherwise but is reappointed or deemed to have been reappointed at the meeting at which he retires, any appointment of an alternate director made by him which was in force immediately prior to his retirement shall continue after his reappointment.

68. Any appointment or removal of an alternate director shall be by notice to the company signed by the director making or revoking the appointment or in any other manner approved by the directors.

69. Save as otherwise provided in the articles, an alternate director shall be deemed for all purposes to be a director and shall alone be responsible for his own acts and defaults and he shall not be deemed to be the agent of the director appointing him.

Powers of directors

70. Subject to the provisions of the Act, the memorandum and the articles and to any directions given by special resolution, the business of the company shall be managed by the directors who may exercise all the powers of the company. No alteration of the memorandum or articles and no such direction shall invalidate any prior act of the directors which would have been valid if that alteration had not been made or that direction had not been given. The powers given by this regulation shall not be limited by any special power given to the directors by the articles and a meeting of directors at which a quorum is present may exercise all powers exercisable by the directors.

71. The directors may, by power of attorney or otherwise, appoint any person to be the agent of the company for such purposes and on such conditions as they determine, including authority for the agent to delegate all or any of his powers.

Delegation of directors' powers

72. The directors may delegate any of their powers to any committee consisting of one or more directors. They may also delegate to any managing director or any director holding any other executive office such of their powers as they consider desirable to be exercised by him. Any such delegation may be made subject to any conditions the directors may impose, and either collaterally with or to the exclusion of their own powers and may be revoked or altered. Subject to any such conditions, the proceedings of a committee with two or more members shall be governed by the articles regulating the proceedings of directors so far as they are capable of applying.

Appointment and retirement of directors

73. At the first annual general meeting all the directors shall retire from office, and at every subsequent annual general meeting one-third of the directors who are subject to retirement by rotation or, if their number is not three or a multiple of three, the number nearest to one-third shall retire from office; but, if there is only one director who is subject to retirement by rotation, he shall retire.

74. Subject to the provisions of the Act, the directors to retire by rotation shall be those who have been longest in office since their last appointment or reappointment, but as between persons who became or were last reappointed directors on the same day those to retire shall (unless they otherwise agree among themselves) be determined by lot.

75. If the company, at the meeting at which a director retires by rotation, does not fill the vacancy the retiring director shall, if willing to act, be deemed to have been reappointed unless at the meeting it is resolved not to fill the vacancy or unless a resolution for the reappointment of the director is put to the meeting and lost.

76. No person other than a director retiring by rotation shall be appointed or re-appointed a director at any general meeting unless –

(a) he is recommended by the directors; or
(b) not less than fourteen nor more than thirty-five clear days before the date appointed for the meeting, notice executed by a member qualified to vote at the meeting has been given to the company of the intention to propose that person for appointment or reappointment stating the particulars which would, if he were so appointed or reappointed, be required to be included in the company's register of directors together with notice executed by that person of his willingness to be appointed or reappointed.

77. Not less than seven nor more than twenty-eight clear days before the date appointed for holding a general meeting notice shall be given to all who are entitled to receive notice of the meeting of any person (other than a director retiring by rotation at the meeting) who is recommended by the directors for appointment or reappointment as a director at the meeting or in respect of whom notice has been duly given to the company of the intention to propose him at the meeting for appointment or reappointment as a director. The notice shall give the particulars of that person which would, if he were so appointed or reappointed, be required to be included in the company's register of directors.

78. Subject as aforesaid, the company may by ordinary resolution appoint a person who is willing to act to be a director either to fill a vacancy or as an additional director and may also determine the rotation in which any additional directors are to retire.

79. The directors may appoint a person who is willing to act to be a director, either to fill a vacancy or as an additional director, provided that the appointment does not cause the number of directors to exceed any number fixed by or in accordance with the articles as the maximum number of directors. A director so appointed shall hold office only until the next following annual general meeting and shall not be taken into account in determining the directors who are to retire by rotation at the meeting. If not reappointed at such annual general meeting, he shall vacate office at the conclusion thereof.

80. Subject as aforesaid, a director who retires at an annual general meeting may, if willing to act, be reappointed. If he is not reappointed, he shall retain office until the meeting appoints someone in his place, or if it does not do so, until the end of the meeting.

Disqualification and removal of directors

81. The office of a director shall be vacated if –

(a) he ceases to be a director by virtue of any provision of the Act or he becomes prohibited by law from being a director; or
(b) he becomes bankrupt or makes any arrangement or composition with his creditors generally; or
(c) he is, or may be, suffering from mental disorder and either –
    (i) he is admitted to hospital in pursuance of an application for admission for treatment under the Mental Health Act 1983 or, in Scotland, an application for admission under the Mental Health (Scotland) Act 1960, or
    (ii) an order is made by a court having jurisdiction (whether in the United Kingdom or elsewhere) in matters concerning mental disorder for his deten-

tion or for the appointment of a receiver, curator bonis or other person to exercise powers with respect to his property or affairs; or

(d) he resigns his office by notice to the company; or
(e) he shall for more than six consecutive months have been absent without permission of the directors from meetings of directors held during that period and the directors resolve that his office be vacated.

Remuneration of directors

82. The directors shall be entitled to such remuneration as the company may by ordinary resolution determine and, unless the resolution provides otherwise, the remuneration shall be deemed to accrue from day to day.

Directors' expenses

83. The directors may be paid all travelling, hotel, and other expenses properly incurred by them in connection with their attendance at meetings of directors or committees of directors or general meetings or separate meetings of the holders of any class of shares or of debentures of the company or otherwise in connection with the discharge of their duties.

Directors' appointments and interests

84. Subject to the provisions of the Act, the directors may appoint one or more of their number to the office of managing director or to any other executive office under the company and may enter into an agreement or arrangement with any director for his employment by the company or for the provision by him of any services outside the scope of the ordinary duties of a director. Any such appointment, agreement or arrangement may be made upon such terms as the directors determine and they may remunerate any such director for his services as they think fit. Any appointment of a director to an executive office shall terminate if he ceases to be a director but without prejudice to any claim to damages for breach of the contract of service between the director and the company. A managing director and a director holding any other executive office shall not be subject to retirement by rotation.

85. Subject to the provisions of the Act, and provided that he has disclosed to the directors the nature and extent of any material interest of his, a director notwithstanding his office –

(a) may be a party to, or otherwise interested in, any transaction or arrangement with the company or in which the company is otherwise interested;
(b) may be a director or other officer of, or employed by, or a party to any transaction or arrangement with, or otherwise interested in, any body corporate promoted by the company or in which the company is otherwise interested; and
(c) shall not, by reason of his office, be accountable to the company for any benefit which he derives from any such office or employment or from any such transaction or arrangement or from any interest in any such body corporate and no such transaction or arrangement shall be liable to be avoided on the ground of any such interest or benefit.

86. For the purposes of regulation 85 –

(a) a general notice given to the directors that a director is to be regarded as having an interest of the nature and extent specified in the notice in any transaction or arrangement in which a specified person or class of persons is interested shall be deemed to be a disclosure that the director has an interest in any such transaction of the nature and extent so specified; and
(b) an interest of which a director has no knowledge and of which it is unreasonable to expect him to have a knowledge shall not be treated as an interest of his.

Directors' gratuities and pensions

87. The directors may provide benefits, whether by the payment of gratuities or pensions or by insurance or otherwise, for any director who has held but no longer holds any executive office or employment with the company or with any body corporate which is or has been a subsidiary of the company or a predecessor in business of the company or of any such subsidiary, and for any member of his family (including a spouse and a former spouse) or any person who is or was dependent on him, and may (as well before as after he ceases to hold such office or employment) contribute to any fund and pay premiums for the purchase or provision of any such benefit.

Proceedings of directors

88. Subject to the provisions of the articles, the directors may regulate their proceedings as they think fit. A director may, and the secretary at the request of a director shall, call a meeting of the directors. It shall not be necessary to give notice of a meeting to a director who is absent from the United Kingdom. Questions arising at a meeting shall be decided by a majority of votes. In the case of an equality of votes, the chairman shall have a second or casting vote. A director who is also an alternate director shall be entitled in the absence of his appointor to a separate vote on behalf of his appointor in addition to his own vote.

89. The quorum for the transaction of the business of the directors may be fixed by the directors and unless so fixed at any other number shall be two. A person who holds office only as an alternate director shall, if his appointor is not present, be counted in the quorum.

90. The continuing directors or a sole continuing director may act notwithstanding any vacancies in their number, but, if the number of directors is less than the number fixed as the quorum, the continuing directors or director may act only for the purpose of filing vacancies or of calling a general meeting.

91. The directors may appoint one of their number to be the chairman of the board of directors and may at any time remove him from that office. Unless he is unwilling to do so, the director so appointed shall preside at every meeting of directors at which he is present. But if there is no director holding that office, or if the director holding it is unwilling to preside or is not present within five minutes after the time appointed for the meeting, the directors present may appoint one of their number to be chairman of the meeting.

92. All acts done by a meeting of directors, or of a committee of directors, or by a person

acting as a director shall, notwithstanding that it be afterwards discovered that there was a defect in the appointment of any director or that any of them were disqualified from holding office, or had vacated office, or were not entitled to vote, be as valid as if every such person had been duly appointed and was qualified and had continued to be a director and had been entitled to vote.

93. A resolution in writing signed by all the directors entitled to receive notice of a meeting of directors or of a committee of directors shall be as valid and effectual as if it had been passed at a meeting of directors or (as the case may be) a committee of directors duly convened and held and may consist of several documents in the like form each signed by one or more directors; but a resolution signed by an alternate director need not also be signed by his appointor and, if it is signed by a director who has appointed an alternate director, it need not be signed by the alternate director in that capacity.

94. Save as otherwise provided by the articles, a director shall not vote at a meeting of directors or of a committee of directors on any resolution concerning a matter in which he has, directly or indirectly, an interest or duty which is material and which conflicts or may conflict with the interests of the company unless his interest or duty arises only because the case falls within one or more of the following paragraphs –

(a) the resolution relates to the giving to him of a guarantee, security, or indemnity in respect of money lent to, or an obligation incurred by him for the benefit of, the company or any of its subsidiaries;
(b) the resolution relates to the giving to a third party of a guarantee, security, or indemnity in respect of an obligation of the company or any of its subsidiaries for which the director has assumed responsibility in whole or part and whether alone or jointly with others under a guarantee or indemnity or by the giving of security;
(c) his interest arises by virtue of his subscribing or agreeing to subscribe for any shares, debentures or other securities of the company or any of its subsidiaries, or by virtue of his being, or intending to become, a participant in the underwriting or sub-underwriting of an offer of any such shares, debentures, or other securities by the company or any of its subsidiaries for subscription, purchase or exchange;
(d) the resolution relates in any way to a retirement benefits scheme which has been approved, or is conditional upon approval, by the Board of Inland Revenue for taxation purposes.

For the purposes of this regulation, an interest of a person who is, for any purpose of the Act (excluding any statutory modification thereof not in force when this regulation becomes binding on the company), connected with a director shall be treated as an interest of the director and, in relation to an alternate director, an interest of his appointor shall be treated as an interest of the alternate director without prejudice to any interest which the alternate director has otherwise.

95. A director shall not be counted in the quorum present at a meeting in relation to a resolution on which he is not entitled to vote.

96. The company may by ordinary resolution suspend or relax to any extent, either generally or in respect of any particular matter, any provision of the articles prohibiting a director from voting at a meeting of directors or of a committee of directors.

97. Where proposals are under consideration concerning the appointment of two or more directors to offices or employments with the company or any body corporate in which the company is interested the proposals may be divided and considered in relation to each

director separately and (provided he is not for another reason precluded from voting) each of the directors concerned shall be entitled to vote and be counted in the quorum in respect of each resolution except that concerning his own appointment.

98. If a question arises at a meeting of directors or of a committee of directors as to the right of a director to vote, the question may, before the conclusion of the meeting, be referred to the chairman of the meeting and his ruling in relation to any director other than himself shall be final and conclusive.

Secretary

99. Subject to the provisions of the Act, the secretary shall be appointed by the directors for such term, at such remuneration and upon such conditions as they may think fit; and any secretary so appointed may be removed by them.

Minutes

100. The directors shall cause minutes to be made in books kept for the purpose –

(a) of all appointments of officers made by the directors; and
(b) of all proceedings at meetings of the company, of the holders of any class of shares in the company, and of the directors, and of committees of directors, including the names of the directors present at each such meeting.

The seal

101. The seal shall only be used by the authority of the directors or of a committee of directors authorised by the directors. The directors may determine who shall sign any instrument to which the seal is affixed and unless otherwise so determined it shall be signed by a director and by the secretary or by a second director.

Dividends

102. Subject to the provisions of the Act, the company may by ordinary resolution declare dividends in accordance with the respective rights of the members, but no dividend shall exceed the amount recommended by the directors.

103. Subject to the provisions of the Act, the directors may pay interim dividends if it appears to them that they are justified by the profits of the company available for distribution. If the share capital is divided into different classes, the directors may pay interim dividends on shares which confer deferred or non-preferred rights with regard to dividend as well as on shares which confer preferential rights with regard to dividend, but no interim dividend shall be paid on shares carrying deferred or non-preferred rights if, at the time of payment, any preferential dividend is in arrear. The directors may also pay at intervals settled by them any dividend payable at a fixed rate if it appears to them that the profits available for distribution justify the payment. Provided the directors act in good faith they shall not incur any liability to the holders of shares conferring preferred rights for any loss they may suffer by the lawful payment of an interim dividend on any shares having deferred or non-preferred rights.

104. Except as otherwise provided by the rights attached to shares, all dividends shall be declared and paid according to the amounts paid up on the shares on which the dividend is paid. All dividends shall be apportioned and paid proportionately to the amounts paid up on the shares during any portion or portions of the period in respect of which the dividend is paid; but, if any share is issued on terms providing that it shall rank for dividend as from a particular date, that share shall rank for dividend accordingly.

105. A general meeting declaring a dividend may, upon the recommendation of the directors, direct that it shall be satisfied wholly or partly by the distribution of assets and, where any difficulty arises in regard to the distribution, the directors may settle the same and in particular may issue fractional certificates and fix the value for distribution of any assets and may determine that cash shall be paid to any member upon the footing of the value so fixed in order to adjust the rights of members and may vest any assets in trustees.

106. Any dividend or other moneys payable in respect of a share may be paid by cheque sent by post to the registered address of the person entitled or, if two or more persons are the holders of the share or are jointly entitled to it by reason of the death or bankruptcy of the holder, to the registered address of that one of those persons who is first named in the register of members or to such person and to such address as the person or persons entitled may in writing direct. Every cheque shall be made payable to the order of the person or persons entitled or to such other person as the person or persons entitled may in writing direct and payment of the cheque shall be a good discharge to the company. Any joint holder or other person jointly entitled to a share as aforesaid may give receipts for any dividend or other moneys payable in respect of the share.

107. No dividend or other moneys payable in respect of a share shall bear interest against the company unless otherwise provided by the rights attached to the share.

108. Any dividend which has remained unclaimed for twelve years from the date when it became due for payment shall, if the directors so resolve, be forfeited and cease to remain owing by the company.

Accounts

109. No member shall (as such) have any right of inspecting any accounting records or other book or document of the company except as conferred by statute or authorised by the directors or by ordinary resolution of the company.

Capitalisation of profits

110. The directors may with the authority of an ordinary resolution of the company –

(a) subject as hereinafter provided, resolve to capitalise any undivided profits of the company not required for paying any preferential dividend (whether or not they are available for distribution) or any sum standing to the credit of the company's share premium account or capital redemption reserve;

(b) appropriate the sum resolved to be capitalised to the members who would have been entitled to it if it were distributed by way of dividend and in the same proportions and apply such sum on their behalf either in or towards paying up the amounts, if any, for the time being unpaid on any shares held by them respectively, or in paying up in full unissued shares or debentures of the company of a nominal amount equal to that sum, and allot the shares or debentures credited as fully paid to those members, or as they may direct, in those proportions, or partly in one way and partly in the other: but the share premium account, the capital redemption reserve, and any profits which are not available for distribution may, for the purposes of this regulation, only be applied in paying up unissued shares to be allotted to members credited as fully paid;

(c) make such provision by the issue of fractional certificates or by payment in cash or otherwise as they determine in the case of shares or debentures becoming distributable under this regulation in fractions; and

(d) authorise any person to enter on behalf of all the members concerned into an agreement with the company providing for the allotment to them respectively, credited as fully paid, of any shares or debentures to which they are entitled upon such capitalisation, any agreement made under such authority being binding on all such members.

Notices

111. Any notice to be given to or by any person pursuant to the articles shall be in writing except that a notice calling a meeting of the directors need not be in writing.

112. The company may give any notice to a member either personally or by sending it by post in a prepaid envelope addressed to the member at his registered address or by leaving it at that address. In the case of joint holders of a share, all notices shall be given to the joint holder whose name stands first in the register of members in respect of the joint holding and notice so given shall be sufficient notice to all the joint holders. A member whose registered address is not within the United Kingdom and who gives to the company an address within the United Kingdom at which notices may be given to him shall be entitled to have notices given to him at that address, but otherwise no such member shall be entitled to receive any notice from the company.

113. A member present, either in person or by proxy, at any meeting of the company or of the holders of any class of shares in the company shall be deemed to have received notice of the meeting and, where requisite, of the purposes for which it was called.

114. Every person who becomes entitled to a share shall be bound by any notice in respect of that share which, before his name is entered in the register of members, has been duly given to a person from whom he derives his title.

115. Proof that an envelope containing a notice was properly addressed, prepaid and posted shall be conclusive evidence that the notice was given. A notice shall be deemed to be given at the expiration of 48 hours after the envelope containing it was posted.

116. A notice may be given by the company to the persons entitled to a share in consequence of the death or bankruptcy of a member by sending or delivering it, in any manner authorised by the articles for the giving of notice to a member, addressed to them by name, or by the title of representatives of the deceased, or trustee of the bankrupt or by any like description at the address, if any, within the United Kingdom supplied for that purpose by the person claiming to be so entitled. Until such an address has been supplied, a notice may be given in any manner in which it might have been given if the death or bankruptcy had not occurred.

Winding up

117. If the company is wound up, the liquidator may, with the sanction of an extraordinary resolution of the company and any other sanction required by the Act, divide among the members in specie the whole or any part of the assets of the company and may, for that purpose, value any assets and determine how the division shall be carried out as between the members or different classes of members. The liquidator may, with the like sanction, vest the whole or any part of the assets in trustees upon such trusts for the benefit of the members as he with the like sanction determines, but no member shall be compelled to accept any assets upon which there is a liability.

Indemnity

118. Subject to the provisions of the Act but without prejudice to any indemnity to which a director may otherwise be entitled, every director or other officer or auditor of the company shall be indemnified out of the assets of the company against any liability incurred by him in defending any proceedings, whether civil or criminal, in which judgement is given in his favour or in which he is acquitted or in connection with any application in which relief is granted to him by the court from liability for negligence, default, breach of duty or breach of trust in relation to the affairs of the company.

Table B

A Private Company Limited by Shares

Memorandum of Association

1. The company's name is 'The South Wales Motor Transport Company cyfyngedig'.

2. The company's registered office is to be situated in Wales.

3. The company's objects are the carriage of passengers and goods in motor vehicles between such places as the company may from time to time determine and the doing of all such other things as are incidental or conducive to the attainment of that object.

4. The liability of the members is limited.

5. The company's share capital is £50,000 divided into 50,000 shares of £1 each.

We, the subscribers to this memorandum of association, wish to be formed into a company pursuant to this memorandum; and we agree to take the number of shares shown opposite our respective names.

Names and Addresses of Subscribers		Number of shares taken by each Subscriber
(a) Thomas Jones, 138 Mountfield Street Tredegar.		1
(b) Mary Evans, 19 Merthyr Road, Aberystwyth.		1
	Total shares taken	2

Dated 19 .

Witness to the above signatures,
Anne Brown, 'Woodlands', Fieldside Road, Bryn Mawr.

Table C

A Company Limited by Guarantee and Not Having a Share Capital

Memorandum of Association

1. The company's name is 'The Dundee School Association Limited'.

2. The company's registered office is to be situated in Scotland.

3. The company's objects are the carrying on of a school for boys and girls in Dundee and the doing of all such other things as are incidental or conducive to the attainment of that object.

4. The liability of the members is limited.

5. Every member of the company undertakes to contribute such amount as may be required (not exceeding £100) to the company's assets if it should be wound up while he is a member or within one year after he ceases to be a member, for payment of the company's debts and liabilities contracted before he ceases to be a member, and of the costs, charges and expenses of winding up, and for the adjustment of the rights of the contributories among themselves.

We, the subscribers to this memorandum of association, wish to be formed into a company pursuant to this memorandum.

Names and Addresses of Subscribers.

(a) Kenneth Brodie, 14 Bute Street, Dundee.
(b) Ian Davis, 2 Burns Avenue, Dundee.

Dated 19 .

Witness to the above signatures.
Anne Brown, 149 Princes Street, Edinburgh.

Articles of Association

Preliminary

1. Regulations 2 to 35 inclusive, 54, 55, 57, 59, 102 to 108 inclusive, 110, 114, 116 and 117 of Table A, shall not apply to the company but the articles hereinafter contained and, subject to the modifications hereinafter expressed, the remaining regulations of Table A shall constitute the articles of association of the company.

Interpretation

2. In regulation 1 of Table A, the definition of 'the holder' shall be omitted.

Members

3. The subscribers to the memorandum of association of the company and such other persons as are admitted to membership in accordance with the articles shall be members of the company. No person shall be admitted a member of the company unless he is approved by the directors. Every person who wishes to become a member shall deliver to the company an application for membership in such form as the directors require executed by him.

4. A member may at any time withdraw from the company by giving at least seven clear days' notice to the company. Membership shall not be transferable and shall cease on death.

Notice of general meetings

5. In regulation 38 of Table A –

  (a) in paragraph (b) the words 'of the total voting rights at the meeting of all the members' shall be substituted for 'in nominal value of the shares giving that right' and
  (b) the words 'The notice shall be given to all the members and to the directors and auditors' shall be substituted for the last sentence.

Proceedings at general meetings

6. The words 'and at any separate meeting of the holders of any class of shares in the company' shall be omitted from regulation 44 of Table A.

7. Paragraph (d) of regulation 46 of Table A shall be omitted.

Votes of members

8. On a show of hands every member present in person shall have one vote. On a poll every member present in person or by proxy shall have one vote.

Directors' expenses

9. The words 'of any class of shares or' shall be omitted from regulation 83 of Table A.

Proceedings of directors

10. In paragraph (c) of regulation 94 of Table A the word 'debentures' shall be substituted for the words 'shares, debentures or other securities' in both places where they occur.

Minutes

11. The words 'of the holders of any class of shares in the company' shall be omitted from regulation 100 of Table A.

Notices

12. The second sentence of regulation 112 of Table A shall be omitted.

13. The words 'or of the holders of any class of shares in the company' shall be omitted from regulation 113 of Table A.

Table D

Part I

A Public Company Limited by Guarantee and Having a Share Capital

Memorandum of Association

1. The company's name is 'Gwestai Glyndwr, cwmni cyfyngedig cyhoeddus'.

2. The company is to be a public company.

3. The company's registered office is to be situated in Wales.

4. The company's objects are facilitating travelling in Wales by providing hotels and conveyances by sea and by land for the accommodation of travellers and the doing of all such other things as are incidental or conducive to the attainment of those objects.

5. The liability of the members is limited.

6. Every member of the company undertakes to contribute such amount as may be required (not exceeding £100) to the company's assets if it should be wound up while he is a member or within one year after he ceases to be a member, for payment of the company's debts and liabilities contracted before he ceases to be a member, and of the costs, charges and expenses of winding up, and for the adjustment of the rights of the contributories among themselves.

7. The company's share capital is £50,000 divided into 50,000 shares of £1 each.

We, the subscribers to this memorandum of association, wish to be formed into a company pursuant to this memorandum; and we agree to take the number of shares shown opposite our respective names.

Names and Addresses of Subscribers	Number of shares taken by each Subscriber
(a) Thomas Jones, 138 Mountfield Street, Tredegar.	1
(b) Andrew Smith, 19 Merthyr Road, Aberystwyth.	1
Total shares taken	2

Dated 19 .

Witness to the above signatures,
Anne Brown, 'Woodlands', Fieldside Road, Bryn Mawr.

Part II

A Private Company Limited by Guarantee and Having a Share Capital

Memorandum of Association

1. The company's name is 'The Highland Hotel Company Limited'.

2. The company's registered office is to be situated in Scotland.

3. The company's objects are facilitating travelling in the Highlands of Scotland by providing hotels and conveyances by sea and by land for the accommodation of travellers and the doing of all such other things as are incidental or conducive to the attainment of those objects.

4. The liability of the members is limited.

5. Every member of the company undertakes to contribute such amount as may be required (not exceeding £100) to the company's assets if it should be wound up while he is a member or within one year after he ceases to be a member, for payment of the company's debts and liabilities contracted before he ceases to be a member, and of the costs, charges and expenses of winding up, and for the adjustment of the rights of the contributories among themselves.

6. The company's share capital is £50,000 divided into 50,000 shares of £1 each.

We, the subscribers to this memorandum of association, wish to be formed into a company pursuant to this memorandum; and we agree to take the number of shares shown opposite our respective names.

Names and Addresses of Subscribers		Number of shares taken by each Subscriber
(a) Kenneth Brodie, 14 Bute Street, Dundee.		1
(b) Ian Davis, 2 Burns Avenue, Dundee.		1
	Total shares taken	2

Dated 19 .

Witness to the above signatures,
Anne Brown, 149 Princes Street, Edinburgh.

Part III

A Company (Public or Private) Limited by Guarantee and Having a Share Capital

Articles of Association

The regulations of Table A shall constitute the articles of association of the company.

Table E

An Unlimited Company Having a Share Capital

Memorandum of Association

1. The company's name is 'The Woodford Engineering Company'.

2. The company's registered office is to be situated in England and Wales.

3. The company's objects are the working of certain patented inventions relating to the application of microchip technology to the improvement of food processing, and the doing of all such other things as are incidental or conducive to the attainment of that object.

We, the subscribers to this memorandum of association, wish to be formed into a company pursuant to this memorandum; and we agree to take the number of shares shown opposite our respective names.

Names and Addresses of Subscribers		Number of shares taken by each Subscriber
(a) Brian Smith, 24 Nibley Road, Wotton-under-Edge, Gloucestershire.		3
(b) William Green, 278 High Street, Chipping Sodbury, Avon.		5
	Total shares taken	8

Dated 19 .

Witness to the above signatures,
Anne Brown, 108 Park Way, Bristol 8.

Articles of Association

1. Regulations 3, 32, 34 and 35 of Table A shall not apply to the company, but the articles hereinafter contained and, subject to the modification hereinafter expressed, the remaining regulations of Table A shall constitute the articles of association of the company.

2. The words 'at least seven clear days' notice' shall be substituted for the words 'at least fourteen clear days' notice' in regulation 38 of Table A.

3. The share capital of the company is £20,000 divided into 20,000 shares of £1 each.

4. The company may by special resolution –

(a) increase the share capital by such sum to be divided into shares of such amount as the resolution may prescribe;
(b) consolidate and divide all or any of its share capital into shares of a larger amount than its existing shares;

(c) subdivide its shares, or any of them, into shares of a smaller amount than its existing shares;
(d) cancel any shares which at the date of the passing of the resolution have not been taken or agreed to be taken by any person;
(e) reduce its share capital and any share premium account in any way.

Table F

A Public Company Limited by Shares

Memorandum of Association

1. The company's name is 'Western Electronics Public Limited Company'.

2. The company is to be a public company.

3. The company's registered office is to be situated in England and Wales.

4. The company's objects are the manufacture and development of such descriptions of electronic equipment, instruments and appliances as the company may from time to time determine, and the doing of all such other things as are incidental or conducive to the attainment of that object.

5. The liability of the members is limited.

6. The company's share capital is £5,000,000 divided into 5,000,000 shares of £1 each.

We, the subscribers to this memorandum of association, wish to be formed into a company pursuant to this memorandum; and we agree to take the number of shares shown opposite our respective names.

Names and Addresses of Subscribers	Number of shares taken by each Subscriber
(a) James White, 12 Broadmead, Birmingham.	1
(b) Patrick Smith, 145A Huntley House, London Wall, London EC2.	1
Total shares taken	2

Dated 19 .

Witness to the above signatures,
Anne Brown, 13 Hute Street, London WC2.

EDITOR'S NOTE

Section 128 of the Companies Act 1989 inserts a new s 8A into the Companies Act 1985, enabling the Secretary of State to prescribe, by statutory instrument, a Table G containing articles of association appropriate for a partnership company, that is a company limited by shares whose shares are intended to be held to a substantial extent, for or on behalf of its employees. No such table has yet (March 1991) been prescribed.

Appendix 2

Jordans Standard Form of Memorandum and Articles of Association for a Private Limited Company

Settled by Richard Sykes QC and Catherine Roberts of Lincoln's Inn, Barristers at Law

Explanatory Notes

Introduction

This form sets out and comments on a specimen draft memorandum and articles of association for a private company limited by shares under the Companies Act 1985, as amended by the provisions of the Companies Act 1989, s 110, which provides for a company to have general commercial objects and which came into force on 4 February 1991. The objects set out on pages 383 to 386 are a suggested format for use now that the section is operative.

For the purposes of registration, copies of the final draft must be printed for signature by subscribers and for supplying to members in accordance with s 19 of the Companies Act 1985.

Commentary on the form

Notes to Memorandum

Clause 2 The country within Great Britain in which the registered office is situated must be stated – either 'England and Wales' or 'Scotland'. Alternatively, a Welsh registered office may be specified and the Welsh words 'cyfyngedig' or 'cyf' substituted for 'limited' or 'ltd' respectively in the name of the company. The intended situation of the registered office will form part of the Statement of Particulars (Form 10) filed with the Registrar of Companies as part of the incorporation procedure.

Clause 3 – Section 110 of the Companies Act 1989, which came into force on 4 February 1991, inserts a new s 3A into the Companies Act 1985. Section 3A provides that company's memorandum states that where the object of the company is to carry on business as a general commercial company (as set out in the new clause on page 383 at paragraph 3(i)) the object of the company is to carry on any trade or business whatsoever, and the company has power to do all things as are incidental or conducive to the carrying on of any trade or business by it. Section 3A draws a clear distinction between objects and powers and the proper construction of this section cannot be to exclude additional powers. Accordingly, if the wording set out in s 3A(a) is used, it would be sensible to add the wording set out in paragraph 3(ii) to the new clause on page 383, followed by the wording of paragraphs (a) onwards or use other similar means to ensure that provisions in the company's memorandum are sufficient for its purposes.

Clause 3(a) – Law prior to s 110 of the Companies Act 1989 (see Introduction). A suitable 'main objects' clause reflecting the principal business to be carried on by the company was inserted as Clause 3(a). This needs to be carefully and comprehensively drafted, a specimen for which is set out below. This type of main objects clause may still be used and in some circumstances will be more suitable than a general commercial object under s 110.

If an existing business or shares in an existing company are being acquired, reference to such acquisition may be desirable.

Specimen 'Main Objects' Clause

3. The company's objects are:
   (a) To create, establish and maintain an organisation for the export, import, introduction, sale, purchase, distribution, advertising or marketing of products, goods, wares and merchandise of every description; to carry on all or any of the businesses of export marketing specialists, market research advisers and consultants, mail order specialists, manufacturers' agents and representatives, importers and exporters, commission agents, general merchants and traders; and to participate in, undertake, perform and carry out all kinds of commercial, industrial, trading and financial operations and enterprises; and to carry out all of the operations performed by commission and general agents, export, import and general merchants, shippers, traders, capitalists and financiers, either on the company's own account or otherwise; and to carry on all or any of the businesses of haulage and transport contractors, garage proprietors and owners, operators, hirers and letters on hire of, and dealers in motor and other vehicles, conveyances and craft of every description, and all plant, machinery, fittings, accessories and stores required in connection therewith or in the maintenance thereof.

The remaining part of Clause 3 sets out additional objects which are likely to be applicable and necessary for any trading company. It is necessary for these or equivalent clauses to be set out to enable a company to carry out such objects or exercise such powers. These may be identical in format to paragraphs (a) to (v) inclusive, but in the articles of association, clause 10, in so far as it cross-refers to the memorandum, will also require amendment. The remainder of Clause 3 might then be as follows.

'(w) To do all such other things as may be deemed incidental or conducive to the attainment of the Company's objects or any of them.

AND so that:—

(1) None of the objects set forth in any sub-clause of this Clause shall be restrictively construed but the widest interpretation shall be given to each such object, and none of such objects shall, except where the context expressly so requires, be in any way limited or restricted by reference to or inference from any other object or objects set forth in such sub-clause, or by reference to or inference from the terms of any other sub-clause of this Clause, or by reference to or inference from the name of the Company.

(2) None of the sub-clauses of this Clause and none of the objects therein specified shall be deemed subsidiary or ancillary to any of the objects specified in any other such sub-clause, and the Company shall have as full a power to exercise each and every one of the objects specified in each sub-clause of this Clause as though each such sub-clause contained the objects of a separate Company.

(3) The word 'Company' in this Clause, except where used in reference to the Company,

shall be deemed to include any partnership or other body of persons, whether incorporated or unincorporated and whether domiciled in the United Kingdom or elsewhere.

(4) In this Clause the expression 'the Act' means the Companies Act 1985, but so that any reference in this Clause to any provision of the Act shall be deemed to include a reference to any statutory modification or re-enactment of that provision for the time being in force.'

Clause 5 Even if the share capital is to be divided into different classes of shares it is advisable (unless there is a particular requirement to entrench class rights), and usual, to omit any such division or reference to special classes in the memorandum.

Subscription There must be shown in the memorandum against the name of each subscriber the number of shares he takes agreed to be taken by them respectively and, if the capital is divided into shares of different classes, the class subscribed for should also be stated.

The memorandum of association must be signed by at least two subscribers and their signatures must be duly attested by one witness (Companies Act 1985, s 2(6)). Underneath the signature of each subscriber and that of the witness there should be printed the full name and address of the signatory. For registration in Scotland, the occupation of the witness should also be inserted.

Notes to Articles

The first 14 articles are standard articles which are followed by special articles which can be selected and added if appropriate.

Article 1 All the regulations in Table A under the Companies Act 1985 are incorporated in these articles unless specifically stated. Where appropriate, special articles have been substituted or added.

It is convenient to bind a copy of the 1985 Table A with the articles when final prints are made.

Table A to the 1985 Act came into force on 1 July 1985 and is set out in the Companies (Tables A to F) Regulations 1985 (SI 1985/805). It was subject to minor amendment in the Companies (Tables A to F) (Amendment) Regulations 1985 (SI 1985/1052) and this final form applies as from 1 August 1985 and to these articles.

Article 2 Paragraph (a) of this article places the shares in the authorised share capital with which the company is incorporated at the disposal of the directors to allot as they think fit. Shares subsequently created must be offered pro rata to existing members in accordance with paragraph (b). Paragraph (c) excludes the statutory pre-emption rights set out in ss 89(1) and 90(1) to (6) inclusive of the Companies Act 1985. Paragraph (d) gives authority under s 80 of the Act for the allotment of shares in the initial authorised share capital. This authority is effective for five years and may be renewed. Whenever a resolution is passed creating new shares it will be normal at the same meeting to seek new authority under s 80 by ordinary resolution either in relation to that capital alone or in respect of all capital then remaining unissued. Resolutions to increase share capital and resolutions to give s 80 authority have each to be filed at the Companies Registry. The following is a possible form of resolution to give s 80 authority in respect of all unissued capital at the date of the resolution:

'That the directors be and they are hereby generally and unconditionally authorised pursuant to s 80 of the Companies Act 1985 to exercise any power of the company to allot and grant rights to subscribe for or to convert securities into shares of the company up to a maximum nominal amount equal to the nominal amount of the authorised but unissued share capital at the date of the passing of this resolution provided that the authority hereby given:

(a) shall be subject to the provisions of Article 2 of the articles of association of the company:
(b) shall expire five years after the passing of this resolution unless previously renewed, revoked or varied save that the directors may, notwithstanding such expiry, allot any shares or grant any such rights under this authority in pursuance of an offer or agreement so to do made by the company before the expiry of this authority'.

A different form of wording will be required if the company has passed an elective resolution pursuant to s 80A and it is desired to give authority for an indefinite period or for a fixed period greater than five years.

Article 3 This article extends the company's lien conferred by clause 8 in Table A.

Article 4 This article increases the liability on defaulted calls imposed by Table A to include costs.

Article 5 This serves as a reminder of the statutory requirements (in s 372 of the Companies Act 1985).

Article 6 This article alters Clause 41 in Table A so as to require a quorum to be present at an adjourned meeting and provides for the dissolution of the meeting if a quorum is not then present.

Article 7

(a) Section 13 provides that the persons named in the statement of directors filed on incorporation are to be the first directors. There is no other method of appointment.
(b) Under paragraphs (a) and (b) the number of directors may be fixed by ordinary resolution of the company. Table A is modified to provide for a sole director if required. It should be noted that a sole director may not act as secretary.
(c) Retirement of directors by rotation is excluded. If it is desired to provide for retirement by rotation the whole of paragraph (c) and the following paragraphs (d) to (f) inclusive should be deleted.

Article 8 Clause 70 of Table A gives the directors authority to exercise all the powers of the company but this article is added to clarify that they may exercise unfettered borrowing powers and should be read in conjunction with Clause 3(ii)(g) of the memorandum. If it is proposed to issue loan capital giving rights of conversion into share capital the issuing company should ensure that authority to allot rights to convert into shares has been given under s 80 of the Companies Act 1985.

Article 9 This article makes some practical modifications to Clauses 65 and 66 of Table A in connection with alternate directors.

Article 10 The powers of the company as to payment of pensions conferred by Clause 3(ii)(s) of the memorandum are wide and extend to directors whether or not they hold or have held any executive office. This article replaces Clause 87 in Table A which limits payment of pensions to directors who have held executive office.

Article 11 This article varies Table A to enable directors to vote at Board meetings without restriction on matters in which they have an interest. Such provision is commonly included in the articles of private companies, but the directors must still comply with s 317 of the Companies Act 1985 in disclosing interests.

Article 12 Section 130 of the Companies Act 1989 inserts a new s 36A into the Companies Act 1985 which provides that a company does not have to have a common seal (although many companies may continue to have one). This article replaces Clause 101 and modifies Clause 6 in Table A so that it will be appropriate whether or not the company has a common seal. These new provisions regarding common seals came into force on 31 July 1990. Paragraph (b) enables the company to have an additional seal for use abroad in accordance with s 39 of the Companies Act 1985.

Article 13 the indemnity given by this clause is wider than that provided by Clause 118 in Table A. Paragraph (b) empowers directors to purchase and maintain insurance against liability of officers in accordance with the new permissive power in s 310(3) of the Companies Act 1985 as altered by s 137 of the Companies Act 1989.

Article 14 This restores the directors' absolute discretion to refuse to register transfers previously contained in Clause 3 of Part II of Table A to the Companies Act 1948 which clause was repealed by the Companies Act 1980. Suggestions for more elaborate transfer articles appear in the optional clauses in this form, and these, when used, replace draft Article 14. Unless the standard Article 14 is deleted or replaced by an alternative form it will be included in the articles of the company.

Optional articles

The following optional forms may be adopted:

I Transfer articles

Type A Paragraph (a) of this article allows freedom of transfer by a member or trustees of a member's family trust to his family and in sub-paragraph (a)(v) to other members of the company.

Transfer in these circumstances may be prevented by the directors only if the company has a lien on the share, or the share is not fully paid.

The directors have absolute discretion as to whether or not to register any other transfer.

If unrestricted transfer between members is not required, sub-paragraph (a)(v) should be deleted.

Type B This alternative article sets out a full and detailed pre-emption procedure in favour of existing members: some amendment would be required for a company with more than one class of shares. A member wishing to transfer shares is required to give a transfer notice and to indicate the price which he regards as the fair value. Any would-be purchaser may request that the fair value be certified by the auditor and the auditor's 'fair value' will be adopted as the selling price if lower than the price stated by the proposing transferor (see paragraph (a)). In determining the fair value of shares comprised in a transfer notice, the auditor will act as an expert and has a total discretion but is directed to fix the value of the shares as a proportion of the value of all issued shares.

Under the procedure laid down in the article the order of events may be summarised as follows:

(1) Any member wishing to transfer any of his shares must give a transfer notice to the company.

(2) Not more than seven days after receipt of the transfer notice, the company issues an 'offer notice' to its members specifying a closing date not less than 21 days and not more than 42 days after the date of the offer notice.

(3) Within eight days from the date of the offer notice, a would-be purchaser may ask that the auditor certify 'fair value'. If this is requested the offer must be left open until 14 days after the company advises members of the definitive price at which the shares included in the offer notice may be purchased.

(4) If at the close of the offer period, the company has received applications for *all* the shares, it must, within seven days, notify the proposing transferor by a 'sale notice'.

(5) Unless the company has received applications from other members for *all* the shares, the company cannot give a sale notice. If for this or any other reason the company does not give a sale notice within the due time to the proposing transferor, the proposing transferor may within a period of 30 days sell all or any of the shares included in his transfer notice to any person at any price, but the directors have an absolute right to refuse to register any such transfer.

Paragraph (g) is designed to prevent shares remaining registered for long periods in the name of a deceased or bankrupt member. Six months is a suggested limit.

Paragraph (h) enables the directors to deem the shares held by an employee (including a director) who has ceased to be employed to be subject to a transfer notice. This clause may be deleted if not required.

Type C This article is in essence an amalgam of Types A and B.

Paragraph (j) is an additional power given to the directors to deem shares to be under a transfer notice where they become aware that there is a non-family interest in a trust. It should be deleted if not required.

Paragraph (k) is similar to paragraph (g) of Type B. It should be noted that if an employee attempts to transfer his shares pursuant to paragraph (a), eg to his wife, before ceasing to be employed, paragraph (c)(ii) gives the directors power to decline to register the transfer. Both paragraphs (c)(ii) and (l) may be deleted if not required.

II Enhanced voting rights for directors

This article reinforces the position of a director who is also a shareholder by giving such director additional votes per share on a resolution to remove him from office or amend or delete this article. Please check that 10 votes for each share is sufficient for this purpose.

III Casting vote

This article removes the chairman's casting vote which is normally exercisable under Table A if there is an equality of votes at a general meeting or a meeting of directors. Such a provision can be useful but additional provisions may be appropriate if the articles are designed to cover a 'deadlock' situation with intentionally evenly balanced representation of specific shareholding interests.

IV Associate directors

For management purposes it may be appropriate to create a class of associate directors who are given additional authority to that of an employee but are not members of the Board. Such can be useful when the appointee is in contact with customers. This additional article makes appropriate provisions for a class of associate directors.

The Companies Acts 1985 to 1989

Private Company Limited by Shares

Memorandum of Association of

1. The Company's name is: ' Limited'.

2. The Company's registered office is to be situated in England and Wales.

3. (i) The object of the Company is to carry on business as a general commercial company.

(ii) Without prejudice to the generality of the object and the powers of the company derived from section 3A of the Act, the Company has power to do all or any of the following things:—

(a) To purchase or by any other means acquire and take options over any property whatever, and any rights or privileges of any kind over or in respect of any property.

(b) To apply for, register, purchase, or by other means acquire and protect, prolong and renew, whether in the United Kingdom or elsewhere any patents, patent rights, brevets d'invention, licences, secret processes, trade marks, designs, protections and concessions and to disclaim, alter, modify, use and turn to account and to manufacture under or grant licences or privileges in respect of the same, and to expend money in experimenting upon, testing and improving any patents, inventions or rights which the Company may acquire or propose to acquire.

(c) To acquire and undertake the whole of any part of the business, goodwill, and assets of any person, firm, or company carrying on or proposing to carry on any of the businesses which the Company is authorised to carry on and as part of the consideration for such acquisition to undertake all or any of the liabilities of such person, firm or company, or to acquire an interest in, amalgamate with, or enter into partnership or into any arrangement for sharing profits, or for co-operation, or for mutual assistance with any such person, firm or company, or for subsidising or otherwise assisting any such person, firm or company, and to give or accept, by way of consideration for any of the acts or things aforesaid or property acquired, any shares, debentures, debenture stock or securities that may be agreed upon, and to hold and retain, or sell, mortgage and deal with any shares, debentures, debenture stock or securities so received.

(d) To improve, manage, construct, repair, develop, exchange, let on lease or otherwise, mortgage, charge, sell, dispose of, turn to account, grant licences, options, rights and privileges in respect of, or otherwise deal with all or any part of the property and rights of the Company.

(e) To invest and deal with the moneys of the Company not immediately required in such manner as may from time to time be determined and to hold or otherwise deal with any investments made.

(f) To lend and advance money or give credit on any terms and with or without security to any person, firm or company (including without prejudice to the generality of the foregoing any holding company, subsidiary or fellow subsidiary of, or any other company associated in any way with, the Company), to enter into guarantees, contracts of indemnity and suretyships of all kinds, to receive money on deposit or loan upon any terms, and to secure or guarantee in any manner and upon any terms the payment of any sum of money or the performance of any obligation by any person, firm or company (including without prejudice to the generality of the foregoing any such holding company, subsidiary, fellow subsidiary or associated company as aforesaid).

(g) To borrow and raise money in any manner and to secure the repayment of any money borrowed, raised or owing by mortgage, charge, standard security, lien or other security upon the whole or any part of the Company's property or assets (whether present or future), including its uncalled capital, and also by a similar mortgage, charge, standard security, lien or security to secure and guarantee the performance by the Company of any obligation or liability it may undertake or which may become binding on it.

(h) To draw, make, accept, endorse, discount, negotiate, execute and issue cheques, bills of exchange, promissory notes, bills of lading, warrants, debentures, and other negotiable or transferable instruments.

(i) To apply for, promote, and obtain any Act of Parliament, order, or licence of the Department of Trade or other authority for enabling the Company to carry any of its objects into effect, or for effecting any modification of the Company's constitution, or for any other purpose which may seem calculated directly or indirectly to promote the Company's interests, and to oppose any proceedings or applications which may seem calculated directly or indirectly to prejudice the Company's interests.

(j) To enter into any arrangements with any government or authority (supreme, municipal, local, or otherwise) that may seem conducive to the attainment of the Company's objects or any of them, and to obtain from any such government or authority any charters, decrees, rights, privileges or concessions which the Company may think desirable and to carry out, exercise, and comply with any such charters, decrees, rights, privileges, and concessions.

(k) To subscribe for, take, purchase, or otherwise acquire, hold, sell, deal with and dispose of, place and underwrite shares, stocks, debentures, debenture stocks, bonds, obligations or securities issued or guaranteed by any other company constituted or carrying on business in any part of the world, and debentures, debenture stocks, bonds, obligations or securities issued or guaranteed by any government or authority, municipal, local or otherwise, in any part of the world.

(l) To control, manage, finance, subsidise, co-ordinate or otherwise assist any company or companies in which the Company has a direct or indirect financial interest, to provide secretarial, administrative, technical, commercial and other services and facilities of all kinds for any such company or companies and to make payments by way of subvention or otherwise and any other arrangements which may seem desirable with respect to any business or operations of or generally with respect to any such company or companies.

(m) To promote any other company for the purpose of acquiring the whole or any part of the business or property or undertaking or any of the liabilities of the Company, or of undertaking any business or operations which may appear likely to assist or benefit the Company or to enhance the value of any property or business of the Company, and to place or guarantee the placing of, underwrite, subscribe for, or otherwise acquire all or any part of the shares or securities of any such company as aforesaid.

(n) To sell or otherwise dispose for the whole or any part of the business or property of the Company, either together or in portions, for such consideration as the Company may think fit, and in particular for shares, debentures, or securities of any company purchasing the same.

(o) To act as agents or brokers and as trustees for any person, firm or company, and to undertake and perform sub-contracts.

(p) To remunerate any person, firm or company rendering services to the Company either by cash payment or by the allotment to him or them of shares or other securities of the Company credited as paid up in full or in part or otherwise as may be thought expedient.

(q) To distribute among the members of the company in kind any property of the company of whatever nature.

(r) To pay all or any expenses incurred in connection with the promotion, formation and incorporation of the Company, or to contract with any person, firm or company to pay the same, and to pay commissions to brokers and others for underwriting, placing, selling, or guaranteeing the subscription of any shares or other securities of the Company.

(s) To support and subscribe to any charitable or public object and to support and subscribe to any institution, society, or club which may be for the benefit of the Company or its Directors or employees, or may be connected with any town or place where the Company carries on business; to give or award pensions, annuities, gratuities, and superannuation or other allowances or benefits or charitable aid and generally to provide advantages, facilities and services for any persons who are or have been Directors of, or who are or have been employed by, or who are serving or have served the Company, or any company which is a subsidiary of the Company or the holding company of the Company or a fellow subsidiary of the Company or the predecessors in business of the Company or of any such subsidiary, holding or fellow subsidiary company and to the wives, widows, children and other relatives and dependants of such persons; to make payments towards insurance and to set up, establish, support and maintain superannuation and other funds or schemes (whether contributory or non-contributory) for the benefit of any of such persons and of their wives, widows, children and other relatives and dependants; and to set up, establish, support and maintain profit sharing or share purchase schemes for the benefit of any of the employees of the Company or of any such subsidiary, holding or fellow subsidiary company and to lend money to any such employees or to trustees on their behalf to enable any such purchase schemes to be established or maintained.

(t) Subject to and in accordance with a due compliance with the provisions of sections 155 to 158 (inclusive) of the Act (if and so far as such provisions shall be applicable), to give, whether directly or indirectly, any kind of financial assistance (as defined in section 152(1)(a) of the Act) for any such purpose as is specified in section 151(1) and/or section 151(2) of the Act.

(u) To procure the Company to be registered or recognised in any part of the world.

(v) To do all or any of the things or matters aforesaid in any part of the world and either as principals, agents, contractors or otherwise, and by or through agents, brokers, subcontractors or otherwise and either alone or in conjunction with others.

(w) To do all such other things as may be deemed incidental or conducive to the attainment of the Company's objects or any of the powers given to it by the Act or by this Clause.

AND so that:

(1) None of the provisions set forth in any sub-clause of this Clause shall be restrictively construed but the widest interpretation shall be given to each such provision, and none of such provisions shall, except where the context expressly so requires, be in any way limited or restricted by reference to or inference from any other provisions set forth in such sub-clause, or by reference to or inference from the terms of any other sub-clause of this clause, or by reference to or inference from the name of the Company.

(2) The word 'Company' in this clause, except where used in reference to the Company, shall be deemed to include any partnership or other body of persons, whether incorporated or unincorporated and whether domiciled in the United Kingdom or elsewhere.

(3) In this clause the expression 'the Act' means the Companies Act 1985, but so that any reference in this clause to any provision of the Act shall be deemed to include a reference to any statutory modification or re-enactment of that provision for the time being in force.

4. The liability of the Members is limited.

5. The Company's share capital is £ divided into shares of £ each.

WE, the subscribers to the Memorandum of Association, wish to be formed into a

Company pursuant to this Memorandum; and we agree to take the number of shares shown opposite our respective names.

Names and addresses of Subscribers	Number of shares taken by each Subscriber
Total shares taken	

Dated this
Witness to the above Signatures:

The Companies Acts 1985 to 1989

Private Company Limited by Shares

Articles of Association of

Preliminary

1. (a) The Regulations contained in Table A in the Schedule to the Companies (Tables A to F) Regulations 1985 (SI 1985 No 805) as amended by the Companies (Tables A to F) (Amendment) Regulations 1985 (SI 1985 No 1052) (such Table being hereinafter called 'Table A') shall apply to the Company save in so far as they are excluded or varied hereby and such Regulations (save as so excluded or varied) and the Articles hereinafter contained shall be the regulations of the Company.

   (b) In these Articles the expression 'the Act' means the Companies Act 1985, but so that any reference in these Articles to any provision of the Act shall be deemed to include a reference to any statutory modification or re-enactment of that provision for the time being in force.

Allotment of shares

2. (a) Shares which are comprised in the authorised share capital with which the Company is incorporated shall be under the control of the Directors who may (subject to section 80 of the Act and to paragraph (d) below) allot, grant options over or otherwise dispose of the same, to such persons, on such terms and in such manner as they think fit.

(b) All shares which are not comprised in the authorised share capital with which the Company is incorporated and which the Directors propose to issue shall first be offered to the Members in proportion as nearly as may be to the number of the existing shares held by them respectively unless the Company in General Meeting shall by Special Resolution otherwise direct. The offer shall be made by notice specifying the number of shares offered, and limiting a period (not being less than fourteen days) within which the offer, if not accepted, will be deemed to be declined. After the expiration of that period, those shares so deemed to be declined shall be offered in the proportion aforesaid to the persons who have, within the said period, accepted all the shares offered to them; such further offer shall be made in like terms in the same manner and limited by a like period as the original offer. Any shares not accepted pursuant to such offer or further offer as aforesaid or not capable of being offered as aforesaid except by way of fractions and any shares released from the provisions of this Article by any such Special Resolution as aforesaid shall be under the control of the Directors, who may allot, grant options over or otherwise dispose of the same to such persons, on such terms, and in such manner as they think fit, provided that, in the case of shares not accepted as aforesaid, such shares shall not be disposed of on terms which are more favourable to the subscribers therefor than the terms on which they were offered to the members. The foregoing provisions of this paragraph (b) shall have effect subject to section 80 of the Act.

(c) In accordance with section 91(1) of the Act sections 89(1) and 90(1) to (6) (inclusive) of the Act shall not apply to the Company.

(d) The Directors are generally and unconditionally authorised for the purposes of section 80 of the Act, to exercise any power of the Company to allot and grant rights to subscribe for or convert securities into shares of the Company up to the amount of the authorised share capital with which the Company is incorporated at any time or times during the period of five years from the date of incorporation and the directors may, after that period, allot any shares or grant any such rights under this authority in pursuance of an offer or agreement so to do made by the Company within that period. The authority hereby given may at any time (subject to the said section 80) be renewed, revoked or varied by Ordinary Resolution of the Company in General Meeting.

Shares

3. The lien conferred by Clause 8 in Table A shall attach also to fully paid-up shares, and the Company shall also have a first and paramount lien on all shares, whether fully paid or not, standing registered in the name of any person indebted or under liability to the

Company, whether he shall be the sole registered holder thereof or shall be one of two or more joint holders, for all moneys presently payable by him or his estate to the Company. Clause 8 in Table A shall be modified accordingly.

4. The liability of any Member in default in respect of a call shall be increased by the addition at the end of the first sentence of Clause 18 in Table A of the words 'and all expenses that may have been incurred by the Company by reason of such non-payment'.

General meetings and resolutions

5. Every notice convening a General Meeting shall comply with the provisions of section 372(3) of the Act as to giving information to Members in regard to their right to appoint proxies; and notices of and other communications relating to any General Meeting which any Member is entitled to receive shall be sent to the Directors and to the Auditors for the time being of the Company.

6. (a) If a quorum is not present within half an hour from the time appointed for a General Meeting the General Meeting shall stand adjourned to the same day in the next week at the same time and place or to such other day and at such other time and place as the Directors may determine; and if at the adjourned General Meeting a quorum is not present within half an hour from the time appointed therefor such adjourned General Meeting shall be dissolved.

(b) Clause 41 in Table A shall not apply to the Company.

Appointment of directors

7. (a) Clause 64 in Table A shall not apply to the Company.

(b) The maximum number and minimum number respectively of the Directors may be determined from time to time by Ordinary Resolution in General Meeting of the Company. Subject to and in default of any such determination there shall be no maximum number of Directors and the minimum number of Directors shall be one. Whensoever the minimum number of Directors shall be one, a sole Director shall have authority to exercise all the powers and discretions by Table A and by these Articles expressed to be vested in the Directors generally, and Clause 89 in Table A shall be modified accordingly.

(c) The Directors shall not be required to retire by rotation and Clauses 73 to 80 (inclusive) in Table A shall not apply to the Company.

(d) No person shall be appointed a Director at any General Meeting unless either:
(i) he is recommended by the Directors; or
(ii) not less than fourteen nor more than thirty-five clear days before the date appointed for the General Meeting, notice signed by a Member qualified to vote at the General Meeting has been given to the Company of the intention to propose that person for appointment, together with notice signed by that person of his willingness to be appointed.

(e) Subject to paragraph (d) above, the Company may by Ordinary Resolution in General Meeting appoint any person who is willing to act to be a Director, either to fill a vacancy or as an additional Director.

(f) The Directors may appoint a person who is willing to act to be a director, either to fill a vacancy or as an additional Director, provided that the appointment does not cause the number of directors to exceed any number determined in accordance with paragraph (b) above as the maximum number of Directors and for the time being in force.

Borrowing powers

8. The Directors may exercise all the powers of the Company to borrow money without limit as to amount and upon such terms and in such manner as they think fit, and subject (in the case of any security convertible into shares) to section 80 of the Act to grant any mortgage, charge or standard security over its undertaking, property and uncalled capital, or any part thereof, and to issue debentures, debenture stock, and other securities whether outright or as security for any debt, liability or obligation of the Company or of any third party.

Alternate directors

9. (a) An alternate Director shall not be entitled as such to receive any remuneration from the Company, save that he may be paid by the Company such part (if any) of the remuneration otherwise payable to his appointor as such appointor may by notice in writing to the Company from time to time direct, and the first sentence of Clause 66 in Table A shall be modified accordingly.

(b) A Director, or any such other person as is mentioned in Clause 65 in Table A, may act as an alternate Director to represent more than one Director, and an alternate Director shall be entitled at any meeting of the Directors or of any committee of the Directors to one vote for every Director whom he represents in addition to his own vote (if any) as a Director, but he shall count as only one for the purpose of determining whether a quorum is present.

Gratuities and pensions

10. (a) The Directors may exercise the powers of the Company conferred by Clause 3(ii)(s) of the Memorandum of Association of the Company and shall be entitled to retain any benefits received by them or any of them by reason of the exercise of any such powers.

(b) Clause 87 in Table A shall not apply to the Company.

Proceedings of directors

11. (a) A Director may vote, at any meeting of the Directors or of any committee of the Directors, on any resolution, notwithstanding that it in any way concerns or relates to a matter in which he has, directly or indirectly, any kind of interest whatsoever, and if he shall vote on any such resolution as aforesaid his vote shall be counted; and in relation to any such resolution as aforesaid he shall (whether or not he shall vote on the same) be taken into account in calculating the quorum present at the meeting.

(b) Clauses 94 to 97 (inclusive) in Table A shall not apply to the Company.

The seal

12. (a) If the Company has a seal it shall only be used with the authority of the Directors or of a committee of Directors. The Directors may determine who shall sign any instrument to which the seal is affixed and unless otherwise so determined it shall be signed by a Director and by the Secretary or second Director. The obligation under Clause 6 of Table A relating to the sealing of share certificates shall apply only if the Company has a seal. Clause 101 of Table A shall not apply to the Company.

(b) The Company may exercise the powers conferred by section 39 of the Act with regard to having an official seal for use abroad, and such powers shall be vested in the Directors.

Indemnity

13. (a) Every Director, or other officer or Auditor of the Company shall be indemnified out of the assets of the Company against all losses or liabilities which he may sustain or incur in or about the execution of the duties of his office or otherwise in relation thereto, including any liability incurred by him in defending any proceedings, whether civil or criminal, in which judgment is given in his favour or in which he is acquitted or in connection with any application under section 144 or section 727 of the Act in which relief is granted to him by the Court, and no Director or other officer shall be liable for any loss, damage or misfortune which may happen to or be incurred by the Company in the execution of the duties of his office or in relation thereto. But this Article shall only have effect in so far as its provisions are not avoided by section 310 of the Act.

(b) The Directors shall have power to purchase and maintain for any Director, officer or Auditor of the Company, insurance against any such liability as is referred to in section 310(1) of the Act from and after the bringing into force of section 137 of the Companies Act 1989.

(c) Clause 118 in Table A shall not apply to the Company.

Standard transfer article (*please delete if not required*).

Transfer of shares

*14. The Directors may, in their absolute discretion and without assigning any reason therefore, decline to register the transfer of a share, whether or not it is a fully paid share, and the first sentence of reg 24 in Table A shall not apply to the Company.

Names and addresses of Subscribers

Dated this

Witness to the above Signatures:—

EDITOR'S NOTE

*Standard transfer article. See subsequent precedents for alternatives.

Type A Optional transfer article

Transfer of shares

14. (a) The Directors shall, subject to Clause 24 in Table A, register the transfer or, as the case may be, transmission of any shares:
   (i) to a member of the family of a Member or deceased Member;
   (ii) to any person or persons acting in the capacity of trustee or trustees of a trust created by a Member (by deed or by will) or, upon any change of trustees of a trust so created, to the new trustee or trustees (so that any such transfer as aforesaid shall be registered pursuant to this paragraph only if such shares are to be held upon the terms of the trust) provided that there are no persons beneficially interested under the trust other than the Member and members of his family and the voting rights conferred by any such shares are not exercisable by or subject to the consent of any person other than the trustee or trustees of the trust or the Member or members of his family and also the Directors are satisfied that the trust is and is intended to remain a trust the sole purpose of which is to benefit the Member or members of his family;

(iii) by the trustee or trustees of a trust to which sub-paragraph (ii) above applies to any person beneficially interested under the trust being the Member or a member of his family;

(iv) to the legal personal representatives of a deceased Member where under the provisions of his will or the laws as to intestacy the persons beneficially entitled to any such shares, whether immediately or contingently, are members of the family of the deceased Member and by the legal personal representatives of a deceased Member to a member or members of the family of the deceased Member;

(v) to any other Member of the Company.

(b) For the purpose of this Article:

(i) The word 'Member' shall not include a person who holds shares only in the capacity of trustee, legal personal representative or trustee in bankruptcy but shall include a former Member in any case where the person concerned ceased to be a Member as a result of the creation of the relevant trust; and

(ii) the words 'a member of the family of a Member' shall mean the husband, wife, widow, widower, child and remoter issue (including a child by adoption), parent (including adoptive parent), brother and sister (whether of the full or half blood and including a brother or sister related by adoption), and child and remoter issue of any such brother or sister (including a child by adoption), of the Member.

(c) The directors may, in their absolute discretion and without assigning any reason therefor, decline to register any transfer or transmission of a share (whether or not it is fully paid) to which paragraph (a) above does not apply.

(d) Clause 24 in Table A shall be modified accordingly.

Type B Optional transfer article

Transfer of shares

14. (a) Any person (hereinafter called 'the proposing transferor') proposing to transfer any shares shall give notice in writing (hereinafter called 'the transfer notice') to the Company that he desires to transfer the same and specifying the price per share which in his opinion constitutes the fair value thereof. The transfer notice shall constitute the Company the agent of the proposing transferor for the sale of all (but not some of) the shares comprised in the transfer notice to any Member or Members willing to purchase the same (hereinafter called 'the purchasing Member') at the price specified therein or at the fair value certified in accordance with paragraph (c) below (whichever shall be the lower). A transfer notice shall not be revocable except with the sanction of the directors.

(b) The shares comprised in any transfer notice shall be offered to the Members (other than the proposing transferor) as nearly as may be in proportion to the number of shares held by them respectively. Such offer shall be made by notice in writing (hereinafter called 'the offer notice') within seven days after the receipt by the Company of the transfer notice. The offer notice shall state the price per share specified in the transfer notice and shall limit the time in which the offer may be accepted, not being less than twenty-one days nor more than forty-two days after the date of the offer notice, provided that if a certificate of fair value is requested under paragraph (c) below the offer shall remain open for acceptance for a period of fourteen days after the date on which notice of the fair value certified in accordance with that paragraph shall have been given by the Company to the Members or until the expiry of the period specified in the offer notice whichever is the later. For the purpose of this Article an offer shall be deemed to be accepted on the day on which the acceptance is received by the Company. The offer notice shall further invite each Member to state in his reply the number of additional shares (if any) in excess of his proportion which he desires to purchase and if all the Members do not accept the offer in respect of their respective proportions in full the shares not so accepted shall be used to satisfy the claims for additional shares as nearly as may be in proportion to the number of shares already held by them respectively, provided that no Member shall be obliged to take more shares than he shall have applied for. If any shares shall not be capable without fractions of being offered to the Members in proportion to their existing holdings, the same shall be offered to the Members, or some of them, in such proportions or in such manner as may be determined by lots drawn in regard thereto, and the lots shall be drawn in such manner as the Directors may think fit.

(c) Any Member may, not later than eight days after the date of the offer notice, serve on the Company a notice in writing requesting that the Auditor for the time being of the Company (or at the discretion of the Auditor, a person nominated by the President for the time being of the Institute of Chartered Accountants in the country of the situation of its registered office) certify in writing the sum which in his opinion represents the fair value of the shares comprised in the transfer notice as at the date of the transfer notice and for the purpose of this Article reference to the Auditor shall include any person so nominated. Upon receipt of such notice the Company shall instruct the Auditor to certify as aforesaid and the costs of such valuation shall be apportioned among the proposing transferor and the purchasing Members or borne by any one or more of them as the Auditor in his absolute discretion shall decide. In certifying the fair value as aforesaid the Auditor shall be considered to be acting as an expert and not as an arbitrator or arbiter and accordingly any provisions of law or statute relating to arbitration shall not apply. Upon receipt of the certificate of the Auditor, the Company shall by notice in writing inform all Members of the fair value of each share and of the price per share (being the lower of the price specified in the transfer notice and the fair value of each share) at which the shares comprised in the transfer notice are offered for sale. For the purpose of this Article the fair value of each share comprised in the transfer notice shall be its value as a rateable proportion of the total value of all the issued shares of the Company and shall not be discounted or enhanced by reference to the number of shares referred to in the transfer notice.

(d) If purchasing Members shall be found for all the shares comprised in the transfer notice within the appropriate period specified in paragraph (b) above, the Company shall not later than seven days after the expiry of such appropriate period give notice in writing (hereinafter called 'the sale notice') to the proposing transferor specifying the purchasing Members and the proposing transferor shall be bound upon payment of the price due in respect of all the shares comprised in the transfer notice to transfer the shares to the purchasing Members.

(e) If in any case the proposing transferor after having become bound as aforesaid makes default in transferring any shares the Company may receive the purchase money on his behalf, and may authorise some person to execute a transfer of such shares in favour of the purchasing Member. The receipt of the Company for the purchase money shall be a good discharge to the purchasing Member. The Company shall pay the purchase money into a separate bank account.

(f) If the Company shall not give a sale notice to the proposing transferor within the time specified in paragraph (d) above, he shall, during the period of thirty days next following the expiry of the time so specified, be at liberty to transfer all or any of the shares comprised in the transfer notice to any person or persons but in that event the Directors may, in their absolute discretion, and without assigning any reason therefor, decline to register any such transfer and Clause 24 in Table A shall, for these purposes, be modified accordingly.

(g) In the application of Clauses 29 to 31 (inclusive) in Table A to the Company:

  (i) any person becoming entitled to a share in consequence of the death or bankruptcy of a Member shall give a transfer notice before he elects in respect of any share to be registered himself or to execute a transfer;

  (ii) if a person so becoming entitled shall not have given a transfer notice in respect of any share within six months of the death or bankruptcy, the Directors may at any time thereafter upon resolution passed by them give notice requiring such person within 30 days of such notice to give a transfer notice in respect of all the shares to which he has so become entitled and for which he has not previously given a transfer notice and if he does not do so he shall at the end of such thirty days be deemed to have given a transfer notice pursuant to paragraph (a) of this Article relating to those shares in respect of which he has still not done so;

  (iii) where a transfer notice is given or deemed to be given under this paragraph (g) and no price per share is specified therein the transfer notice shall be deemed to specify the sum which shall, on the application of the Directors, be certified in writing by the Auditors in accordance with paragraph (c) of this Article as the fair value thereof.

(h) Whenever any Member of the Company who is employed by the Company in any capacity (whether or not he is also a Director) ceases to be employed by the Company otherwise than by reason of his death the Directors may at any time not later than six months after his ceasing to be employed resolve that such Members do retire, and thereupon he shall (unless he has already served a transfer notice) be deemed to have served a transfer notice pursuant to paragraph (a) of this Article and to have specified therein the fair value to be certified in accordance with paragraph (c) of this Article. Notice of the passing of any such resolution shall forthwith be given to the Member affected thereby.

Type C Optional transfer article

Transfer of shares

14. (a) The Directors shall, subject to Clause 24 in Table A, register the transfer or, as the case may be, transmission of any shares:

  (i) to a member of the family of a Member or deceased Member;

(ii) to any person or persons acting in the capacity of trustee or trustees of a trust created by a Member (by deed or by will) or, upon any change of trustees of a trust so created, to the new trustee or trustees (so that any such transfer as aforesaid shall be registered pursuant to this paragraph only if such shares are to be held upon the terms of the trust) provided that there are no persons beneficially interested under the trust other than the Member or members of his family and the voting rights conferred by any such shares are not exercisable by or subject to the consent of any person other than the trustee or trustees of the trust or the Member or members of his family and also the Directors are satisfied that the trust is and is intended to remain a trust the sole purpose of which is to benefit the Member or members of his family;

(iii) by the trustee or trustees of a trust to which sub-paragraph (ii) above applies to any person beneficially interested under the trust being the Member or a member of his family;

(iv) to the legal personal representatives of a deceased Member where under the provisions of his will or the laws as to intestacy the persons beneficially entitled to any such shares, whether immediately or contingently, are members of the family (as hereinafter defined) of the deceased Member and by the legal personal representatives of a deceased Member to a member or members of the family of the deceased Member;

(v) to any other Member of the Company.

(b) For the purpose of paragraphs (a) and (j) of this Article but not any other paragraph:

(i) the word 'Member' shall not include a person who holds shares only in the capacity of trustee, legal personal representative or trustee in bankruptcy but shall include a former Member in any case where the person concerned ceased to be a Member as the result of the creation of the relevant trust; and

(ii) the words 'a member of the family of a Member' shall mean the husband, wife, widow, widower, child and remoter issue (including a child by adoption), parent (including adoptive parent), brother and sister (whether of the full or half blood and including a brother or sister related by adoption), and child and remoter issue of any such brother or sister (including a child by adoption), of the Member.

(c) Notwithstanding the provisions of this Article, the directors may decline to register any transfer or transmission which would otherwise be permitted hereunder without assigning any reason therefore, if it is a transfer:

(i) of a share (whether or not it is fully paid) made pursuant to paragraph (i) below;

(ii) of a share pursuant to paragraph (a) by a Member of the Company who is employed by the Company in any capacity provided that this restriction shall not apply to such Members' legal personal representatives.

Clause 24 in Table A shall, for these purposes, be modified accordingly.

(d) Save where a transfer is made pursuant to paragraph (a) above any person (hereinafter called 'the proposing transferor') proposing to transfer any shares shall give notice in writing (hereinafter called 'the transfer notice') to the Company that he desires to transfer the same and specifying the price per share which in his opinion constitutes the fair value thereof. The transfer notice shall constitute the Company the agent of the proposing transferor for the sale of all (but not some of) the shares comprised in the transfer notice to any Member or Members willing to purchase the same (hereinafter called 'the purchasing Member') at the price specified therein or at the fair value certified in accordance with paragraph (f) below (whichever shall be the lower). A transfer notice shall not be revocable except with the sanction of the directors.

(e) The shares comprised in any transfer notice shall be offered to the Members (other than the proposing transferor) as nearly as may be in proportion to the number of shares held by them respectively. Such offer shall be made by notice in writing (hereinafter called 'the offer notice') within seven days after the receipt by the Company of the transfer notice. The offer notice shall state the price per share specified in the transfer notice and shall limit the time in which the offer may be accepted, not being less than twenty-one days nor more than forty-two days after the date of the offer notice, provided that if a certificate of valuation is requested under paragraph (f) below the offer shall remain open for acceptance for a period of fourteen days after the date on which notice of the fair value certified in accordance with that paragraph shall have been given by the Company to the Members. For the purpose of this Article an offer shall be deemed to be accepted on the day on which the acceptance is received by the Company. The offer notice shall further invite each Member to state in his reply the number of additional shares (if any) in excess of his proportion which he desires to purchase and if all the Members do not accept the offer in respect of their respective proportions in full the shares not so accepted shall be used to satisfy the claims for additional shares as nearly as may be in proportion to the number of shares already held by them respectively, provided that no Member shall be obliged to take more shares than he shall have applied for. If any shares shall not be capable without fractions of being offered to the Members in proportion to their existing holdings, the same shall be offered to the Members, or some of them, in such proportions or in such manner as may be determined by lots drawn in regard thereto, and the lots shall be drawn in such manner as the Directors may think fit.

(f) Any Member may, not later than eight days after the date of the offer notice, serve on the Company a notice in writing requesting that the Auditor for the time being of the Company (or at the discretion of the Auditor, a person nominated by the President for the time being of the Institute of Chartered Accountants in the country of the situation of its registered office) certify in writing the sum which in his opinion represents the fair value of the shares comprised in the transfer notice as at the date of the transfer notice and for the purpose of this Article reference to the Auditor shall include any person so nominated. Upon receipt of such notice the Company shall instruct the Auditor to certify as aforesaid and the costs of such valuation shall be apportioned among the proposing transferor and the purchasing Members or borne by any one or more of them as the Auditor in his absolute discretion shall decide. In certifying fair value as aforesaid the Auditor shall be considered to be acting as an expert and not as an arbitrator or arbiter and accordingly any provisions of law or statute relating to arbitration shall not apply. Upon receipt of the certificate of the Auditor, the Company shall by notice in writing inform all Members of the fair value of each share and of the price per share (being the lower of the price specified in the transfer notice and the fair value of each share) at which the shares comprised in the transfer notice are offered for sale. For the purpose of this Article the fair value of each share comprised in the transfer notice shall be in its value as a rateable proportion of the total value of all the issued shares of the Company and shall not be discounted or enhanced by reference to the number of shares referred to in the transfer notice.

(g) If purchasing Members shall be found for all the shares comprised in the transfer notice within the appropriate period specified in paragraph (e) above, the Company shall not later than seven days after the expiry of such appropriate period give notice in writing (hereinafter called 'the sale notice') to the proposing transferor specifying the purchasing Members and the proposing transferor shall be bound upon payment of the price due in respect of all the shares comprised in the transfer notice to transfer the shares to the purchasing Members.

(h) If in any case the proposing transferor after having become bound as aforesaid makes default in transferring any shares the Company may receive the purchase money on his behalf, and may authorise some person to execute a transfer of such shares in favour of the purchasing Member. The receipt of the Company for the purchase money shall be a good discharge to the purchasing Members. The Company shall pay the purchase money into a separate bank account.

(i) If the Company shall not give a sale notice to the proposing transferor within the time specified in paragraph (g) above, he shall, during the period of thirty days next following the expiry of the time so specified, be at liberty subject to paragraph (c) above to transfer all or any of the shares comprised in the transfer notice to any person or persons.

(j) In any case where any shares are held by the trustee or trustees of a trust following a transfer or transfers made pursuant to sub-paragraph (ii) of paragraph (a) above and it shall come to the notice of the Directors that not all the persons beneficially interested under the trust are members of the family (as hereinbefore defined) of the Member by whom the trust was created, the Directors may at any time within twenty-eight days thereafter resolve that such trustee or trustees do transfer such shares and such trustee or trustees shall thereupon be deemed to have served a transfer notice comprising such shares pursuant to paragraph (d) above and to have specified therein the fair value to be certified in accordance with paragraph (f) above and the provisions of this Article shall take effect accordingly. Notice of such resolution shall forthwith be given to such trustee or trustees.

(k) In the application of Clauses 29 to 31 (inclusive) in Table A to the Company:
   (i) save where the proposed transfer or transmission is within paragraph (a) above ('a permitted transfer') any person becoming entitled to a share in consequence of the death or bankruptcy of a Member shall give a transfer notice before he elects in respect of any share to be registered himself or to execute a transfer;
   (ii) if a person so becoming entitled shall not have executed a permitted transfer or given a transfer notice in respect of any share within six months of the death or bankruptcy, the Directors may at any time thereafter upon resolution passed by them give notice requiring such person within thirty days to execute permitted transfers or give a transfer notice in respect of all the shares to which he has so become entitled and for which he has not previously done so and if he does not do so he shall at the end of such thirty days be deemed to have given a transfer notice pursuant to paragraph (d) of this Article relating to those shares in respect of which he has still not executed permitted transfers or given a transfer notice;

(iii) where a transfer notice is given or deemed to be given under this paragraph (k) and no price per share is specified therein the transfer notice shall be deemed to specify the sum which shall, on the application of the Directors, be certified in writing by the Auditors in accordance with paragraph (f) of this Article as the fair value thereof.

(l) Whenever any Member of the Company who is employed by the Company in any capacity (whether or not he is also a Director) ceases to be employed by the Company otherwise than by reason of his death the Directors may at any time not later than six months after his ceasing to be employed resolve that such Member do retire, and thereupon he shall (unless he has already served a transfer notice) be deemed to have served a transfer notice pursuant to paragraph (d) of this Article and to have specified therein the fair value to be certified in accordance with paragraph (f) of this Article. Notice of the passing of any such resolution shall forthwith be given to the Member affected thereby.

Additional Optional Articles

Enhanced voting rights for directors

Every Director for the time being of the Company shall have the following rights:

(a) if at any General Meeting a poll is duly demanded on a resolution to remove him from office, to ten votes for each share of which he is the holder; and

(b) if at any General Meeting a poll is duly demanded on a resolution to delete or amend the provisions of this Article, to ten votes for each share of which he is the holder if voting against such resolution.

Clause 54 in Table A shall be modified accordingly.

Casting vote

The Chairman shall not, in the event of an equality of votes at any general meeting of the company, or at any Meeting of the Directors or of a Committee of Directors, have a second or casting vote. Clause 50 in Table A shall not apply to the Company, and Clauses 88 and 72 in Table A shall be modified accordingly.

Associate directors

(a) The Directors may at any time and from time to time appoint any employee of the Company to the position of Associate Director.

(b) An Associate Director shall advise and assist the Directors but shall not attend Board Meetings except at the invitation of the Directors, and when present at the Board Meetings he shall not be entitled to vote, nor be counted in the quorum, but subject as aforesaid he shall as Associate Director have such powers, authorities and duties as the Directors may in the particular case from time to time determine.

(c) An Associate Director shall not be deemed a Member of the Board, nor any committee thereof, nor shall he be a Director for any of the purposes of these Articles of Association or (so far as provision may lawfully be made in this behalf) for any of the purposes of the Companies Act 1985.

(d) Without prejudice to any rights or claims the Associate Director may have under any contract with the Company, any appointment as an Associate Director may be terminated by the Directors at any time and shall ipso facto terminate if the Associate Director shall from any cause cease to be an employee of the Company.

(e) An Associate Director may receive such remuneration (if any) in addition to the remuneration received as an employee of the Company as the Directors shall from time to time determine.

Appendix 3

Companies and Business Names Regulations 1981

The Companies and Business Names Regulations are set out in SI 1981 No 1685 which is printed in full below. This subject is dealt with in Chapter 3.

Companies and Business Names Regulations 1981*

(SI 1981 No 1685, amended SI 1982 No 1653)

1. These Regulations may be cited as the Companies and Business Names Regulations 1981 and shall come into operation on February 26, 1982.

2. In these Regulations, unless the context otherwise requires, 'the Act' means the Companies Act 1981.

BNA 1985, s 2(1)(b) 3. The words and expressions stated in column (1) of the Schedule hereto are hereby specified as words and expressions for the registration of which as or as part of a company's corporate name the approval of the Secretary of State is required by section 22(2)(b) of the Act or for the use of which as or as part of a business name his approval is required by section 28(2)(b) of the Act.

BNA 1985, s 3(2) 4. Subject to Regulation 5, each Government department or other body stated in column (2) of the Schedule hereto is hereby specified as the relevant body for the purposes of section 31(2) and (3) of the Act in relation to the word or expression opposite to it in column (1).

5. Where two Government departments or other bodies are specified in the alternative in Column (2) of the Schedule hereto the second alternative is to be treated as specified,

(a) in the case of the corporate name of a company,
  (i) if the company has not yet been registered and its principal or only place of business in Great Britain is to be in Scotland or, if it will have no place of business in Great Britain, its proposed registered office is in Scotland, and
  (ii) if the company is already registered and its principal or only place of business in Great Britain is in Scotland or, if it has no place of business in Great Britain, its registered office is in Scotland, and

(b) in the case of a business name, if the principal or only place of the business carried on or to be carried on in Great Britain is or is to be in Scotland,

and the first alternative is to be treated as specified in any other case.

EDITOR'S NOTE

*Authority: Companies Act 1981, ss 31 and 32. These regulations have effect as if made under the Companies Act 1985, s 29 and the Business Names Act 1985, ss 3 and 6.

SCHEDULE

Regulations 3–5

SPECIFICATION OF WORDS, EXPRESSIONS AND RELEVANT BODIES

Word or expression	Relevant Body
Abortion	Department of Health and Social Security
Apothecary	Worshipful Society of Apothecaries of London or Pharmaceutical Society of Great Britain
Association	
Assurance	
Assurer	
Authority	
Benevolent	
Board	
Breed	} Ministry of Agriculture, Fisheries and Food
Breeder	
Breeding	
British	
Building Society	
Chamber of Commerce	
Chamber of Industry	
Chamber of Trade	
Charitable	} Charity Commission or Scottish Home and Health Department
Charity	
Charter	
Chartered	
[Chemist	
Chemistry]	
Contact Lens	General Optical Council
Co-operative	
Council	
Dental	} General Dental Council
Dentistry	
District Nurse	Panel of Assessors in District Nurse Training
Duke	Home Office or Scottish Home and Health Department
England	
English	
European	
Federation	
Foundation	
Friendly Society	
Fund	
Giro	
Great Britain	
Group	

Word or expression	Relevant Body
Health Centre Health Service	Department of Health and Social Security
Health Visitor	Council for the Education and Training of Health Visitors
Her Majesty His Majesty	Home Office or Scottish Home and Health Department
Holding	
Industrial and Provident Society	
Institute	
Institution	
Insurance	
Insurer	
International	
Ireland	
Irish	
King	Home Office or Scottish Home and Health Department
Midwife Midwifery	Central Midwives Board or Central Midwives Board for Scotland
National Nurse Nursing	General Nursing Council for England and Wales or General Nursing Council for Scotland
Nursing Home	Department of Health and Social Security
Patent	
Patentee	
Police	Home Office or Scottish Home and Health Department
Polytechnic	Department of Education and Science
Post Office	
Pregnancy Termination	Department of Health and Social Security
Prince Princess	Home Office or Scottish Home and Health Department
Queen	
Reassurance	
Reassurer	
Register	
Registered	
Reinsurance	
Reinsurer	
Royal Royale	Home Office or Scottish Home and Health Department
Royalty	
Scotland	
Scottish	
Sheffield	
Society	
Special School	Department of Education and Science
Stock Exchange	

Word or expression	Relevant Body
Trade Union	
Trust	
United Kingdom	
University	Department of Education and Science
Wales	
Welsh	
Windsor	Home Office or Scottish Home and Health Department

Guidance notes on the above words are contained in the Companies Registry booklet *Company and Business Names: Notes on Sensitive Words and Expressions* (ref C499, March 1985).

Other words and expressions are also covered by a variety of legislation and it may be a criminal offence to use them (s 26(1)(d)). The following list is not exhaustive however and any enquiries should be directed to the Companies Registry Office.

SPECIFICATION OF WORDS, EXPRESSIONS AND RELEVANT BODIES

Word or expression	Relevant body
Architect, Architectural	Architects Registration Council of the UK
Credit Union	Registrar of Friendly Societies
Veterinary Surgeon	Royal College of Veterinary Surgeons
Dentist, Dental Surgeon, Dental Practitioner	General Dental Council
Chemist, Chemistry, Drug, Druggist	Seek the advice of the Companies Registry Office
Pharmacist, Pharmaceutist, Pharmaceutical	
Ophthalmic Optician, Dispensing Optician, Registered Optician	General Optical Council
Bank, Banker, Banking Deposit	Bank of England
Red Cross, Anzac	Seek the advice of the Companies Registry Office
Insurance Broker, Assurance Broker, Reinsurance Broker, Reassurance Broker	Insurance Brokers Registration Council

Appendix 4

Forms Prescribed for Use in Connection with the Companies Acts

The following numerical list of forms are prescribed by the Companies (Forms) Regulations 1985 (SI 1985 No 854) as amended. Other forms are prescribed by the Insolvency Act 1986 and the Company Directors Disqualification Act 1986, but these are outside the scope of this book.

G 6	Notice of application to the Court for cancellation of alteration to the objects of a company
G R7	Application by an old public company for re-registration as a public company
G R7a	Notice of application made to the Court for cancellation of a special resolution by an old public company not to be re-registered as a public company
G R8	Declaration by Director or Secretary on application by an old public company for re-registration as a public company
G R9	Declaration by an old public company that it does not meet the requirements for a public company
10	Statement of first directors and secretary and intended situation of registered office
G 12	Statutory Declaration of compliance with requirements on application for registration of a company
G 30(5)(a)	Declaration on application for the registration of a company exempt from the requirement to use the word 'limited' or its Welsh equivalent
G 30(5)(b)	Declaration on application for registration under section 680 of the Companies Act 1985 of a company exempt from the requirements to use the word 'limited' or its Welsh equivalent
G 30(5)(c)	Declaration on change of name omitting 'limited' or its Welsh equivalent
G 43(3)	Application by a private company for re-registration as a public company
G 43(3)(e)	Declaration of compliance with requirements by a private company on application for re-registration as a public company
G 49(1)	Application by a limited company to be re-registered as unlimited
G 49(8)(a)	Members' assent to company being re-registered as unlimited
G 49(8)(b)	Form of Statutory Declaration by directors as to members' assent to re-registration of a company as unlimited

G 51	Application by an unlimited company to be re-registered as limited
G 53	Application by a public company for re-registration as a private company
G 54	Notice of application made to the Court for the cancellation of a special resolution regarding re-registration
G 88(2) (Revised 1988)	Return of allotment of shares
G 88(3)	Particulars of a contract relating to shares allotted as fully or partly paid up otherwise than in cash
G 97	Statement of the amount or rate per cent of any commission payable in connection with the subscription of shares
G 117	Application by a public company for certificate to commence business and statutory declaration in support
G 122	Notice of consolidation, division, sub-division, redemption or cancellation of shares, or conversion, re-conversion of stock into shares
G 123	Notice of increase in nominal capital
G 128(1)	Statement of rights attachcd to allotted shares
G 128(3)	Statement of particulars of variation of rights attached to shares
G 128(4)	Notice of assignment of name or new name to any class of shares
G 129(1)	Statement by a company without share capital of rights attached to newly created class of members
G 129(2)	Statement by a company without share capital of particulars of a variation of members' class rights
G 129(3)	Notice by a company without share capital of assignment of a name or other designation to a class of members
G 139	Application by a public company for re-registration as a private company following a Court Order reducing capital
G 147	Application by a public company for re-registration as a private company following cancellation of shares and reduction of nominal value of issued capital
G 155(6)a	Declaration in relation to assistance for the acquisition of shares
G 155(6)b	Declaration by the directors of a holding company in relation to assistance for the acquisition of shares
G 157	Notice of application made to the Court for the cancellation of a special resolution regarding financial assistance for the acquisition of shares
G 169	Return by a company purchasing its own shares
G 173	Declaration in relation to the redemption or purchase of shares out of capital
G 176	Notice of application to the Court for the cancellation of a resolution for the redemption or purchase of shares out of capital

G 190	Notice of place where a register of holders of debentures or a duplicate is kept or of any change in that place
G 190a	Notice of place for inspection of a register of holders of debentures which is kept in a non-legible form, or of any change in that place
G 224	Notice of accounting reference date (to be delivered within 9 months of incorporation)
G 225(1)	Notice of new accounting reference date given during the course of an accounting reference period
G 225(2)	Notice of new accounting reference date given after the end of an accounting reference period by a parent or subsidiary undertaking or by a company subject to an administration order
G 244	Notice of claim to extension of period allowed for laying and delivering accounts – oversea business or interests
G 266(1)	Notice of intention to carry on business as an investment company
G 266(3)	Notice that company no longer wishes to be an investment company
G 287	Notice of change in situation of registered office
288	Change of directors or secretary or change of particulars
G 318	Notice of place where copies of directors' service contracts and any memoranda are kept or of any change in that place
G 325	Notice of place where register of directors' interests in shares, etc, is kept or of any change in that place
G 325a	Notice of place for inspection of a register of directors' interests in shares, etc, which is kept in a non-legible form, or of any change in that place
G 353	Notice of place where register of members is kept or of any change in that place
G 353a	Notice of place for inspection of a register of members which is kept in a non-legible form, or of any change in that place
G 362	Notice of place where an overseas branch register is kept, or of any change in that place, or of discontinuance of any such register
G 362a	Notice of place for inspection of an overseas branch register which is kept in a non-legible form, or of any change in that place
363a	Annual Return
363b	Annual Return
363s	Annual Return
G 386	Notice of passing of resolution removing an auditor
M 395	Particulars of a mortgage or charge
M 397	Particulars for the registration of a charge to secure a series of debentures
M 397a	Particulars of an issue of secured debentures in a series

M 398	Certificate of registration in Scotland or Northern Ireland of a charge comprising property situate there
M 400	Particulars of a charge subject to which property has been acquired
M 403a	Declaration of satisfaction in full or in part of mortgage or charge
M 403b	Declaration that part of the property or undertaking charged (a) has been released from the charge; (b) no longer forms part of the company's property or undertaking
M 405(1)	Notice of appointment of receiver or manager
M 405(2)	Notice of ceasing to act as receiver or manager
M 410(Scot)	Particulars of a charge created by a company registered in Scotland
M 413(Scot)	Particulars for the registration of a charge to secure a series of debentures (note 1)
M 413a(Scot)	Particulars of an issue of Debentures out of a series of secured Debentures (note 1)
M 416(Scot)	Particulars of a charge subject to which property has been acquired by a company registered in Scotland
M 419a(Scot)	Application for registration of a memorandum of satisfaction in full or in part of a registered charge
M 419b(Scot)	Application for registration for a memorandum of fact that part of the property charged; (a) has been released from the charge; (b) no longer forms part of the company's property
429 dec	Statutory Declaration relating to a Notice to non-assenting shareholders
429(4)	Notice to non-assenting shareholders
430A	Notice to non-assenting shareholders (pursuant to section 430A(3) of the Companies Act 1985)
M 466(Scot)	Particulars of an instrument of alteration to a floating charge created by a company registered in Scotland
G 600	Notice of appointment of liquidator Voluntary winding up (Members or Creditors)
600a	Notice of appointment of liquidator [Members'] [Creditors']† voluntary winding up
G 680a	Application by joint stock company for registration under Part XXII of the Companies Act 1985, and Declaration and related statements
G 680b	Application by a company which is not a joint stock company for registration under Part XXII of the Companies Act 1985, and Declaration and related statements
G 684	Registration under Part XXII of the Companies Act 1985, List of members – existing joint stock company
G 685	Declaration on application by a joint stock company for registration as a public company

G 686	Registration under Part XXII of the Companies Act 1985 Statutory Declaration verifying list of members
691	Return and declaration delivered for registration by an oversea company
G 692(1)(a)	Return of alteration in the charter, statutes, etc, of an oversea company
692(1)(b)	Return of alteration in the directors or secretary of an oversea company or in their particulars
G 692(1)(c)	Return of alteration in the names or addresses of persons resident in Great Britain authorised to accept service on behalf of an oversea company
G 692(2)	Return of change in the corporate name of an oversea company
G 694(a)	Statement of name, other than corporate name, under which an oversea company proposes to carry on business in Great Britain
G 694(b)	Statement of name, other than corporate name, under which an oversea company proposes to carry on business in Great Britain in substitution for name previously registered
G 701a	Notice of accounting reference date by an oversea company
G 701b	Notice by an oversea company of new accounting reference date given during the course of an accounting reference period
G 701c	Notice by an oversea company of new accounting reference date given after the end of an accounting reference period

INDEX

[references to Precedents are in bold]